WITCHES, WHORES, AND SORCERERS

WITCHES, WHORES, AND SORCERERS

The Concept of Evil in Early Iran

BY S. K. MENDOZA FORREST
FOREWORD AND OTHER CONTRIBUTIONS
BY PRODS OKTOR SKJÆRVØ

UNIVERSITY OF TEXAS PRESS *Austin*

Requests for permission to reproduce material from this work should be sent to:
   Permissions
   University of Texas Press
   P.O. Box 7819
   Austin, TX 78713-7819
   utpress.utexas.edu/about/book-permissions

♾ The paper used in this book meets the minimum requirements of
ANSI/NISO Z39.48-1992 (R1997) (Permanence of Paper).

LIBRARY OF CONGRESS CATALOGING-IN-PUBLICATION DATA

Forrest, S. K. Mendoza.
   Witches, whores, and sorcerers : the concept of evil in early Iran / by
S. K. Mendoza Forrest ; with contributions by Prods Oktor Skjærvø. — 1st ed.
     p.   cm.
   Includes bibliographical references and index.
   ISBN 978-0-292-74767-8
    1. Good and evil—Religious aspects—Zoroastrianism.   2. Avesta—Criticism,
interpretation, etc. I. Skjærvø, Prods O.   II. Title.
   BL1590.G66F67   2011
   295′.5—dc22

                                        2011005491

ISBN 978-0-292-73540-8 (E-book)

CONTENTS

THE AVESTA AND ITS TRANSLATION

PRODS OKTOR SKJÆRVØ

THE TERM *Avesta* refers to a relatively small group of orally composed and transmitted texts written down only in the Islamic period, some of them perhaps around the year 600. We have no evidence that all the known texts were written down at the same time, however. The texts are in Avestan, an Iranian language related to Old Persian (the ancestor of modern Persian or Farsi), which was spoken in the northeast of the later Persian (Achaemenid) empire (550–330 BCE), in the areas of modern Afghanistan and the Central Asian republics. The language is known in two linguistic forms: an older form, similar to the oldest Indic language of the Rigveda, and a younger form, slightly antedating that of Old Persian (known from about 520 BCE). The extant texts were therefore probably committed to memory sometime in the second half of the second millennium and the first half of the first millennium BCE, respectively. We have considerable archeological evidence from these areas dating to these periods, but with lack of written evidence it is impossible to correlate this evidence with the Avestan texts. This means that we do not know their precise historical contexts.

The Old Avesta contains the "Gāthās of Zarathustra," five hymns ascribed to the (mythical) prophet of Zoroastrianism, and the Young(er) Avesta, miscellaneous ritual texts, among them the Yasna, the text that accompanies the morning ritual (*yasna*); the Yashts, hymns to individual deities; and the Videvdad, rules for keeping the *daēwa*s, demons, away, a text inserted in the Yasna and recited at important purification ceremonies.

The texts are known from manuscripts dating from the thirteenth to the nineteenth centuries, all of which apparently go back to individual prototypes written around the year 1000 (known from colophons), which means that there is a considerable gap in the written tradition between the time the texts were first committed to writing and the earliest known and extant manuscripts. It should be noted that the Avesta is not a single "book" like the Bible, but individual texts transmitted in separate manuscripts. These became a book only in Western editions during the nineteenth and twentieth centuries.

That the translation of these texts presents problems should be apparent. The translations in this book have been smoothed by leaving out discussions of problematic translations and marking uncertain or conjectural ones by a bracketed query: [?]. Hopelessly corrupt or incomprehensible passages have been left out, sometimes marked by ellipses.

I WAS IN BENGAL staying at a small village doing research several years ago, when one evening I decided to walk along a shadowy road. Like most foreigners, I was unaware of the dangers lurking in the dark. The sky was already a rich dark blue against the almost black trees, and the few people who were hurrying home gawked at me as if I had three heads. Being quite used to this, I continued to make my way to a grove I had discovered earlier in the day. Luckily, one of my little English students was passing by with her mother. They looked quite worried, despite my happy greeting.

"Don't go there," the girl warned when I explained my quest. "It is a place where jinn live. They will offer you anything your heart desires, but then your soul will belong to them."

I was most interested in meeting a jinni (genie), so I asked her if she had ever seen one. She had not, but she warned me, "You can recognize them by their feet—that's one thing they can't hide. Their feet look like giant bird claws."

I hardly had time to thank them as they scurried off. As for me, I went to see if I could meet a jinni, but they had apparently taken the day off. Jinn are the sometimes-demonic spirits that inhabited the Arab wastelands and deserts, howling on dark nights and often possessing a hapless passerby. How they ended up in Bengal, we will never know, but I suspect that the Muslim imagination that brought the other delightful stories of the Arabs was responsible.

It was in this way that I became fascinated with the things people consider evil. Evil is not always something to do with morality, as we in the West often think. When I once foolishly attempted to catch a large crab-like insect awkwardly scuttling across a temple floor in India, I saw the looks of horror people gave me. They warned me not to touch it, but their expressions told me that it was not just the poison they feared. They regarded the creature with a kind of awe they reserve for evil. Indeed, later I was told that it was an "inauspicious" creature.

When I started to study Zoroastrianism, evil ultimately hooked me. Evil, I found, was simple yet complex, disgusting at times, yet attractive. The sources available for the study of this tradition are scarce, however. I envy scholars of the Indian traditions for their rich sources, yet there were reasons for the scholar in the study of religion to revel in the fact that so few of their brethren have tackled the early Iranian material. I found the study of the Zoroastrian tradition to be the realm of the philologists, who were, and are, making valiant attempts to translate and make available the difficult texts. The study of the Iranian texts by scholars of religion has been hampered for several reasons. The most vexing is the corruption of the texts by scribes. The Avesta, for example, was an oral text passed down since perhaps the first half of the second millennium BCE. It was finally put into writing toward the end of the Sasanian period (224–651 CE), but the extant manuscripts date only from the thirteenth through fourteenth centuries. The priests who transmitted the texts orally and in writing, but who did not understand the original language, had corrupted these texts.

Most translations in this book are from the Avesta. In some cases, to avoid lengthy translated passages, I have paraphrased and shortened some translations from various works I have used, and I have given the English translation sources for the benefit of the reader wishing to investigate them further. I concentrate on the period of the Avesta and the earlier Pahlavi texts, with the exception of a few passages from the later texts, especially the Persian Rivāyats. With apologies to all of the learned scholars of Iranian traditions before me, I have had to lighten the text for print and have not been able to acknowledge all of the opinions that have been offered in the past in the understanding of the Avesta. I wanted above all to share my love of these fascinating myths with my students and with the public so that they too can enjoy the world of evil.

ACKNOWLEDGMENTS

THIS WORK WAS MADE POSSIBLE by the generous support of the Ford Foundation. I also thank Harvard University and its Department of Near Eastern Languages and Civilizations for allowing me the facilities I needed to complete this work. I am grateful to Centre College for support in the last phase of my writing. Professor Prods Oktor Skjærvø provided the translations of the Avesta, for which I am eternally indebted. These new translations will surely improve our understanding of the Zoroastrian religion.

When I first began studying Zoroastrianism, I realized that an interdisciplinary approach to this religion was essential. The linguists and philologists working on the very difficult and often cryptic Avestan and Pahlavi texts have dedicated lifetimes to deciphering them. Scholars in the study of religion, likewise, have developed methodologies to guide themselves in approaching the interpretation of religious phenomena. I am honored to have had the opportunity to work with Professor Prods Oktor Skjærvø, a leading scholar and philologist in the field of Iranian studies. My hope is that this study will prove to be a fruitful one; however, any shortcomings in this work are mine alone.

Professor Diana Eck of Harvard's Committee on the Study of Religion and Professor Kimberley Patton of Harvard Divinity School deserve my thanks for their comments and suggestions. I am also grateful to Professor James Russell of Harvard University for being an outstanding source of knowledge and inspiration. I thank Professor Laurie Cozad of the University of Mississippi for her many helpful suggestions. Finally, I acknowledge my student assistant, Gary Andrews.

I dedicate this book to my advisor and friend Professor Prods Oktor Skjærvø, who labored to teach me the difficult Gathic Avestan, Young Avestan, Pahlavi, and Sogdian languages; and to my mother, Maria Mendoza, who was never able to finish high school but wanted a better life for her children.

Danville, Kentucky
September, 2010

WITCHES, WHORES, AND SORCERERS

A SERIOUS PROBLEM in the study of Zoroastrianism is the notion of Zara-thustra[1] as a prophet, a reformer of what is often referred to as the pagan Iranian tradition. The result is the "textbook" understanding of Zoroastrianism, which distinguishes between a corrupt period of lawlessness and polytheism punctuated by a golden age of Zarathustra's teachings, followed again by a return to the old polytheistic state where superstitions reigned.

Most scholars of religion have long since abandoned the type of thought that pits "ethical" monotheists against "superstitious" polytheists. Traditions are just traditions, and one is no better than another. It is our task to observe, not to judge. It is with this thought that I approach the texts. Unfortunately, for scholars of early Iranian traditions, there is very little beyond the texts. Therefore, we have to let the texts "talk" to us. We have no idea of what opposing and marginalized groups and individuals practiced and believed. However, in an oblique way the Avesta reveals the identities and some of the practices of the outsiders to these traditions—at least those that bothered the authors the most.

I found it fruitful to examine and catalog ideas concerning evil in these texts because they reveal many things. In addition to the worldviews of the elite priests, the texts can also shed some light on the problems people in general faced when they dealt with the elite, who were often state-sponsored. For example, while scholars may know very little about the practices of women during the time of the creation of the Avesta, we can know the rules they were expected to follow, the attitudes of the priests toward women, and what the sanctions were against them. When the texts deal with the subject of women, I believe we can learn something very important about the concept of evil itself. It is precisely when addressing the subject of the female that the ambiguity of evil in Iran is revealed.

At first glance, one may assume that the concepts of good and evil are simple for dualists. This does not seem to be the case at all when we examine their views on humans. The Young Avesta sees a clear separation between the good god Ahura Mazdā (called Ohrmazd in the Sasanian and later texts) and the Evil Spirit, Angra Mainyu (Ahriman in the Sasanian and later texts), and their respective creations. Humans throw a wrench into the picture. Humans, and women in particular, have a strange status. Although created by the good god Ahura Mazdā, humans, like the great deities, have the power of choice: they can choose good or evil.

While women can choose good over evil, the problem becomes complex because, according to these texts, a woman's body is naturally linked to evil by blood pollution. I will deal with this interesting notion in my discussion on female evil beings. Female beings also appear in the Avesta as important demons or classes of demons. The sanctions against things evil also give us some insights on their occupations, such as providing for women's health, and at times abortions, which put these female health providers under the suspicion of witchcraft. What was the "magic" or witchcraft that these women used? Was it herbal medicine, or was it a combination of herbal medicine and spells?

Given such limited resources, we have to make some conjectures, but there is still quite a bit to learn by what is forbidden in a tradition. If the Avesta condemns abortion providers, then we must assume that they existed. When the texts forbid the eating of dogs, we can safely assume that some people may have eaten dogs. This is certainly not unheard of in other cultures. Similarly, when the texts complain about sorcerers and other evildoers, we will have to speculate on what they meant. Were they followers of other traditions? Were they actually practicing alternative magic?

At this point, it is important to say a few words about terms. The word "magic," for one, is fraught with a long history of verbal wrangling. It is a word similar to the term "religion," a definition of which will never satisfy every scholar, and will therefore remain elusive. Until recently, magic had a pejorative meaning. In the past, scholars made a distinction between magic and religion, and there were numerous attempts to differentiate the two. There is no consensus, even after many attempts, as to what, if anything, differentiates magic and religion. As I already mentioned, the study of early Iranian traditions has been mainly the field of philologists, rather than scholars in the study of religion or anthropology. Because of this, we see that some scholars in Iranian studies still use terms that today's religion scholars consider antiquated when describing various rituals and beliefs.

Religions can employ magical formulas, attempt coercion, be public or private, and so on. Therefore, perhaps looking at the magical part of any religion, we can separate a few aspects that may be contrasted to purely theological thought. My idea is not to single out the Avestan religion as magical, as opposed to other religions. Indeed, all religions could be analyzed in the same manner. In the case of the religion of the authors of the Avesta, we have only the extant texts to guide us, and considering the incredible antiquity of the religion, they are scant indeed. The elements we can separate as magical were still to have a great influence on the later development of theology in Zoroastrianism as it began to coalesce during the interaction with Islam in the seventh century CE and onwards. Magic and magical beings were important for the Zoroastrian theologians in the elucidation of evil in their dualistic system as opposed to the omnipotent power of the god of Islam.

I have gleaned the following definition from older anthropological works, from Malinowski to Van Gennep's "magico-religious," which ends up positing a definition of magic as a *part* of a religious process, not as opposed to it. I have adapted it for this book, although in no way do I claim that it can be used as a universal definition. It seems preferable to tediously using quotation marks around words like "magic," "spell," "curse," "sorcerer," etc.

1. Magic consists of words and rites meant to produce a desired result by the coercion or supplication of forces beyond the realm of humans. This is basically the same as prayer except that the aims are as below, in point 2.

2. The realm of magic is predominantly practical, because the use of magic usually has a goal, especially for the aim of suppressing disease, misfortunes, and evil beings. This can be opposed to simple praise and prayer, which are also features of the Avesta.

3. Magical rituals are usually private or secret and carried out by specialists in nonpublic settings. The *manthras* (*mantras* in Sanskrit), or spells, to use a broad, although loaded term, are passed down through a line of priests thought to be kin somehow to Zarathustra.

4. Magic revolves around a mantra or spell that uses special language and quite often contains mythological allusions. It is often simply the use of words from the Gāthās, which, by their antiquity, have acquired sacred status.[2]

There are always many exceptions to every rule, as scholars in the history of religion and anthropology will surely point out. To complicate matters, certain terms that have acquired a pejorative meaning will always be problematic. Can we totally avoid these terms? I agree with H. S. Versnel that this may prove impossible and that the "only realistic alternative is to devise at least a working definition of the concept you are going to employ."[3] While being careful not to allow old meanings to color our words, it is awkward to have to somehow avoid them. When we look at Avestan curses, I could use Versnel's term "judicial prayers" because, as he notes, the author is the injured party and so feels justified when appealing to the gods, as opposed to the demons.[4] This is indeed the case with the Avestan counterparts. However, Versnel is opposing his judicial prayers to *defixiones*, curses, from Graeco-Roman cursetexts. It would be problematic to make that sort of distinction concerning the composers of the Avesta as opposed to the so-called sorcerers and other demonic things they oppose, for the reason that we do not know who these sorcerers were, and we certainly do not have any examples of their texts. If we are to posit some continuity between the approaches of the composer or composers of the Gāthās and the later Avesta, at least in the way they chose their enemies (and this, I realize is dubious, and poses many challenges), there are a few ways to look at demons. They would include the so-called evil beings that plagued the authors of the Avesta and were of three kinds: unseen demons, persons who actually practiced black magic (or *abhicāra* as it is called in Sanskrit), and also ordinary people of opposing sects or religions. Another inevitable reason to think in these terms is that the authors of the Avesta themselves thought in terms of good and bad magic. They called performers of bad magic sorcerers, witches, and various other names. They also accused these people of usurping their own rituals and using them for bad purposes. This points to a conclusion that the actual methods of good and bad magic were not always different.

In analyzing the Avestan treatment of evil and how to combat it, my definition of "magic" works reasonably well. As far as the words "spell" and "curse" are concerned, these are mantras[5] that, in an effort to bring about the desired result of what I have termed "magic," will be discussed later.

Another problem in identifying evil in the Avesta is the obscurity of references in the early Avestan texts. Sometimes they are explained in post-Avestan texts, and sometimes the myths are fleshed out. We have no way of knowing if these elaborations are later additions invented to explain the bits and pieces offered by the early compositions, or explanations passed down orally and incorporated into the later compositions. Following the example of Wendy Doniger in her work on evil in the Hindu tradition,[6] I will use a thematic scheme, referring to the earliest compositions and then following them with any appropriate related later compositions. While it is important to keep in mind that concepts change and develop over time, this approach may help in several ways. For instance, one can examine what may be a foundational idea in the Avesta, or even as early as the Gāthās, and then observe the ways in which the concepts are interpreted by later authors. This is especially interesting considering that the authors of the Pahlavi compositions were working at a time when they were grappling with polemic arguments during the period of Muslim domination.

Using this method, we might ask for example, "What did the Avesta have to say about women?" How does this persist or change as the tradition responds to outside forces? While it may not be prudent to use later sources to fully explain earlier ones, looking at references in the earlier compositions to particular themes such as the disposal of dead bodies, and relating them to later texts that appear influenced by them, is a valid form of inquiry. Presenting the material in a thematic manner will also help to give us a more complete picture of the tradition as it developed.

This book deals with the question of how evil is understood and categorized, and then finally combated in early Iranian traditions. Very important in this study is the investigation into the lives of the witches, whores, sorcerers, and other people thought to embody evil. The priestly incantations are directed at these people. These "evil" beings are even more interesting than the priests, but they cannot speak. One can only discover something about them through the very people who hated them.

CHAPTER I

THE STUDY OF AN ANCIENT TRADITION

IN SOME FORM, Zoroastrianism was the state religion in Iran, perhaps even by the time of Cyrus the Great (550–530 BCE), although this has been an area where few scholars agree.[1] By the time of Darius I, the Achaemenid religion as seen through limited sources such as inscriptions, appears to be Zoroastrianism as known from the Avesta. This great religion had been dominant in Iran since antiquity. However, it began a steady decline, perhaps even before the assassination in 651 of the last Sasanian ruler, Yazdegird. One outcome of the contact with Islam was the realization on the part of the Zoroastrian priesthood that they needed to rethink and organize their theology if they hoped to sustain their weakening religion.

Zoroastrian clergy in the ninth and early tenth centuries were exposed to an Islam whose theology had been developing rapidly. Considering the theological issues that they had to tackle, one of the most obvious weaknesses in Zoroastrianism, as seen by Muslim theologians, was its dualistic stance, something very different from Islam. Zoroastrians were faced with arguments that made it necessary for them to systematize and clarify their belief system. Zoroastrian theologians, rather than alter their dualistic theology, employed novel strategies by which they updated it in ways that allowed them to answer many of the troubling questions posed by Islam. In this attempt, the Evil Spirit, Ahriman as he was called by then, attained a prominent position in the theological debate.

Jewish and Christian theologians before Islam had argued over the problem of theodicy, the dilemma that arises when one tries to defend an omnipotent god's goodness in the face of his apparent tolerance of evil. Muslim theologians were less perturbed by the question of theodicy as compared with their Jewish and Christian counterparts, yet the issue of the free will of humans was contentious. Islam does not give an important role to Iblīs, the devil figure. Iblīs has the job of tempting humans, but has no real power over them. Some see him as a helper of God, in as much as God gave him his job. He has no power independent of God. If this is the case, do humans choose to be evil?

The Qur'ān expresses the notion that God is the cause of everything, as seen, for example, in 6:125. At the same time it stresses human accountability. The Qur'ān makes no attempt to reconcile these divergent views. Muslim theologians produced much complex speculation on the matter, but common believers are, in general, content with the Qur'ānic god, who is the cause of everything, while simultaneously leaving humans to be responsible for their own actions.

Muslim theologians grappled with the question of theodicy particularly as it relates to the doctrine of predestination. Especially in the eighth and ninth centuries, there were acrimonious disputes among the Mu'tazilites, who as rationalists refused to believe that God could act in an unjust manner, and the Ash'arites, who attributed everything, including human acts, to the will of God. This period also approximately coincides with the reorganization of the Zoroastrian theological stance, as we see it in the Pahlavi texts, written down from the ninth century onward.

Zoroastrian theologians saw the matter of theodicy as a fault in the Abrahamic traditions—one that could serve them well in their polemical and apologetic works. They used their well-developed ideas regarding evil to form an argument against the Abrahamic religions with their omnipotent god.[2] In turn, they had to deal with the Islamic critique of the Zoroastrian god as a weakling. One might assume that, being dualists who believed that evil and good had separate sources, Zoroastrian theologians did not encounter the problem of theodicy in their tradition. However, we will find this to be simplistic. They had to grapple with the question, especially when it came to free will in humans—precisely the same problem that vexed Muslim theologians. Zoroastrians, who took the position that God never wills evil, still had to explain why humans choose to be evil.

From the beginning of the Islamic era of dominance in Iran, Zoroastrian theologians shifted toward an approach that involved theological argumentation, as is evident from the many apologetic texts that were produced. However, the authors of the Pahlavi texts did not abandon the older forms of religious expression, which consisted of rituals aimed at promoting order and purity, as well as inhibiting disorder and pollution. These rituals were apotropaic, that is, meant to ward off evil, or exorcistic, to remove demons. They comprised the nucleus of the Zoroastrian tradition in practice. The Avesta and specifically the ancient Gāthās were the primary source for their spells and apotropaic or exorcistic instructions.

The Zoroastrian theologians of the ninth and early tenth centuries not only used the earlier Avestan concepts as a basis for their apologetics, but they also attempted to find in them solutions to many problems intrinsic to the Avestan and early Pahlavi texts. As Zoroastrian theologians struggled to classify and codify their ancient theology, they employed the idea of evil as an important element of their arguments. When there was a need, they looked to the Avesta for their arguments. In order to understand Zoroastrian theology as it develops in the Pahlavi texts, one must attempt to comprehend the unfolding of the notion of evil in earlier texts.

Examining how the idea of evil developed entails investigating its roots from the Gāthās, where evil appears at first glance to be a rather vague force, to the post-Gathic Avestan texts, where evil takes an active role in the lives of people, and indeed, of the universe. In the Videvdad, strict rules are formed to protect against evil by the performance of ritual and by the observance of taboos.[3] The Zoroastrian response to evil was very practical. Until the time of the composition of the Pahlavi work, the predominant methods that priests, and presumably the community, used to control evil were apotropaic and exorcistic spells and rites. Few scholars can agree on when these practices came into being and if they ran counter to the presumed teachings of Zarathustra.

A quick look at almost any textbook on world religions will most likely reveal a simplistic view of the Zoroastrian tradition, which, like any tradition, is naturally highly complex. When Western scholars first began in-depth studies of Zoroastrianism, it was mainly among the Parsis in India. Parsis were Iranian Zoroastrians who had fled Muslim persecution in their homeland before settling in India. According to tradition, they started about one hundred years after the Muslim conquest of Iran in 642 CE. During the British occupation of India, Parsis rose in rank above many other Indians, and, perhaps like their Hindu brethren who began the organization called the Brahmo Samaj, were keen on presenting their tradition as progressive and advanced.[4] Wendy Doniger calls the tendency to accept Protestant elements "a kind of colonial and religious Stockholm syndrome."[5]

Western scholars, hampered as they were by the obscure languages of the texts, tended to make an artificial separation between the oldest of the Zoroastrian texts, the Gāthās, and later texts. They interpreted the Gāthās as ethical and abstract, while they considered other texts as presenting a corruption of the older ethical religion. The same approach was used regarding the Vedic texts. Scholars viewed the highly philosophical texts of the Upanishads as superior to the Purānas, which were younger and presented much of the mythology of the tradition.[6]

Thus we find that both many modern scholars and many members of the modern Zoroastrian community have elevated the Gāthās to the status of "the real teachings of Zarathustra,"[7] while they relegate the rest of the Avesta to evidence of a loss of the true teachings.[8] Instances of "magic" and myth tend to be dismissed as not being part of the prophet's teachings. Early scholars of Zoroastrianism were attracted to the notion of a "pure" Zoroastrianism, which meant to them a "rational, non-legalistic and non-ritualistic religious tradition."[9] The parts of the Avesta that seemed to contradict this idea were disturbing and had to be somehow explained away. Christian Bartholomae, the leading Avestan scholar in the late nineteenth and early twentieth century, asserted that the sole author of the Gāthās was Zarathustra, a prophet with an ethical message.[10] Bartholomae believed that Zarathustra had a revelation of monotheism, but later had to compromise on strict monotheism because of all of the resistance he encountered.[11]

The Zarathustra embodied in this idea was an ethical teacher and a prophet. Max Weber, writing in the 1920s, had obviously read these accounts of Zarathustra, and this led Weber to class him as an "ethical prophet," along with Muhammad. He postulated that this type of prophet "demands obedience as an ethical duty."[12] Weber writes: "In the case of Zoroaster too it can be asserted that the range of his vision was also oriented to the views of the civilized lands of the West."[13] One cannot blame him for coming to these conclusions, given the expert scholarly opinions he had at his disposal.

If the Gāthās were the only extant work of the "prophet" Zarathustra, then scholars were faced with the problem of how to explain the rest of the Avesta. To this end, the Magi of the Greek authors were resurrected, with many scholars postulating that the Median Magi were behind what Jacques Duchesne-Guillemin called a "gross, rigid dualism."[14] Later scholars such as Gherardo Gnoli, however, dismissed the idea that dualism was "nothing but a vicious inheritance of the primitive superstitious mentality of the Median Magi."[15] The Magi, with their reputation as magicians, thus became important in the argument concerning the perception of the changing nature of Zoroastrianism.

In an early publication, Gnoli rejected the standard explanation of a discontinuity between the "old Iranian" religion and the supposedly revolutionary Zoroastrianism delivered by a prophet teaching a new, radical message. Instead, he proposed that "Mazdeism is not the result of a revolution or of a reformation, but the final product of a slow process of transformation of a kind of more ancient Aryan religiosity; a process that has developed this side of the Indus, parallel with and analogous to what happened at the other side of the big historical stream with the Vedic religion and its successive developments."[16] Gnoli also attacked the notion that the Gāthās were a "theological synthesis of Zoroastrianism" or a "complete theory of the many aspects, doctrinal, liturgical and ethical, that a religion is made of." Rather, he noted that they are ritual texts centering on the *haoma* sacrifice. The attempt to find every aspect of the religion in the Gāthās was therefore pointless and could only serve to further obscure what was already unclear.

The theory of the reformation of Zarathustra was rooted in the notion that Zarathustra was an ethical, monotheistic prophet and that whatever came after him was a disgraceful fall from the "true" religion. R. C. Zaehner lamented that

> [n]ever has a religious thinker been more grossly travestied—travestied by his own followers who straightway obscured the purity of his monotheistic vision, travestied by the Magi in the Levant who presented him to the Graeco-Roman world not only as the author of a rigid religious dualism which made good and evil two rival and co-eternal principles, but also as a magician, astrologer, and a quack.[17]

This statement is a good reflection of the past scholarly approaches to Zoroastrianism that have produced the textbook definitions of the religion today. As opposed to the earlier scholars of Zoroastrianism, if we follow Gnoli in his rejection of the notion that "ethical Zoroastrianism" was somehow distorted and poisoned by outsiders (the Magi), we are still faced with the problem of a seeming lack of continuity between the Gāthās and the rest of the Avesta. Some of this has to be attributed to the translators who assume meanings for words about which we still know very little. Even taking that into account, there is a difference in language, style, and content between the Gāthās and the Young Avesta.[18] The attempt to find a totally smooth transition of religious thought throughout the Zoroastrian texts, which span an enormous time period, is methodologically unsound, because religions change constantly. Seeking to find an evolutionary growth in complexity of thought will lead to an equally flimsy conclusion.

This study will not be based on the assumption of a historical Zarathustra, prophet, reformer, philosopher, etc., and thus will not try to determine whether the ideas discussed in it belonged to the prophet's teaching or not. Indeed, the very notion of a historical Zarathustra was seriously challenged in the second half of the twentieth century, beginning with the work of Marijan Molé, and continued by Jean Kellens and most recently Prods Oktor Skjærvø.[19] The question and its answer are irrelevant for the present study, since the analysis of the texts does not depend on them.

The foci of this book are the ideas of their authors concerning evil and how these notions influenced their lives. I begin with a survey of early Zoroastrian literature and then I discuss the relationship between the Magi and magic.

After a general discussion of the notion of evil, I embark on an examination of varieties of evil, from what we consider natural occurrences, such as old age and death, to evildoers. These include the supernatural demons, people who practice evil arts, such as sorcerers and sorceresses, witches, and evil magicians. An interesting addition to this list of evildoers is the category of people who did not intentionally practice evil, such as those who became polluted. The varieties of evildoers are fascinating because they span a wide spectrum from whores to demon worshippers, from givers of the evil eye to two- and four-legged wolves.

The remainder of the book covers methods that the Avestan people employed to free themselves, or protect themselves from the evil they seemed to see everywhere. These can take the form of spells, exorcisms, and curses meant to drive demons out of the body, the home, and the land. It also explains which gods could be implored for help. The grammatical structure of Avestan incantations is also examined, as are rituals for their execution.

Rather than being an intrusion into the ethical system represented by the Gāthās, concern for evil seems instead to be central to the Avestan worldview. It has its roots in the Gāthās, but it displays its complexities in the later Avestan compositions. We will see that the Gāthās continue to have a central role in the battle against evil as the most powerful and sacred of all spells.

CHAPTER 2

THE IRANIANS AND THEIR LITERATURE

ARCHEOLOGICAL EVIDENCE SHOWS the existence of a large complex of settlements in what is today's Uzbekistan at the end of the third and beginning of the second millennium BCE, which Victor Sarianidi has baptized the Bactrian-Margiane Archeological Complex. This culture is the only one at this early time whose artifacts found their way onto the Iranian Plateau.[1] It is therefore tempting to identify it with the proto-Iranians, but "stones do not speak," so we cannot be certain. Linguistic evidence combined with the geographical references found in the Avesta, however, points strongly to eastern Iranian populations having lived in this area in the second millennium.[2] They must have split up from the Indians, to whom they were closely related, before this. A date *ante quem* is perhaps given by the end of the Indus civilization in 1900 BCE, if this was caused by the incoming Indians.[3]

Persians are first mentioned in the Assyrian annals in the area of Urartu in the ninth century[4] BCE and Medes and Persians in more southerly areas of the western Plateau during the eighth and seventh centuries.[5] This means that the migrations into the Plateau cannot have taken place any later than 1000 BCE. The Median king Deiokes may have formed an empire around 700 BCE,[6] but our most detailed account is in Herodotus, which cannot be used as a secure historical source. We know, however, that the Median king Cyaxares, whom the Achaemenid inscriptions call Uvaxštara (and the Babylonian Chronicles, Umakištar), conquered Assyria and its capital Nineveh on the Tigris in 612 BCE, two years after the destruction of Ashur (614).[7]

The literatures of the earliest Iranians and their Indian neighbors comprise the Old Indic Vedas (oldest of which is the Rigveda), the East-Iranian Avesta, and the Southwest-Iranian Old Persian cuneiform inscriptions of the Achaemenid kings (from ca. 520 BCE).

The Rigveda and the Old Avestan texts are in languages that are very similar in respect to grammar, vocabulary, and especially literary style and formulas,[8] which means that they are probably contemporary compositions (from about 1400 to 200 BCE).[9] The Young Avestan texts, according to the linguistic criteria (the language is relatively close to Old Persian) and the geographical evidence (names from northeastern Iran), probably date to the beginning of the first millennium BCE. These dates are today fairly securely established, though there has been much debate about them, but since they are compositions transmitted orally for millennia before they were written down, they cannot be dated with any high degree of exactitude.[10]

There is little information in the Old Avestan texts about the society in which they were composed. Molé stresses that these are religious, not historical texts.[11] They are ritual texts accompanying the daily ritual and annual events, such as the observance of the new year. There are references to pastures, camels, chariot races, and a few other concrete issues, which are of traditional literary nature and prove nothing much about social and political conditions.[12]

The Young Avesta, on the other hand, at least contains geographical names from the area of Central Asia (the modern Central Asian republics, northeast Iran, and Afghanistan), as well as the names of the river Helmand and its tributaries in Sistan, today's southern Afghanistan.

There are two lists of geographical names in the Young Avesta, one in Yasht 10, in which Mithra surveys his lands, and the other in the Videvdad, which lists the land Ahura Mazdā created. The list in Yasht 10 traces—relatively speaking—the path of the sun from the east to the west:

YASHT 10.13–16

(We sacrifice to Mithra . . .)
who, as the first of the beings worthy of sacrifice in the world of thought,
rises beyond Mount Harā
in front of the immortal sun with fleet horses,—
who as the first seizes the gold-adorned, beautiful heights.

From there he looks upon the entire area inhabited by the Aryans,
he, the most rich in life-giving strength,— [13]
in which brave rulers lay out in straight lines their many palisades,
in which tall mountains with plenty of grass further the . . . for the cow,
in which there stand deep, surging lakes,
in which rivers in spate rush broad with a swell to Ishkata and Pouruta,
to Merv, Herat, and Gawa, to Sogdiana and Choresmia,
toward Arzahi and Sawahi,[14]

toward Fradadafshu and Vidadafshu,
toward Vourubarshti and Vourujarshti,
toward this continent, radiant Khwaniratha.

Mithra rich in vitalizing strength surveys the area where Gawas dwell,
the healing settlement of the Gawas,
he, worthy of sacrifice in the world of thought,
who flies over all the continents bestowing Fortune,[15]
he, worthy of sacrifice in the world of thought,
who flies over all the continents bestowing command.
He increases the obstruction-smashing strength of these
who, qualified (and) knowing Order,[16] sacrifice to him with libations.

The first chapter of the Videvdad describes how Ahura Mazdā created the lands inhabited by Iranians,[17] while the Evil Spirit brought forth evils, plagues, and scourges for them. Most of those listed are still unidentified, but apparently the lands become more afflicted by evil as one moves west:

VIDEVDAD 1.2–19

As the best of places and settlements I, Ahura Mazdā, first fashioned the Aryan Expanse with the Good Lawful (river).
Then the Evil Spirit, full of destruction, whittled forth as its antagonist a dragon, the red, and the winter made by the evil gods (daēwas). There, ten months are winter, two summer. Water, earth, and plants are frozen . . .

As the second best of places and settlements I, Ahura Mazdā, fashioned Gawa settled by Sogdians.
Then the Evil Spirit full of destruction whittled forth as its antagonists thistles and other destructive things.

As the third best of places and settlements I, Ahura Mazdā, fashioned Merv, abiding by Order, rich in life-giving strength.
Then the Evil Spirit full of destruction whittled forth as its antagonists [unknown words].

As the fourth best of places and settlements I, Ahura Mazdā, fashioned Bactria with upraised banners.
Then the Evil Spirit. . . .

As the fifth best of places and settlements I, Ahura Mazdā, fashioned Nisa which is between Merv and Bactria.

Then the Evil Spirit full of destruction whittled forth as its antagonist bad confusion [?].

As the sixth best of places and settlements I, Ahura Mazdā, fashioned Herat. . . .
Then the Evil Spirit full of destruction whittled forth as its antagonist spittle and phlegm.

As the seventh best of places and settlements I, Ahura Mazdā, fashioned Vaēkerta, the lair of hedgehogs.
Then the Evil Spirit full of destruction whittled forth as its antagonist the witch Khnanthaitī, who followed Kersāspa.

As the eighth best of places and settlements I, Ahura Mazdā, fashioned Urwā with abundant pasture.
Then the Evil Spirit full of destruction whittled forth as its antagonist bad overseers.

As the ninth best of places and settlements I, Ahura Mazdā, fashioned Khnanta, settled by Hyrcanians.
Then the Evil Spirit full of destruction whittled forth as its antagonist bad inexpiable acts: male intercourse.

As the tenth best of places and settlements I, Ahura Mazdā, fashioned beautiful Arachosia.
Then the Evil Spirit full of destruction whittled forth as its antagonist bad inexpiable acts: exposure of corpses.

As the eleventh best of places and settlements I, Ahura Mazdā, fashioned Helmand, wealthy and munificent.
Then the Evil Spirit full of destruction whittled forth as its antagonists bad sorcerers.
And this shall be a clear sign and a clear [?]: Wherever they come . . . the one possessed by sorcerers. Then those are the most possessed by sorcerers. Then those come up for destruction and . . . and locusts.

As the twelfth best of places and settlements I, Ahura Mazdā, fashioned Ragā of three tribes.
Then the Evil Spirit. . . .

As the thirteenth best of places and settlements I, Ahura Mazdā, fashioned Cakhra, abiding by Order, rich in life-giving strength.
Then the Evil Spirit full of destruction whittled forth as its antagonist bad inexpiable acts: burning of corpses.

As the fourteenth best of places and settlements I, Ahura Mazdā, fashioned four-cornered Varna, in which Thraētaona was born, who struck down the giant dragon (Azhi Dahāka).
Then the Evil Spirit full of destruction whittled forth as its antagonist untimely menses and the un-Aryan teachers [?] of the land.

As the fifteenth best of places and settlements I, Ahura Mazdā, fashioned the Seven [world] Rivers.
Then the Evil Spirit full of destruction whittled forth as their antagonist untimely menses and untimely heat.

As the sixteenth best of places and settlements I, Ahura Mazdā, fashioned [the lands] by the falls [?] of the river Ranghā. . . .
Then the Evil Spirit full of destruction whittled forth as its antagonist the demon-made winter and the . . . teachers of the lands.

These lists have been used by scholars to identify the Aryan Expanse (Airyana Vaējah), the mythical homeland of the Iranians, with Choresmia. Such attempts, however, are linked with the pseudo-problem of the "time and place" of Zarathustra and have been shown to have little merit. It has also been suggested that these lists imply that the authors of the Young Avesta were acquainted with western India (Hapta Hindu "Seven Rivers")[18] but did not yet know the western area of Greater Iran, and that they may have come from the north, slowly moving south and west.

It is a reasonable assumption that the Young Avestan corpus and the religion it represented was at some stage established in the area of Sistan, or ancient Arachosia, and that from there it spread westward, perhaps during the Median period, to be firmly established in Persia (the Greek Persis) by the time the Achaemenids came to power (Cyrus the Great 559–530, Cambyses II 530–522, etc.; the last king was Darius III 336–330, conquered by Alexander of Macedonia).[19] The corpus of inscriptions,[20] mainly from Persepolis, Susa, and Hamadan, comprise several long inscriptions from the reigns of Darius I (522–486 BCE) and his successor, Xerxes (486–465 BCE), and several short ones, among them a relatively substantial one from Artaxerxes II (405–359 BCE).[21] Several (or most) of the inscriptions have Elamite or Accadian translations (or both), and Darius' great inscription at Bisotun has Aramaic translation.[22] They are often accompanied by reliefs depicting a king and his activities, notably in the posture of sacrificing to god.[23] As far as they go, the inscriptions show that the religion of the Achaemenids was that of the Avesta.[24] The evidence of the Greek historians, notably of Herodotus, is also little at variance with our picture of the Zoroastrian religion.

Of the later Iranian literatures, we should mention the inscriptions written in Middle Persian, the official language of the Sasanian state, a language descended from Old Persian and the ancestor of modern Persian. Most important are the inscriptions from the third century CE,[25] which open a window onto the religion of this period, and the numerous Zoroastrian texts written in Pahlavi, a late stage of the Middle Persian language, including translations of and commentaries on the Avesta, what is traditionally referred to as the Zand,[26] in addition to numerous other, mostly religious, texts. Among these, several will be cited below, such as the Dēnkard,[27] an encyclopedic text containing many subjects from proper religious conduct to eschatology; the Bundahishn ("how everything was set in place in the beginning"),[28] the Zoroastrian creation myth; the Dādestān ī Dēnīg ("judgments according to the religious tradition");[29] the Mēnōy ī Khrad ("the otherworldly wisdom");[30] and the Ardā Wīrāz-nāmag ("the book of the righteous Wirāz [or Wirāf]"),[31] a visionary text with eschatological material. Many of these are instructional texts in question-and-answer format (a common form in the Pahlavi texts). Also of importance is the Shkand-gumānīg Wizār ("the exposition that smashes all doubts"),[32] an apologetic work.

It must be kept in mind that the final versions of the Pahlavi texts were mostly written down in the ninth and tenth centuries, far into the Muslim period, and therefore they contain literature formed over several centuries. It is especially problematic to use this literature as evidence for earlier forms of the religion. However, it will serve to demonstrate how the earlier material was used in the reformulation of later variations on similar subjects.

It was also in the Sasanian period that the Avesta was written down for the first time, probably sometime in the sixth to seventh centuries BCE.[33] The earliest manuscripts date only from the thirteenth and fourteenth centuries, however.[34] Note also that the manuscript tradition is extremely weak. In fact, it has been proven that all extant manuscripts of each text of the Avesta are descended from single manuscripts that were in existence around 1000 CE. According to the Zoroastrian tradition, as told in the Dēnkard, the Avesta at the time of Xosrow I (531–579) consisted of twenty-one *nasks* (approximately "books").[35] These books are summarized in Dēnkard book 8, and show that we have lost many of the Avestan texts known then, but also that some text had been lost already before that time and that only the Pahlavi translation was known to the compiler.[36]

Some work was written later than this time, but most of what was produced was written in the new Persian language, such as the Zarātusht-nāmah,[37] a vita of Zarathustra, which I will have the occasion to quote below. Of great importance is also the correspondence (*rivāyat*s) among the Iranian communities (the Pahlavi *rivāyat*s) and between the Iranian and Indian Zoroastrian communities (the Persian *rivāyat*s) on questions of religious practice.[38]

Among other Iranian languages, we may mention Khotanese and Sogdian in the far northeast, both of which contain much material for the reconstruction of the ancient religion of the Sogdians and Khotanese,[39] although, with few exceptions, all the literature is non-Zoroastrian (Manichean, Christian, Buddhist). There is, however, a fragment of the Ashem Vohū prayer in Sogdian, which shows that Zoroastrian texts were being written in Sogdiana in the first millennium of our era.[40]

THE ZOROASTRIAN TEXTS

According to the Zoroastrian tradition as told in the Pahlavi books, during the reign of Dārā, son of Dārā, that is, under the Achaemenids (barely remembered in the later tradition), the Avesta had been written down in gold letters on the skins of oxen, but the "accursed" Alexander destroyed it, and the remnants were brought to Rome.[41] They also mention that the Avesta was repeatedly recompiled, with a succession of commentaries being added. According to the tradition, this took place once under the Arsacids (Parthians; ca. 247 BCE–224 CE) and at least four times during the reign of the Sasanians: under Ardashir, the first Sasanian monarch (224–240), by the legendary high priest Tansar (or Tōsar); under Shahpur I (240–270?); under Shahpur II (309–379) by his high priest Ādurbād; and finally under Khosrow I (531–579). It is commonly assumed that it was under Khosrow that the twenty-one *nasks* (books) of the Avesta were written down along with their Zand.[42]

The Avesta contains two chronological layers of texts, which we refer to as the Old Avesta and the Young (Younger) Avesta.[43] The Old Avesta contains the five Gāthās, "songs, hymns," and the Yasna Haptanghāiti, the "sacrifice in seven sections."[44] The Old Avestan hymns are all addressed to Ahura Mazdā.[45] They are recited about halfway through the Yasna, the text that accompanies the *yasna* ritual, the principal sacrificial ceremony, at the time of the pressing of the *haoma*, the most important component of the sacrifice. This special position in the *yasna* liturgy may have assured their survival. It is not known why only the Gāthās and the Yasna Haptanghāiti survive out of all the Old Avestan compositions that must at one time have existed. The Gāthās may have originally been recited during the five days (named after the five Gāthās) leading up to the important new year celebrations. If this was their original function, it may be the reason for their importance.[46]

Among the Young Avestan texts are two that follow the ritual, the longer Yasna and the shorter Vispered, a text used to supplement the Yasna for the seasonal Vispered ritual.[47] They include invocations and texts of praise, as well as sections describing the ritual procedures. One such ritual was the preparation of the *barsom*, the holy grass on which the implements of the ritual are laid out and, originally at least, served as a seat for the gods when they arrived to the sacrifice. Other rituals included the pressing of the *haoma*; the offering of the holy bread, the holy plant, and the waters; and the tending of the fire. The Young Avesta further contains the Yashts,[48] hymns to deities, among which are the long hymns to the river goddess Anāhitā, the sun god Mithra,[49] the weather god Tishtriya,[50] the war god Verthragna, the god Divine Fortune (Khwarnah),[51] and several others. Two important hymns are included in the Yasna: the hymn to Haoma (Yasna 9–11) and the hymn to Sraosha (Yasna 56–57).[52]

The Khorda Avesta,[53] or "little Avesta," contains a selection of prayers, including short versions of the principal Yashts and calendrical litanies. Finally, there are several "instructional" texts, among them the Videvdad, concerned with purity rituals and exorcisms; the Ērbedestān,[54] containing questions and answers regarding the behavior of priestly students and priests; and the Nīrangestān,[55] which contains rules for how to perform the ritual. Among the remaining texts we may mention the Hādōxt Nask[56] and Aogemadaēca,[57] which among other things tell about the fate of the soul after death: its journey to the Bridge of the Accountant, where the soul's thoughts, words, and deeds determine whether it should go to paradise, go to hell, or stay in the intermediary sphere.

The texts drawn upon in this book are mainly from the Gāthās, the Yasna, the Yashts, and the Videvdad. In all these texts, the human involvement in the control of evil in this world is given ample room, but we also find the intervention of the gods in the suppression of evils on a greater cosmic scale. Thus, we find "recipes" for how to deal with sorcerers, witches, and other magicians, as well as with robbers, diseases, and—especially in the Videvdad—pollution caused by contact with dead matter.

The Videvdad is fundamentally a law book that details ritual cleanliness and laws pertaining to pollution. Its name means literally "the law about how to keep the evil gods [demons] away,"[58] that is, the demons that cause defilement and thus sin. Most of the Videvdad deals with pollution caused by the dead matter of corpses and blood, notably from menstruation, the two most serious afflictions caused by demons.

The strategies described for dealing with these various manifestations of evil include simple curses and spells, but also more elaborate magical rituals, which all fall under the general rubric of "magic." The following chapter deals with the manifestations of evil in the Avesta, before I show how these rituals are put to actual use.

CHAPTER 3

MAGIC AND THE MAGI

THE ROLE OF THE MAGI and their association with magic influenced ideas about the early Zoroastrian tradition. In antiquity, if Zoroastrians were known for anything, it was the Magi's purported use of magic. The term "magic" itself is derived from the Greek adjective *magikos* and noun *mageia*, which in turn are derived from *magos*, the Greek rendition of Old Persian *magu*, "magus."[1] This word is attested in Old Iranian in Avestan and in Old Persian, as well as in Median by Herodotus' statement that the "Magoi" were one of the six Median tribes. No convincing etymology of the word has yet been proposed. Molé tentatively suggested that *magu* is derived from Avestan *magawan-*. This term designates a person connected in some way with ritual.[2] However, this in turn is derived from *maga-*, which probably denotes the ritual exchange of gifts between the sacrificers and the gods.[3] Other proposals are pure speculation. These include that of Émile Benveniste, who suggested that the word might have originally meant "member of the tribe."[4] Its only attestation in the Avesta (in the form *mogu-*) is in Yasna 65.7:

YASNA 65.7

Do not, O waters, [give] us [over] to the one with evil thought,
nor to the one with evil speech,
nor to the one with evil acts,
nor to the one with evil *daēnā*,
nor to him who is hostile to his companion,
nor to him who is hostile to the *magu*,
nor to him who is hostile to the members of community,
nor to him who is hostile to the members of the family,
and do not give us over to this one,
O good, best, Orderly waters set in place by Ahura Mazdā,

who wishes to collect the debt of our livestock, which are not owed as
   debt, [?]
nor give us over to this one,
O good, best, Orderly waters set in place by Ahura Mazdā,
who wishes to collect the debt of our bodies, which are not owed as debt. [?]

In his inscription at Bisotun, Darius describes the alleged usurper of Cambyses' throne, whom he (Darius) fought, overcame, and killed, Gaumāta the *magu*. In later Zoroastrianism, however, *magu* is a positive term for a priest (Middle Persian *mow*), and the highest clerical office in the early Sasanian period is that of the "chief of the magus" (Middle and modern Persian *mowbed*), later also *mowbedān mowbed*, fashioned on the model of *shāhān shāh*, "king of kings."

The Greek and Latin authors regarded the Magi as magicians, astrologers, and conjurers. Herodotus mentions that the Magi practiced divination, and gives several examples of their skill in interpreting dreams, etc. Magic had many forms, and in the ancient world it could be used for curses and spells against enemies, so that it came to be regarded with suspicion. In classical culture and religion, however, magic and magicians were important elements in the everyday lives of people, for many legitimate reasons. If we approach the texts without the untenable notion of the historical reformer, we will see that the Avesta, like other Near Eastern literature of the second and first millennia BCE, reflects the society of that time, in which magic was a part of both daily life and ritual.

The classical authors must have had some basis for their beliefs that the Iranian Magi practiced magic. Thus, Herodotus describes the Magi as interpreters of dreams and diviners, both of which practices were regarded as magical. According to him, on several occasions, kings consulted the Magi about dreams, notably the Median king Astyages[5] and Xerxes, son of Darius I.[6] However, they were not always right in their interpretations. On the other hand, Agathias credited the Magi with the ability to divine by staring into a fire (*Historiae* 2.25), and other sources describe how they used sticks or rods for divination purposes (*Scholia in Nicandri Theriaca* 613).[7] Albert de Jong conjectures that the idea of divining by staring into a fire was based upon a combination of the fact that Zoroastrian priests tended fires as part of their priestly function and "an interpretation based upon their reputation." The claim that the Magi divined using sticks, Jong points out, was another such "amalgam of information,"[8] whereby the *barsom* sticks carried by the Zoroastrian priests were confused with sticks for divination (perhaps used by the

Scythians). Finally, the classical authors refer to shamanic soul travel into the other world, a clearly magical practice (Lucian Menippus 6–8).[9]

The term also found its way into Semitic languages such as Hebrew and Aramaic. The rabbinical stereotype of the magus, according to Jonathan Seidel, was "a malicious grave-robber and mumbler."[10] In Qur'ān 22:17, Zoroastrians, and indeed Iranians in general, are called "Majūs," and are considered marginally to be *ahl al-kitāb*, or "people of the book," the Muslim designation for those people to whom a book has been delivered by God.

The magical practices of dream interpretation, divination, and soul travel are common in the later Zoroastrian texts, in the Pahlavi books, and also in still later literature, often with a combination of two or all three. Thus, in the thirteenth-century Persian Zarātusht-nāmah (71–181), it is related that Zarathustra dreamt that he was overwhelmed on all sides by armies of hostile men and had the dream interpreted. In the same passage, Zarathustra is taken on a soul journey to meet Ahura Mazdā and his companions. Only then can he learn all the truths of the religion. This journey is remarkably similar to the shamanic journeys involving a kind of "death" and return to the body.[11]

Soul travel is often a reaction to a spiritual crisis, as we see in the cases of Wishtāspa,[12] Ardā Wīrāz,[13] and Kerdīr.[14] In the cases of Ardā Wīrāz and Wishtāspa, their stories clearly state that they took a drug to induce their visions. In the case of Kerdīr, the fragmentary text is not clear about how he achieved soul travel.[15] In the Selections of Zādspram, Zarathustra appears as an opponent of the wizards and sorcerers. In Chapter 17.1–6 of the same, Zarathustra divines the future by looking into the sky and the earth. He sees the "best existence" for the good (after death) and hell for the demons, fiends, wizards, and witches. He also overcomes a wizard who wants to destroy him with the evil eye.[16]

How much of this was known to the classical authors we do not know, but probably enough to warrant their impression of Zoroastrians as magicians. More importantly, in the classical world, the Zarathustra image itself was closely connected with astrology. Jong notes, "[T]o judge from the surviving [classical] literature, he was considered to have been the inventor of astrology and magic and to have written books on these subjects."[17]

The later Zoroastrian texts, notably the Bundahishn,[18] the Mēnōy ī Khrad (7.1–27), Kār-nāmag ī Ardashīr ī Pābagān, and Shkand-gūmānīg Wīzār (4.1–60) contain numerous astrological passages and horoscopes, as well as mentions of astrologers and their art. The Avesta does not contain clear references to astrology and astrologers,[19] but several heavenly phenomena are considered to have evil effects on Ahura Mazdā's cosmos.

When we look at the development of the concept of evil in Iran, as I already mentioned, some of the problems we face are the scarcity of sources beside what remains of the Zoroastrian texts, and further, that we know only the priestly interpretations. The "enemies" of the priests, who include witches and sorcerers, may have represented popular traditions, but, lacking any evidence, there is no way to determine this. When we look at the earliest texts, the Gāthās, there is some indication that various groups of priests were at odds with each other. If this attitude of demonizing the other camp was continued, practitioners of popular traditions might have been targeted as evil, as happened with the Druidic tradition in Europe. It is very important, in this dualistic picture, to identify the players in the "battle" between good and evil. The linear nature of Zoroastrian "history" means that there is an end to the battle. "Good" and "bad" players help to create "points" for the two opposing forces. In effect, the end will be decided by tallying the scores for each side.

Another important issue is the role of magical language and ritual in the early Iranian tradition. Anti-evil rites—spells, curses, and exorcisms with their accompanying rituals in the Avesta—are strongly tied to the attempt to control evil. The most common types of rituals in the Avesta are those used to remedy evil, either apotropaic or exorcistic. The utterances that accompany these two are spells and curses. The problems addressed by this kind of magical ritual are mostly practical and personal, though not exclusively so.

The nature of the practical concerns is complex. While the priest may perform acts of sacrifice to uphold and preserve the ordered universe, the householder performs acts on a microcosmic level in the home. The maintenance of an ordered home that safeguards the sacred fire is essential to the preservation of good. Even following the rules of cleanliness adds to the macrocosmic mass of good on the side of the gods. Conversely, disregarding such things will only add to the hoard of evil. While the fight against evil in the Avesta is waged in a practical manner at times, the reasons for that fight are strongly linked to the belief system.

Who performed the high rituals? The Zoroastrian religion, however it may have changed throughout the ages, has always accepted the need for an elite priesthood. We might say that these priests saw themselves as the "good" counterparts of the "evil" sorcerers and witches they so often denounced. This function remains fairly steady as the tradition develops. The function of the Gathic poet-sacrificer can be most closely compared to that of the Rigvedic poet-sacrificer. Their function was social in that it fulfilled a need in a society whose beliefs centered on the sacrifice.

The Young Avestan picture, dating from perhaps half a millennium or more later than that of the Gāthās, may have differed considerably; however, the priest as a person one hired to perform a ritual remained the same. The Videv-dad explains that a priest must be trained and qualified to perform purifica-tions.[20] This traditional role of the priest has remained the same even among modern Zoroastrians.[21] The priest, by the time of the writing of the late Pah-lavi texts, was expected to abide by the traditions of the "church," as is evident by the verbal attacks on the priest Zādspram by his brother, the higher ranking Manushchihr, when Zādspram attempted some small innovation.[22]

On the other hand, the rituals performed by the priests have always taken place in a private setting. Today the *yasna* ceremony is still a private ritual, un-like the Christian Mass, although there are other rituals for the daily religious life of the laity.[23] Few can attend the sacrifice, and some, notably women, never do attend,[24] presumably for fear that the ritual might be nullified by the pres-ence of outsiders or those ritually impure, even if they are Zoroastrians. In short, the *yasna* ceremony is not a community event and has never been one.

The application of the term "magic" to some of the practices in the Zoroas-trian texts must be further clarified. The authors of the Avesta saw themselves as staunch enemies of sorcerers, etc., but they considered their own practices to be within the realm of orderly, beneficial behavior. In fact, the instances where it is most clear that they are practicing their "good magic" is when they are attacking the very same sorcerers with words and actions akin to those of their enemies. To distinguish between the two, it may be useful to apply the standard terminology of "good versus evil" magic.[25] The authors of the Avesta considered good and evil to be contrasting elements in the worship of spiri-tual forces: the good sacrifice to and worship of (the real) gods versus the evil sacrifice to and worship of false gods (demons). The "good" priests sacrificed to the gods either just before dawn or during the day[26] to bring back light and life, Order, and fertility to the world of Ahura Mazdā. I translate the word *asha* and its Old Indic equivalent *rita* as "Order," with a capital letter, because it designated something more than "order" in the English sense of the word. For these ancients, the word *asha* meant a power that upheld and organized the ordered cosmos. It was a power even beyond that of the gods, who were also subject to its laws. "Order" also meant the ritual of the sacrifice, and order on earth, which meant that *asha* operated on a cosmic and a microcos-mic level.[27]

Sacrifice to the demons produced a similar cosmic power that opposed that of the good Order. It was carried out under the cover of night and brought chaos, infertility, disease, and death. In the Gāthās, however, there was even less distinction between the good and bad sacrifices and sacrificers. The Gāthās present bad sacrificers not as demons, but as greedy or incompetent men.

The two kinds of "magic" are the same in method, as they are both coercive and use spells, curses, and magical rites. The authors of the Avesta thought that they practiced the "good" faith tradition, while others were necessarily agents of the Lie: all kinds of sorcerers and demon worshippers. This is similar to the biblical attitudes to other religions as evil and magical. We do not know who the practitioners of "evil magic" of the Avesta actually were; they could have included herbal healers, female health specialists, common magicians, and anyone who prayed to a different god or in a different language.

I must point out that for the authors of the Avesta, often it was not the method of ritual "magic" that was evil; it was the intention that was evil. Like other ancient peoples, the authors of the Avesta relied not only on the help of the gods, but also on the power of spells, curses, exorcisms, and magical rites. These protective methods were in no way considered to be sorcery, or the magic of evildoers, but rather a means of overcoming sorcery to protect the home and family. Thus, in the Avesta, "good magic" was often retaliatory. It was most often used when someone suspected that an evildoer had used magic against one's household and goods. Accordingly, because it sent the evil back to its source, only the witch or sorcerer was to blame if he or she was killed, or suffered some loss as we see below in Yasna 65.8.

Many of the curses in the Yasna are of this type; they are reverse curses that return a planned evil onto the head of its originator, and order evil against a sorcerer or other evildoer whose identity has not yet been determined. For example, Yasna 65.8 specifically asks that the evils be returned to those who were its sources:

YASNA 65.8

The thief, the violator, the robber,
the striker of the Orderly,
the one possessed by sorcerers,
the one who throws a corpse [where he should not],
the covetous [?], the ungenerous,
the one who does not sustain Order, who darkens Order,
the man who is a false teacher possessed by the Lie—
By [this] invigorant let the hostilities go back against him!
By [this] invigorant let the dangers [go back against him] who made them!
Let the dangers go [against him] who made them!

Aside from protecting people against sorcery, rituals were performed for the purpose of renewing and refreshing the cosmic situation and for strengthening good. These rituals were said to be *humaya*, that is, containing "creative magic,"[28] that used the most venerated old spells, such as those from the Gāthās and rituals such as the *haoma* sacrifice. *Haoma*, or *soma* in Vedic ritual, was a plant that was crushed and made into an infusion to be offered to the gods and later drunk by the priests and participants in the sacrifice.[29] There has been much speculation concerning the identity of this plant, which is unknown today. Judging by the evidence, particularly the Vedic evidence, it is likely that this plant was some sort of stimulant. This sacrifice served not only to invigorate the gods, but also to disperse the demons, who seemed to be sensitive to the ringing sound produced by the pounding of the mortar used for crushing the *haoma*.[30] The Vispered extols the "creative magic" of the sacrifice:

VISPERED 12.2–5

We select the ties [?] of good creative magic of the *Ahuna vairiya*,
proclaimed in Orderly fashion [before
and now again] being proclaimed
and of the mortar and pestle pounding the *haoma*,
[the mortar and pestle] moved forth in Orderly fashion [before
and now again] being moved forth, —
and of the words correctly spoken
and the famous words of those like Zarathustra
and of the well-performed deeds,
and of the *barsom* spread out in Orderly fashion
and of the *haoma* pressed in Orderly fashion
and of the Texts of Sacrifice and Praise [the *Gāthās*?]
and of the *daēnā* of the Mazdayasnians[31]
and of the [thoughts] to be thought, the [words] to be spoken,
and the [deeds] to be performed.
For in that way they shall have greater creative magic for us.

We accept these creations as having good creative magic.
We select them as having good creative magic.
We think of them as having good creative magic,
which Ahura Mazdā, sustainer of Order, established,
made prosper [?] by Good Thought, and made grow by Order,
which are the greatest, best, and most beautiful of all things that are.
For in that way they have even greater creative magic for us,
and we shall be more worthy of being invoked
by the Creations of the Life-giving Spirit

when we shall point them out as having creative magic and worthy of being invoked.

May you have good creative magic for us,
O stone mortar, O metal pestle,
when you are turned around, when you are moved forth,
in the house, in the town, in the tribe, and in the land,
in this house, in this town, in this tribe, in this land,
and for us Mazdayasnians when we sacrifice
with firewood, incense, and pleasing of the ritual models.
For in that way they shall be of even greater creative magic for us.

The rituals of the Avesta were thus used both for the direct intervention against evil and as an intrinsic part of the sacrifice performed in order to further the prosperity of the good world, which depended on it. The authors of the Avesta were convinced that sorcerers and other demon worshippers were conducting sacrifices using evil magic for fortifying the Evil Spirit. They considered this most offensive because demon worshippers were using rituals and words just like the worshippers of the gods, but their result was evil. This sort of thinking was very much akin to what we find in the Gāthās, where competing poets use the same techniques, but according to the Gathic poets, their competitors did so for the sake of evil.

The Avestan sacrificer thought that, by his use of "creative magic," he waged an ongoing war with the people who practiced evil magic, but that his own rituals were superior to the evil magic in that their motive was good and pure. Being powerful in magic was a dangerous situation, for only qualified individuals could perform good magic without great risks. For this reason too, we will see that priests in the Avesta were sometimes themselves suspected of performing sorcery. There was, according to the Avesta, a temptation to use magic for evil purposes, or simply because of greed, as we shall see when we review the Avestan categories of evildoers.

CHAPTER 4

GENERAL CONCEPTS OF EVIL IN THE AVESTA

WHAT WAS GOOD and what was evil for the authors of the Avesta? What were their responses to evil? Without delving extensively into the texts at this point, a very simple and general definition of evil in Zoroastrianism is that it is an eternal principle that is opposed to good.[1] Good can be described as an eternal principle that is opposed to evil. "Good" is what is in accordance with Ahura Mazdā's Order (*asha*) and sustains it, and "evil" that which is not in accordance with Order (*asha*) and endeavors to undo it. There is no fundamental distinction between moral and natural evils, because they are both aspects of a single phenomenon. All evil has its source in a force distinct from good.

Ahura Mazdā put preexisting, "fashioned" or "generated" things in their proper places to make an ordered cosmos, and afterward he maintains the universe. The idea of a *creatio ex nihilo*, as we see in Genesis, was not an aspect of early Zoroastrianism.[2] Ahura Mazdā's creative act is therefore to some extent similar to that of the creator god in the Enuma Elish (second millennium BCE), who makes order out of chaos. The Mesopotamian myth, however, features an ancient combat myth with a conflict between the creator god and his opponent, Tiamat, the female Dragon of Chaos, which is not apparent in Iran, although Indic parallels suggest it may have been a feature of Indo-Iranian mythology.[3] Finally, in the Enuma Elish, the gods are also conceived as having their source in chaos, as the dragon is the progenitor of Marduk, the order-producing entity, and they both have bodies made of preexisting matter. In Iran, the source of evil is entirely separate from Ahura Mazdā, the producer of order, and his creations.

The problem of evil is a constant in the Avesta, whether we are examining the oldest texts, the Gāthās, or the relatively later texts that make up the balance of the Avestan corpus. In both, evil is the transgression against or denial of the Order (*asha*) of Ahura Mazdā, or its absence. In the divine world, which in the Gāthās is called that of thought, evildoers are the *daēwa*s, the old Indo-

Iranian gods. In the Young Avesta, they become demons and "those possessed by the Lie"[4] in the world of living beings, which in the Gāthās is called "that which has bones" (e.g., Yasna 28.2). All of these evildoers wish to replace Order with chaos, whose principal expression is the Lie;[5] that is, a lie or deception about what, and whose, the true Order is. One of the purposes of the ritual is to ensure that certain individuals, gods and men, who are possessed by the Lie, are restrained from doing damage or, preferably, are completely suppressed.

The Young Avestan texts convey the same basic message, but because of their much larger volume, in greater detail than the Old Avesta. The Young Avesta contains hymns to numerous gods other than Ahura Mazdā, all of whom play their special roles in combating evil. It also contains stories from the mythical past about hero-sacrificers who upheld Order by their sacrifices, which were accepted by the gods. The Young Avesta also includes the myths of those demons or devious humans whose sacrifices the deities rejected.

The return of chaos caused by the Lie poses a permanent threat to both humans and the gods. In the Gāthās, we find the clear message, well known from the Vedic religion, that humans are instrumental in maintaining Order by the performance of the order-producing ritual. The ritual is represented as a microcosmos corresponding to the macrocosmos of the universe.[6] Its function is to influence or assist the gods in restoring the cosmic order, societal harmony, life, and growth in the world; while removing disorder: death, illness, and other afflictions caused by the Lie.

For their successful sacrifice, the performers expect to be rewarded by tangible goods and boons such as success and happiness, as well as horses, camels, and cows. Part of this reward is that their enemies will be destroyed, and other obstacles to a content and fruitful life removed. The ritual is a means of communicating directly with the gods, and it is a crucial instrument for upholding the Order created originally by God, who needs the sacrifice as much as the humans who perform it.[7]

The authors of the Avesta, seeing themselves as the only legitimate performers of sacrifice, considered other sacrificers illicit usurpers of the ritual. They thought that the "evil sacrificers and poets" wanted to promote disorder, because they were intrinsically bad, having interests at odds with the gods, or because they were incompetent, producing inefficient sacrifices that would therefore backfire and produce the opposite of the desired result.[8] Consequently, there was a microcosmic conflict among sacrificers over the performance of the sacrifice, which mirrored the macrocosmic struggle between good and evil gods. It is evident that, at least in some cases, the rituals and liturgy of both camps were very close, if not identical. What makes one poet "bad" and the other "good" is only the opinion of the author of the poem. We are therefore only looking at the views of the surviving faction.

Poets in both the Rigvedic and Avestan periods were free agents, priests who made a living by offering sacrifices and composing verses for their well-to-do patrons. They received payment in the form of goods, but they also expected rewards from the gods. Thus, they had to convince their benefactors that they were the right men to hire. The priests and poets had to persuade their human patrons to believe that they were more skillful and truthful than their rivals were, and they had to convince the gods that they alone were righteous and deserving of the blessing the gods could bestow. It is important to understand that at this stage in the development of the tradition, just as the priests requested material things from their employers, their requests to the gods were for usable goods and freedom from illnesses and suffering caused by demons and bad humans. Many of these goods were limited. There just was not enough to go around, which resulted in competition.

EVIL IN THE GĀTHĀS

Even without Gnoli's warning that the Gāthās are by no means a complete repository of the religious beliefs of the people who composed them,[9] the small size of the corpus (five poems) makes us realize that they express only a small part of the religion of early Iranians, and a fortiori, of their notions of evil. Nevertheless, it is clear that the Gathic solution to evil was a ritual response.

However, the message of the Gāthās was also very important to the authors of the subsequent Iranian religious literature. The authors of the Young Avesta used selected passages of the Gāthās as powerful mantras, to borrow the Sanskrit term. Many major themes that became prominent in the ninth- and early-tenth-century texts are based on the interpretations of issues found in the Gāthās as well. The Gāthās contain curses too, most often overlooked because scholars have assumed that the poems are the exalted utterances of the prophet, and curses would not be part of his repertoire. As a background to the subsequent discussion, it will be helpful to briefly consider two questions: What solutions did the Gāthās offer to the problems of evil, and how did these arise and develop throughout the text?

The Gāthās approach evil as a force, rather than as an individual; in fact, they do not mention the Evil Spirit as we know him in the later texts (Angra Mainyu).[10] Instead we have the notion of two opposing mental forces (*mainyu*s), which in Yasna 30.3 are called "the twin sleeps," that is, presumably, two dormant or embryonic forces that awake in gods and men much like an in-*spir*-ation:

YASNA 30.3

Thus, those two spirits in the beginning,
which have been renowned as the two twin 'sleeps',[11]
the two thoughts and speeches—
they are two actions: a good and a bad one.
And between those two those who give good gifts
have discriminated rightly, not those who give bad gifts.

When these two spirit forces, one good, and one bad, come together, each individual decides the future and terms of his life, death, and reward or punishment after death by choosing between them.

These two forces are primordial, but at this point they seem to be formless inspirations for good and evil thoughts, words, and deeds, which in the Avesta become the foundations of the theology. This triad is ever-present in the Young Avestan and Pahlavi compositions. It is interesting to note that the actions of either camp are nearly always the same, just infused with what the authors consider good or bad. There are good thoughts, words, and deeds, and bad thoughts, words, and deeds.

Thus, choice became another important component of the Avestan belief system. In this and the following strophe (Yasna 30.4), we find expressed the concept of the total separation of good and evil, which is so prominent from the Old Avestan to the late Pahlavi texts:

YASNA 30.4

Thus, also: whenever the two spirit/inspirations come together
one receives for the first time
both life [for the good] and lack of survival [for the bad]
and [learns] how the existence will be at last:
the worst [existence will be that] of those possessed by the Lie,
while for the sustainer of Order [there will be] best thought.[12]

The two initial *mainyu*s, spirits, though not yet explicitly personified, were themselves able to make choices. This implies that the "good" spirit was capable of making the wrong choice. To what extent the authors of the Gāthās allowed the *mainyu*s to "choose" remains uncertain, however.

In later texts, the Young Avesta and the Pahlavi texts such as the Bunda-hishn, it seems that the authors have decided to make the issue clear. The two *mainyu*s took on more distinct personalities, one *spenta*, "life-giving," the other *angra*, "destructive." They also became surrounded by increasingly concrete myths, so that when the Evil Spirit was given a choice, because of his inherent evil nature he could only "choose" evil, as much as the Good Spirit could only "choose" good. The authors of the Pahlavi texts were of the firm opinion, however, that the Evil Spirit made a conscious evil choice that reflected his nature. In the creation myth in the Bundahishn, the meeting of the two spirits marks the beginning of a battle:

BUNDAHISHN 1.2–3

As it is manifest in the Mazdayasnian tradition[13]:
Ohrmazd was in the highest place in omniscience and goodness for an unlimited time in the light. That light is the throne and place of Ohrmazd. Some say the "Endless Lights." That omniscience and goodness was there for an unbounded time, that is, there were Ohrmazd, his goodness, the Tradition, and the Time of Ohrmazd.[14]
Ahriman was in darkness in the depths with backward knowledge [after the fact?] and desire to kill. His desire to kill is his nature and that darkness his place. Some say "Endless Darkness."

The opposition between pairs is clear in this later text. Ohrmazd, the Avestan Ahura Mazdā, the Good Spirit, is here "omniscient" and good. An omniscient being cannot make wrong choices. The Evil Spirit Ahriman is the opposite: rather than being omniscient, he is "anti-knowledge." The desire to kill is his "nature," not something he chooses. Perhaps the ambiguity of the above Gathic passage was uncomfortable for these later authors, and they were able to clear it up by making the issue of choice just one for the humans, rather than one for both the gods and the humans. In the Gāthās, however, this primordial choice made by the two *mainyu*s foreshadows the state of gods and mortals to come, who never cease having to make choices. According to the Gāthās, the *daēwa*s, or bad gods, made the wrong, evil choices, because they were overcome by the Lie while deliberating—that is, while trying to choose between the two "inspirations." By this choice, they cause damage to the universal Order through bad words, thoughts, and deeds.

YASNA 30.5–6

At the choosing between these two spirits
you, who are possessed by the Lie, would produce the worst [words/actions].
The most Life-giving spirit, which is clad in the hardest stones,
[chose to produce] Order,
and so do whoever shall favor the Ahura by [their] *true* actions,
him, Mazdā, again and again.

Especially the old gods (*daēwa*s) did not discriminate
straight between these two, because deception
would come over them as they were asking one another,
so that they would choose the worst thought.
Thus, they would scramble together to wrath,
with which mortals sicken this existence.[15]

The necessity of making a choice is clear. However, choosing evil does not *produce* evil, rather it allows evil to overtake good. Good is the result of Order, and bad is the result of Disorder, or the Lie. Humans, being inherently good, cannot create evil, a preexisting quality, but they can allow it entrance into their arena. In the Pahlavi texts, the idea of choice is illustrated in the myth of the first man and woman. In this myth from the Bundahishn 15.6–9, reminiscent of the Biblical account of Adam and Eve, the first man and woman make the right choice at first, but under the influence of the Evil Spirit, they finally choose to lie:

BUNDAHISHN 15.6–9

Ohrmazd said to Mashī and Mashiyānī: You are humans. You are the parents of the world of the living. You must perform work and law with perfect thought! Think good thought, speak good speech, perform good action, do not sacrifice to the evil gods [*dēw*s]!
The two of them first thought as follows, when they thought about one another: He/She is human.
And the first deed they did was as follows: When they walked they urinated.
And the first speech they spoke was as follows: Ohrmazd gave [us][16] the water, the earth, the plants, the cattle, the stars, the moon, the sun, and all prosperity whose appearance is from Orderliness.—[That is,] he mentions origin and fruit [cause and effect].
Then the Adversary rushed into their thoughts, and he made their thought

sinful, and they howled: The Foul Spirit gave [us] the water, the earth, the plants, and the other things.

As it is said: that was the first lying speech of theirs that went astray. It was said at the instigation of the evil gods. This was the first bliss the Foul Spirit took from them. By that lying speech they both became possessed by the Lie, and their souls will be in Hell until the Final Body.[17]

The lie they told was that the Evil Spirit, not Ohrmazd, created good things. How they came to lie does not seem to be totally volitional, even in this late text. They were corrupted by evil and fell from their innocent state.

Humans, according to these later Zoroastrian texts, were created by a force devoid of evil, but they could be influenced by the Evil Spirit, who was the originator of evil thoughts, words, and deeds. God's humans were not independently capable of evil; instead, evil was caused by unseen demonic powers.

In the Young Avestan texts, total evil was realized in one entity, the personified Evil Spirit, Angra Mainyu, who had a completely independent will. He was entirely evil because it was his choice to be evil. The malevolent power of the Evil Spirit represented opposition to Order and therefore to the absolute goodness of Ahura Mazdā, which was Order. The human poet-sacrificers assisted the Good Spirit in maintaining this order, but if they did not adhere perfectly to their duties, the disorder of the Evil Spirit would be the result.

Disorder, or chaos, was a fact of the universe, however, and it was represented by darkness, destruction, and death. For the Avestan authors, it was a permanent threat to Order. The scenario presented by the Avesta is one in which there is a constant struggle for dominance between good and evil. There was no opportunity to slacken regarding the sacrifice and other rituals, for maintaining Order required the attentions of both humans and the gods on a regular basis. Disorder, represented by disease and death, was constantly threatening the world, and the only way to maintain Order was by revitalizing the world through sacred ritual and sacrifice. Both gods and humans had to take part in this continuous resistance. Otherwise, the universe would be lost to chaos.[18]

The battle between good and the demonic forces of an evil realm was fought not only by means of the sacrifice, but also by apotropaic and exorcistic practices, as they are prescribed in the Young Avestan texts. Evil, having its source in the Evil Spirit, was not internalized in humans. The authors of the Avesta saw themselves as warriors in the army of the gods, fighting against their enemies, who could be supernatural or real beings in league with the Evil Spirit, such as demons (daēwas), "sorcerers," "witches," and various human evildoers, or unseen enemies like old age, disease, and death. Thus, dualism in the Young Avesta is clearer than in the Gāthās: the two Young Avestan spirits act in opposite ways, and they correspond as complete opposites. The Gāthās do not present such a systematic scheme, as the Evil Spirit is not mentioned by name as such, rather the two *mainyu*s are usually referred to as one "good" or "vitalizing" and performing good deeds, etc., the other "bad" and performing bad deeds.[19] Nevertheless, this was the origin of the later, more developed myth.

Who, then, were the individuals in the divine and human domains who made bad choices, and thereby threatened, and still constantly threaten, Ahura Mazdā's order in the divine and human worlds? The Gāthās answer this question relatively substantially. In the divine world, it is the *daēwa*s, bad gods or demons, who have chosen wrongly, and so contribute to the worsening of existence, and in the human world it is their followers. In Yasna 32.3, the origin of the *daēwa*s is said to be "an evil thought," that is, the opposite of the order that was thought by Ahura Mazdā. However, who thought this bad thought? Logically it would be Ahura Mazdā's evil counterpart, which would seem to point to the existence of a prototypical Evil Spirit, who in the same strophe seems to be identified with the Lie and a "distraught mind."

YASNA 32.3

But you, O old gods, are [all] the seed [issued] from an evil thought,
and [so is] the great one who is sacrificing to you:
[issued] from the Lie and [your] distraught mind, —
ever since [your] ancient *or* duplicating[?] blunders[?],
on account of which you have been heard on [only] a seventh of the earth.

The identity of "the great one" in this strophe, who sacrifices to the *daēwa*s, is not clear. Conceivably it is the Evil Spirit who sacrifices to the *daēwa*s in the same way that, in the Young Avesta, Ahura Mazdā sacrifices to lesser gods such as Anāhitā, the Frawashis, Mithra, Tishtriya, Vayu, and others,[20] to help increase their powers. If this is another example of the opposition between pairs, then this act would fit in well, but that must remain a speculation for now.

The most devastating deed gods or humans can do is the performance of a wrong or inefficient sacrifice,[21] because that would strengthen the forces of evil, as in Yasna 45.3:

YASNA 45.3

And so I shall proclaim the *first* [announcement?] of [= about?] this existence,
[the ordinance?] which the knowing one, Mazdā Ahura, has spoken to me:
those of you who shall *not* produce it in this way, the poetic thought,
the way this [ordinance?] is and I shall think and speak it,
for those the last word of this existence will be "woe!"

The Gathic poet blamed these bad priests and poets for a bad performance, but it is not clear who they were. Certainly they were not only those who offered sacrifices to the *daēwa*s, for elsewhere not only are the *daēwa*s themselves portrayed as trying to obtain Ahura Mazdā's favor, presumably by a sacrifice (Yasna 32.1), but also other human sacrificers, who, according to the Gathic poet, do not produce good hymns but rather ruin the ritual (Yasna 32.9):[22]

YASNA 32.1

And for his [bliss?] the family implores him
and the household together with the community [implores him for] his [bliss].
The old gods [*daēwa*s], to my resentment, [implore him] for that bliss of *his*,
    Ahura Mazdā's.
Let *us* be *your* messengers, but you keep a firm hold on *them*,
[because they are the ones] who are being hostile to you all.

YASNA 32.9

The one of bad announcing diverts [my] songs of fame;
he [diverts my] guiding thought, [source?] of [my] livelihood, by [his]
    "announcements."
He has robbed me of [the gain of my] ritual, the esteemed[?] gain[?] of my
    good thought.
By that utterance of *my* inspiration I am now complaining to you all,
to you, O Mazdā, and to Order.

These are "hymns" of complaint against competitors. How did the follower of Order get the gods to hear his plea? As is the case in the later texts, the Gāthās present gods who are good, yet they can be tempted or coerced by sacrifice. The Gathic poet lodged his complaint against both the "bad" sacrificer and the "old gods" who could also ask favors. The result of the sacrifice by the "bad" sacrificer was that there were fewer benefits for the Gathic poet. He resented this and tried, by his good counsel, to make the gods recognize him and to reject his rivals.

The poet of the Gāthās also claimed that the rival poet ruined his hymns by reciting a bad hymn because of his desire to "see the cow and the sun," and to make the one possessed by the Lie appear seemly.[23] It is likely that the idea of the evil eye was present at this time. The Gathic poet accused the rival poet of wishing to look upon the cow and the sun, which represented sustenance derived from the animal world, and that derived from the plant world, with the evil eye.[24] The evil eye is a power produced from envy. Again, the dispute was over worldly resources. The "good" poet, representing truth and orderliness, was contrasted with the "bad" poet, who represented lies and chaos. The complaint went on to claim that the one possessed by the Lie is he who squanders away the pastures and who physically attacked the follower of Order. The Avestan poet appealed to the gods that the cow was being abused and that the sacred *haoma*, a plant central to the sacrifice, was being burned under the pretext of purifying it (Yasna 32.10–14).

YASNA 32.10

That "hero" diverts *my* songs of fame who declares the worst in order to see with his evil eyes[25] the cow and the sun,—
and who makes out those possessed by the Lie
to be the ones abiding by the established rules,
and who lays waste the pastures and who holds unyieldingly his weapon
against the sustainer of Order.

YASNA 32.11

Just those shall divert [my] livelihood from me
who have distinguished those possessed by the Lie with great [gifts?],
the "ladies" and "lords." The possession of wealth/heritage[?] shall go away
for those who shall, O Mazdā, from the best thought of the sustainer of
     Order.

YASNA 32.12

[Because it is] a "renown" by which mortals
move [their] men away from the best action,
Mazdā says to these, who will divert the livelihood of [my] cow

[that those utterances/actions are] "bad"
by which the "mumbler" has chosen gluttony to Order[26]
and [that their] command over bad desires[?] [is nothing but] the Lie, —

YASNA 32.13

the command by which the glutton seeks a seat in the abode of worst thought,
[as do] the [other] destroyers of this state of existence and those who,
     O Mazdā, ever complain—to my pleasure—
about [*my*] messenger-smoke, that of *your* master of the poetic thought,
     which shall keep them from the sight of Order.

YASNA 32.14

The "glutton" and the "poets" deposit [their] "guiding thoughts" here in *his*
     cord-work,
[their] "miracle-works," by daily pouring,
when they are ready to be help for the one possessed by the Lie
and when the cow has been mistreated
to [the point of] being killed [by him] who "purifies" the *haoma* by burning.[27]

The *daēwa*s of the Gāthās are ambiguous without the interpretations that
the Young Avestan and Pahlavi texts offer. In the Gāthās, there is a contest between poets, but we hear only one side. They presumably accuse each other of
bad poetry and rituals, and entreat the gods to accept their own good poetry.[28]
The very idea that the gods have to choose between rival poets is important.
This is reflected in later Young Avestan texts where the demons perform sacrifices for the gods so that they may gain boons. This is a common theme in
the Vedas as well.[29] The poet-sacrificers fight using their poetry, and the win-
ner is chosen, not so much on moral reasons but the fact of victory itself. The
sacrifice that the Gathic authors speak of is a real contest, just like the chariot
race.[30] The gods should win in the cosmic battle, just as their supporters, the
good priests, should win rewards for the performance of the sacrifice. The
characteristic of the Vedic and Avestan poet-sacrificer that made him so different from the demon-besieged supporter of Order (*ashawan*), in the post-
Gathic texts, is that in the Gāthās the opponents are basically alike. It is for
the gods to recognize the advantages of choosing one over the other.[31]
     How was the poet-sacrificer to deal with these beings, the evil gods and
bad humans? One way was to include disparaging remarks about them in his
poetry, what may be described as the precursors of curses or spells that appear

in the Young Avesta. Thus, in Yasna 49.3, the poet says he will "ban from the community" teachers of such evil doctrine and their followers, and, in Yasna 49.4, he describes the effect of their actions:

YASNA 49.3

And thus, O Mazdā, Order has been deposited for this one[?]
for [it to be his] chosen belief, for it to be vitalized,
but the Lie in order for [it to be his] false teaching in order to cause harm.
Those [are the things] to be expected from the union of [= with] good
    thought.
I am banning [here and now] from [their] following all those possessed by
    the Lie.

YASNA 49.4

Those who by [their] bad "guiding thought"
shall increase fury and obstruction
by [the utterances of] their own tongues,
who tend no cattle among those who do,
and not one of whom has overcome bad deeds by good deeds,
they shall determine as old gods [what is in reality]
the vision-soul of the one possessed by the Lie.

The result of the bad thoughts and words of the rival poets is that the "Lie" is vitalized, increasing fury and obstructing the good things in life. The remark about "those who do not raise cattle among those who do" hints at the conflicts there may have been between the pastoral and the agricultural communities. Naturally, this assumes the existence of an agricultural community, but this rebuke could also be meant for those who steal cattle.[32]

Particularly significant for the development of later doctrine is Yasna 49.2, where we are told that the one possessed by the Lie is forever separate from Order:

YASNA 49.2

Thus, the evil belief of this "binder"[33] is making me angry.
The one possessed by the Lie is ever separated from Order!
He has *not* seen [as he pretends?] that life-giving Ārmaiti is for *him/this one*[?]
nor, O Mazdā, has he consulted a good thought.

There may be an early manifestation of dualism in the above verse. It declares that the Lie is always distinct from Order. It is likely that the doctrine was developing even at the time of the composition of the Gāthās, rather than being a later innovation, as some scholars have theorized.[34] We only hear one side of the argument here, yet in the complaint we learn a lot about the "opposing group." They have similar means of appealing to the gods, and they seem to have a similar goal—that is, the acquisition of goods. It is clear from the appeal to the gods that they choose well, and that they do not accept the rival poet's offerings, that the opposing groups were more similar than different. This was apparently the reason for having to point out the differences.

In reality, the Gāthās, being only five poems of one strain of an early Iranian tradition, cannot possibly give definitive answers about the ideas of the time. We may be able to deduce some models from them, but ultimately much of it is speculation. However, the Gāthās were foundational to the Young Avesta, where we see the possible interpretations of these archaic poems. The explanations I have offered are based on those ideas found in the Young Avesta. Interpreting early compositions based on later ones is not wholly reliable. However, one may certainly consider the influence of the older compositions upon the younger.

For the authors of the Young Avesta, the most important aspect of the Gāthās was their place in the ancient times: in the beginning of mythic history. This lent them authority and miraculous power, for the poems were thought to have been given to Zarathustra in early mythical times for him to use to combat evil. Not only the spells of the Gāthās, but any part of them could be used as powerful mantric formulas against agents of evil in both worlds, the visible and the invisible. In one sense, then, by becoming the first human poet-sacrificer, Zarathustra also became the first human (good) magician, who was instructed by Ahura Mazdā, the primeval poet-sacrificer and magician.[35] Together they used their magico-ritual powers to fight and overcome the Evil Spirit, the primeval and most powerful sorcerer, along with his minions, the *daēwa*s and evil human poet-sacrificers and sorcerers. The practical value of the Gāthās was thus its magical potency, as will be apparent in what follows.

EVIL IN THE YOUNG AVESTA

The Young Avesta provides us with a rich source for the study of the concept of evil in early Iran. Now we finally get to meet the evil beings and natural evils that the Iranians feared. Harmful, or potentially harmful, supernatural beings comprise, on the one hand, evil gods, or demons (*daēwa*s), and the supernatural variants of "sorcerers" and "witches," as well as agents of sickness and death, notably the female demon of pollution or dead matter (Nasush). On the other hand are what we might term evil natural phenomena—that is, celestial beings that cause drought and other natural disasters.

The *daēwa*s are the Indo-Iranian gods (Indic *deva*), who came to be regarded as causing chaos rather than cosmos, apparently for making bad choices and performing a bad sacrifice,[36] but the details of the switch from good to evil beings are not known.

The female demon of pollution, Nasush (Carrion)—female because of its grammatically female gender—attacks the body when it comes into contact with dead matter, particularly in the case of dead bodies and bleeding, notably menstruation and other female bleeding, but also in connection with the trimming of hair and nails.[37]

The text that discusses evil in the greatest detail is the Videvdad. It is the longest book in the Avesta (twenty-one chapters), and it is the only one that has been preserved in its entirety, judging by the description of it in Dēnkard 8. Its main concern is how to avoid impurity and pollution—as defined in Zoroastrianism—and how to punish transgressors and violators of the purity laws.

The collections of purity laws proper are framed by several chapters of myths of an etiological nature, explaining how evil entered human society and how it can be removed. Chapter 1 contains the most explicitly "dualistic" text in all of the Avesta: the account of how Ahura Mazdā made the Iranian lands and the good things he gave to them, after which the Evil Spirit created terrible evils to oppose Ahura Mazdā's goodness.[38] Among these are, in this order: the Dragon, the ten months of winter, agnosticism,[39] spittle and phlegm,[40] the witch that followed the hero Kersāspa, anal intercourse, the exposure of corpses, sorcerers, magicians, the burning of corpses, untimely menses and untimely heat, and the winter created by demons (Videvdad 1.2–19).[41]

Chapter 2 contains the myth of Yima, first king, and his eugenic *vara*, a kind of fortress in which the best specimens of humanity, animals, etc., were enclosed to avoid being killed by terrible winters, while all individuals with flaws were excluded, as their defects were regarded as marks put on them by the Evil Spirit.[42]

Chapter 3 continues the "dualistic" description of the world, this time the things that please and displease the earth. These first three chapters set the stage for the more technical chapters to come.

The Videvdad is concluded by four more mythological chapters. Chapter 19 contains the myth of Zarathustra's overcoming the Evil Spirit, and chasing him and his minions back into hell. Chapter 20 contains the story of how Ahura Mazdā gave the first healer, Thrita, healing powers. Chapter 21 consists of curses of evil and blessings of good things. Chapter 22 contains the myth of how the Evil Spirit, upon seeing Ahura Mazdā's perfect creation, made 99,999 illnesses and how the god Airyaman managed to heal the creation.[43] The evils introduced in the three introductory chapters are of various types: pollutions, evil beings (both supernatural and natural), and natural disasters.

As if setting the scene for the bulk of the Videvdad, for the first time we encounter the sins of anal intercourse, exposure of corpses, burning of corpses, and untimely menses, as evils of great consequence. Anal intercourse, in particular, is never mentioned in the Yasna or the Yashts. The goddess Ashi made it clear that she was opposed to men who were infertile, and although that was in connection with their inability to impregnate women, the fact remains that infertility seemed to bother her the most:

YASHT 17.59

The third complaint that she complained, good Ashi, the tall:
This is the grossest act that men perform when commanded,
[namely] that they lead girls [from their homes]
[and then] for a long time approach them without making them pregnant.
What shall I do about these!
Shall I go forth to heaven? Shall I burrow into the earth?

The Pahlavi text the Dādestān ī Dēnīg (questions 71–76), explains that anal intercourse was instituted by the forces of evil to prevent the semen of men from mingling with women and producing the desired result: the renewal and furthering of life in the service of good, and instead causes the progress of mankind to come to an end.[44]

Although menses in general was a demon-given condition, as was illness, untimely menses was considered a particularly ominous state of being.[45] By this time, it was well understood that a woman was fertile after the passing of her menstrual period, so there was some good gained by this condition, but untimely menses was a sign of an illness that produced infertility. The fear of a state of infertility was thus most likely the force that inspired the classification of homosexuality and untimely menses as great evils.

Almost as harmful was the burial of the corpses of men and dogs in the earth (Videvdad 3.8). Although the Yasna and the Yashts mention "corpse throwers" as a great evil, what they were is not explained.[46] The next chapter deals not with evildoers, but with naturally occurring evils. I have presented it first so that the reader may have a clearer picture of the range of things that are considered evil. While we may tend to associate evil with a moral or volitional decision, this was not the case in the Avesta.

CHAPTER 5

"NATURALLY" OCCURRING EVILS

IN THE TITLE OF THIS CHAPTER I have placed the word "naturally" in quotes because what we consider natural occurrences, such as old age, disease, and death, as well as natural disasters, were not at all "natural" for the authors of the Avesta. For them, these things were caused by demons, or they were initiated by the Evil Spirit himself. Ahura Mazdā, the Good Spirit, produced only good things, while the Evil Spirit, Angra Mainyu, countered his good acts with evil acts. What modern insurance policies term as "acts of God" — that is, floods, tornados, droughts, etc. — the authors of the Avesta would call "acts of the demons." Naturally occurring evils were thought to be the result of demonic influence, rather than the fault of humans. Nevertheless, humans could still cause pollutions that displeased the gods. Some natural conditions, especially menstruation, could be the cause of harshly punishable offenses if the pollution were not contained according to the law. Natural disasters could sometimes be the result of offending a good god by withholding a sacrifice, or by an improper sacrifice. Any naturally occurring evil can thus have serious consequences beyond the evil itself.

Humans were considered responsible in most cases for the control of evil if it had to do with the body. A woman was responsible for keeping her menstrual and birth blood under control. She was to blame if it contaminated anything. In the case of a dead body, the person who died was no longer responsible for what happened to his or her body, but family, villagers, or even a passerby who saw a body became the responsible party or parties. Disease, as we will see, was caused by demonic possession and had to be treated by exorcism.[1]

OLD AGE AND DISEASE

In view of such concepts, the infirmities of old age, disease, and death were obviously great concerns of the authors of the Avesta. These plagues of humanity were thought to be the creation of the Evil Spirit: as Ahura Mazdā gave health, youth, and life, Angra Mainyu gave disease, old age, and death. Although old age and death could not be prevented, at least premature death could be avoided. During the "golden age" when Yima reigned as the first king, humanity was not cursed with these afflictions. Even old age and death were nonexistent, and both Yima and his father never looked more than fifteen years old, the age Zoroastrians considered the peak of strength and beauty:

YASNA 9.5

Under Yima the brave's command
there was never cold, never heat,
there was never old age, never death,
never envy set in place by the *daēwa*s.
Fifteen [years] in shape the two went forth,
father and son each,
as long as Yima with good herds, Vīwanghwant's son,
would stay in command.

The appearance of old age was another victory for evil, because the disabilities and breaking down of the body presaged demon-given death.

In Bundahishn 4.10, we see that disease and death entered the world because of the contamination of the Evil Spirit. Although this is a later text, it contains many of the older myths, among them the Zoroastrian story of creation. Its description of the entrance of the Evil Spirit into Ahura Mazdā's world echoes the plight of the body upon death. The image of the fly was the form in which Nasush (Carrion), the demon of dead matter, entered the body. The Evil Spirit caused disease to befall the bodies of the first human, the first animal, and the first plant.

The pure beings created by Ahura Mazdā were thus contaminated by a demonic entry into the previously trouble-free world. From the sky to the earth, the entire world became polluted by the entering evil creatures so that the creation became broken and sick. The cures found in the Avesta can thus be better understood if one recognizes the Avestan beliefs concerning the etiologies of diseases.

According to the authors of the Avesta, disease has its source in the Evil Spirit alone, and being diseased meant that one was possessed by the demon who was the vehicle of that particular disease. For this reason, exorcism was the main cure for illnesses. In much the same way, on the macrocosmic level, sacrifice on a regular basis was necessary for the health of the universe. Purity on the personal level was a similar means for achieving health and ousting the demons that caused disease. In the Bundahishn, the entrance of the Evil Spirit into the pristine world of Ahura Mazdā caused a "sickening" of the world by attacking each part of it with disease, pestilence, or corruption:[2]

BUNDAHISHN 4.15–20

And [the Foul Spirit] let loose evil animals [*khrafstar*s][3] upon the earth. In that manner, the bony [creations] were filled with them,[4] biting and venomous evil animals, such as dragons and snakes, scorpions and lizards, tortoises and frogs, so that the earth was not free from evil animals even [the amount of] a needle-point.

And the earth said: "For this creation they set in place, my revenge will come upon these vengeful ones!"

And he brought poison upon the plant in such a manner [that] it dried out immediately.

And the spirit of the plant said: "It was by that respect[5] of his that Ohrmazd made the plant grow."

And he let loose upon the kine[6] and Gayōmard greed and need, danger, pain and disease, lust, and sloth.

Before he came to the kine, Ohrmazd gave the kine healing bang to eat, and he smeared it before its eyes so that the evil, damage, and discomfort from the striking might be less. It immediately became weak and sick, and its milk came out, and it passed away.

The notion of an evil spirit causing sickness to the creation is thus part of the cosmic scheme, because as the world becomes sickened, being possessed by the Evil Spirit, so the individual is sickened when possessed by a demon. The purification and renewal of the world by sacrifice was recreated on a microcosmic scale in the ritual purification of the body.

Videvdad 22 tells the history of the creation of disease by the Evil Spirit. Ahura Mazdā explains to Zarathustra that when he created the beautiful material world, the evil Angra Mainyu looked at it and created 99,999 diseases to spoil it. Ahura Mazdā himself explains that the Evil Spirit, by giving the "evil eye" to the creation of Ahura Mazdā, was able to sicken it:

VIDEVDAD 22.1–2

Ahura Mazdā said to Spitāma Zarathustra:
I, Ahura Mazdā, who set in place good things,

when I made that house, beautiful, luminous, visible afar,
going up, going far away,
then the villain looked at me,
then the villain made against me 99 diseases, 9,900, and 90,000,
he, the Evil Spirit full of destruction.
So may you heal me, Life-giving Sacred Thought,[7]
you of great munificence!

Although the Yashts do not mention it in the below passage where the sick
or deformed are banned from taking part in the sacrifice, and from receiving
libations offered to the goddess, the next passage from the Videvdad offers
the reason. It is the special origin of old age and decrepitude that is given as
the reason for keeping diseased, malformed, and decrepit individuals from the
sacrifice, which they would spoil:

YASHT 5.92

Let not drink of this my libation:
. . . someone with fever, a fat person, . . . someone with pimples,[8]
or a woman or a qualified [man] who does not perform the Gāthās,
or a leper whose body has been secluded.

YASHT 5.93

I do not accept those libations of which [females] drink for my sake
who are blind, deaf, . . . epileptic,
carrying the mark [made] with *that* mark . . .

YASHT 17.54

Thus said good Ashi, the tall:
May no one partake in these libations of mine
which they repay me [for my favors]:
neither a man with blocked semen,
nor a whore beyond her period,
nor a tender child,
nor girls not yet approached by men.

and out of Yima's eugenic *vara*:

VIDEVDAD 2.29

May no one with humps, in front or in the back,
nor an impotent or a . . . ,
nor a driveling one, deceitful one,
one with pustules, or a crooked one,
nor one with irregular teeth,
or one with blotches whose body has been excluded,
nor any of the other marks that are the marks
of the Evil Spirit placed on man.

Priestly concern that the sacrifice should be perfect and, in addition, reach the god for whom it was intended, resulted in priests' strict regulations governing who should be allowed to participate. We see that they excluded several types of persons from the sacrifice, especially those with bodily defects of some kind, ostensibly the mark of the Evil Spirit upon them. There were also several aspects of human evil discussed above, notably infertility, which were disqualifications. While Yasht 5.87, a hymn to Ardwī Sūrā Anāhitā (a goddess who presides over many female functions) invites requests from healthy women and girls, this does not mean that they can take part in the performance of the sacrifice.

The interesting idea here is that these conditions are by no means considered the fault of the afflicted person. There is no sense that they are caused by sin (or karma, as the Hindus would say). A person need not have been "deserving" of these sufferings, so why would such a person be banned from receiving the libations of the goddess? This is a uniquely Zoroastrian view. Although willful disregard of the pollution taboos was a moral downfall, becoming afflicted by any pollution, which all have their source in the Evil Spirit, was being "marked" and thus fouled by evil. Moral faults or "sins" were not necessary elements. Pollution itself was an unfortunate and at times inadvertent condition that reflected one's connection with the demonic to some degree or other. Pollutions were offensive to the gods, but there were rituals that could remove many of them. Some pollutions—such as bodily deformities, leprosy, blindness, deafness, etc.—were, however, permanent. Old age, although a condition caused by the Evil Spirit, was not a polluting condition, perhaps because of its universal nature.

Along with conditions we generally recognize as disease, the Avesta included natural female states such as menstruation, menopause, infertility, and perhaps virginity[9] as undesirable. Women, we shall see, were subject to suspicions because of the perception that they were easily allied with evil. They were good and useful to the creation in that they could produce offspring; therefore, infertile states, such as menopause or prepubescence, were considered less desirable. Although the above natural female states such as menstruation are what the Avesta would consider "natural" evils, I have explained them under the section on female agents of evil. The reason is that they were very often linked with a more volitional evil.[10]

Beauty was also valued as good, not just because of aesthetics. The creation was originally good and beautiful, so all ugliness had to have come from the Evil Spirit. Irregularities such as crooked teeth or limbs thus came under the label of deformity and disease. Although the persons suffering from the above defects may otherwise have been believers, the authors of the Avesta considered these maladies and cosmetic differences a mark of the Evil Spirit. Therefore, they excluded persons thus affected from the sacrifice and from receiving its benefits.

The Yasna, the Yashts, and the Videvdad generally agree that disease is caused not by the gods, but by demons. In the Yashts, however, we are warned that the gods, too, may cause disease among their opponents. Thus, Verthragna, as Mithra's helper and enforcer, strides between the battle lines, consulting with Mithra and Rashnu, deliberating:

YASHT 14.47

We sacrifice to Verthragna, set in place by Ahura [Mazdā],
who strides between the ordered battle lines back and forth,
consulting with Mithra and Rashnu:
Who belies Mithra/the contract?
Who transgresses against Rashnu?
To whom shall I apportion, having the power [to do so], sickness and
    destruction?

These martial gods could bring various diseases as well as death to their enemies. However, the origin of these misfortunes was the Evil Spirit alone. The gods only acted as judges, and dispensed punishments in this way. Ahura Mazdā, however, was never depicted meting out such punishments.

THE CONTAMINATION OF DEATH

The Videvdad, the most important Avestan source of knowledge of evil and its causes, defines evil largely in terms of purity and pollution. Just as evil originally entered the world through contamination from the Evil Spirit, so evil continues to plague the world by the possession of good things by demons. This is most vividly expressed in the attitudes toward death.

The methods the Zoroastrians used for dealing with corpses has been a subject of great interest because of laws forbidding the burial or burning of corpses. Dead bodies are considered impure in most cultures for the good reason that they are a source of disease and that putrefaction is repellent. Corpses are the source of ritual pollution as well in most religions, but the Videvdad presents perhaps the most rigid and complex system of beliefs and rituals regarding the dead. The reasons are many, but most importantly, while in many religions ritual pollution is a sort of dirtiness, for the authors of the Avesta it was more serious. The body is pure in itself, unless it is somehow ritually contaminated. However, when it dies, Carrion, the demon of dead matter, is free to enter it, causing the dead body to become entirely polluted. Death was thus the possession of the body by a demon. Therefore, the rituals surrounding it were precise and dangerous. Death was a problem involving the community as a whole, because the contamination could endanger not just the priests, but also anyone who might be exposed to the body, or even have indirect contact through some other person. Ritual specialists undertook the perilous task of the disposal of a corpse. These were the corpse bearers, the priests who performed exorcistic rituals, and dogs, who were considered demon-repellant.[11]

Videvdad 7 explains how and when the corpse demon comes to invade a body, and what it looks like. Directly after death, as soon as the soul leaves the body, the corpse demon rushes in from the northern lair of the demons. It is an ugly demon in the form of a raging fly, knock-kneed and with flat buttocks. It buzzes endlessly, like the foulest of *khrafstars* (Videvdad 7.2). It stays in the dead body until the performance of the *sagdīd* (literally "dog-view") ritual, in which a dog is taken to look upon the corpse. The dog, being the helper of the gods who drive away demons, is by his glance able to scare off and repel the corpse demon.

VIDEVDAD 7.2A

Until a dog looks at [them] or nibbles [at them]
or a flesh-eating bird flies up at him.
Then, when a dog looks at them or nibbles [at them]
or a flesh-eating bird flies up at him,
this lie-demon Carrion rushes back to the northern directions
in the form of a disgusting fly, knob-kneed, flat-assed, . . . driveling,
like the most repulsive evil animals.

Another way to expel the corpse demon was to place the corpse on a high place where the carrion-eating birds could fly onto it and dispose of the contaminated flesh (Videvdad 7.2a). The proper way to dispose of a corpse was to take it off to a rocky area away from any life, and especially away from water and fire, then to tie down the corpse by its own hair or its feet so that the bones could not be dragged around by animals (Videvdad 6.45–47). After carrion eaters consumed the body, the bones were most likely collected and carefully buried. Protection of the purity of the earth was the main goal, but water might also be affected; therefore, burial of a body in the ground was a great sin. Although the Videvdad forbade this transgression in the strongest of terms, it allowed for expiation until the period of two years was over, then it became an inexpiable offence (Videvdad 3.36–39).

This held for the bodies of both dogs and humans, because dogs, with their important demon-repelling skills, had nearly the same status as humans. The demon was then forced out of the body and it had to return to its lair in the northern regions, where evil had its stronghold. After the demon of dead matter was expelled, the body remained ritually impure, but more in the sense of being filthy, rather than being capable of contagion via demonic possession. It was still treated with extreme care because of the possibility for repossession. The exorcistic rituals concerning dead bodies took on overwhelming importance because they were central to the fight against the Evil Spirit in this world, death being his most powerful weapon.

Moving the corpse to the proper area was a most dangerous job. After the *sagdīd* ritual was performed, the corpse bearers would move the body. Although the Videvdad does not mention exactly how the corpse was to be carried, later traditions required two men, joined together by a string, to move the body. Carrying a body alone was considered a certain invitation to the corpse demon to enter the living body from any of the openings:

VIDEVDAD 3.14

Let no one carry alone what is dead.
But if he carries alone something that is dead,
for certain the corpse will contaminate [him]
from the nose, from the eye, from the tongue,
from the jaw, from the penis, from the anus.
This lie-demon, Carrion, will then rush upon their nails.
Afterward they become impure forever and eternity.

A person who attempted to carry a body alone was considered impure for eternity, with the exception of dire circumstances, such as if one had to save a body of water from a corpse by removing it, yet one had no companion to help (Videvdad 6.26–29).

VIDEVDAD 6.26–29

O Orderly maker of the world of the living with bones,
if these Mazdayasnians, while walking, running, riding, or driving,
come upon a body in running water,
how should these Mazdayasnians behave?

Then Ahura Mazdā said:
Having loosened the shoes, laid down the clothes,
they should wait, O Zarathustra.
One should go forth, take up the dead from the water,
from water reaching him to the calves,
from water reaching him to the knees,
from water reaching him to the waist,
from water the depth of a man,
until he reaches the dead body.
O Orderly maker of the world of the living with bones,
and if this corpse is dissolving and rotting,
how should these Mazdayasnians behave?
Then Ahura Mazdā said:
However much of it they can grasp by the hands,
this much they should take out of the water,
they should deposit on dry earth,
and they will not incur sins against the waters
for throwing the bones or hairs about,
or throwing excrements, urine, or blooded matter about.

A person who touched a corpse needed to be purified through the *barshnūm*,[12] a nine-night purification and exorcism ceremony. An area contaminated by a corpse could become purified after a year, as long as the corpse was not buried. A buried corpse rendered the area impure for fifty years, and it was thought to introduce demons into the earth (Videvdad 3.8). Although a rocky hill would be the preferable place to dispose of a demon-infested body, such a place was not always available to the community. The alternative was a tall structure called a *dakhma*. It was built in such a way as to try to contain dead matter, and at the same time make the bodies available to carrion-eating birds. If a corpse was placed on a *dakhma*, the spot was rendered impure until the corpse was fully reduced to dust:

VIDEVDAD 7.53–54

O Orderly maker of the world of the living with bones,
Where is the *daēwa*, where is he who sacrifices to the *daēwa*s?
Where is it the *daēwa*s run together?
Where is it the *daēwa*s come together?
Where do the *daēwa*s run together in the Turian lands
for the striking of fifty by striking a hundred,
for the striking of a hundred by striking a thousand,
for the striking of a thousand by striking ten thousand,
for the striking of ten and by striking countless ones.

Then Ahura Mazdā said:
In these *dakhma*s, O Zarathustra of the Spitāmas,
these structures that are built up all over this earth,
in which dead men are deposited,
there is the *daēwa*, there is he who sacrifices to the *daēwa*s.
That is where the *daēwa*s run together.
That is where the *daēwa*s come together.
There the *daēwa*s run together in the Turian lands
for the striking [of] . . . countless ones.

VIDEVDAD 7.55–58

In these *dakhma*s, O Zarathustra of the Spitāmas,
these *daēwa*s chew and throw away,
just as in this life you men might prepare
cooked food and eat cooked meat . . .
For this is the supporter [?] of the *daēwa*s
as long as this stench is with them.
In these *dakhma*s there arise pain, itch, fever, stings . . .
In these *dakhma*s men become
the most destructive of one another after the sun has set.

Considering that dead bodies contained powerful demons, the *dakhma* was a place of great evil. It may be possible that the word *dakhma* referred to above-ground tombs, but we cannot be certain. However, it was thought that these places attracted demons, demon-sacrificers, and other demonic people, such as witches and sorcerers. They were meeting places for these evil forces, especially after nightfall, when the powers of evil were believed to naturally increase. Judging by the contents of Videvdad 7.58, it is possible that the demons ate dead bodies and chewed the bones of the dead. This is a common belief in India concerning crematoriums, which were haunted at night by fiends and flesh-eating demons, the Rākshasas. The *dakhmas* were also breeding places of disease and ill will.

A serious problem concerning women was the stillbirth of a baby, a condition that necessarily exposed the mother to a dead body; in fact, her body contained dead matter, as did a *dakhma* (Videvdad 5.51).[13] Because of the intimate contact with the dead infant, a mother was in effect possessed by a demon, as contact with dead matter was believed to cause a demon to enter the body.

Fascinating and unexpected details arise concerning death, including the concept that dead bodies are not all equally contaminating. Some dead bodies were never considered dead matter (Avestan *nasu*, Middle Persian *nasay*) in a ritual sense. For example, animals butchered ritually or animals that were hunted by a Mazdayasnian (a Zoroastrian) were never *nasu*. In an unexpected twist, the most highly contaminated bodies were those of the most righteous, starting with the holy priests of the religion and continuing down the scale via the other members of the good religion and dogs,[14] down to the least impure: the corpse of an evil man (Videvdad 5.28–38).[15]

One would naturally think that the bodies of the evil people would be more contaminating, but this is not the case, as we saw above in Videvdad 5.36. The Videvdad also tells us that the dead bodies of "people of other beliefs, other teachings" defile no more than that of a dried frog who has been dead for a year.

Clearly, the cause of the contamination was the demon of dead matter that possessed the body. Therefore, we may try to think as a demon would. It is a greater victory for the demon to possess the body of a person who during life has carefully avoided pollution and evil, such as a priest. Later texts explained why the bodies of the faithful and those of dogs were possessed by this demon, while those of evil men and animals were not. This, indeed, was a criticism voiced by the heretic Abālish in the ninth-century text, Gizistag Abālish:[16]

> The sixth question [the heretic Abālish asked] was, "It is clearly revealed, and everyone is of the same opinion, that the [dead] bodies of the righteous, who are honest and doers of good deeds, are more pure and holy than those of the sinful doers of evil deeds. [But] you say that the dead bodies of the evil ones,

the non-Iranian doers of sin, are purer than those of the righteous. This is illogical and unacceptable."

The Mowbed said, "It is like this, not like you think: When evil people die, the demon that was with them in life grabs hold of them and leads them before Ahriman in Hell, and when the demon is no longer with the dead body, it is [more] pure. When the righteous, who are honest and doers of good deeds pass away, the *amahrspands*[17] take hold of their souls and receive them, bringing them back before Ohrmazd, the Lord. Carrion, the demon of decomposition makes her home in the body [of the righteous] when it perishes, and makes it corrupt. It is like when an enemy comes into a city, and if the king of that city falls into the hands of the enemy, he takes and binds him [the king], and carries him before his own king. If he [the enemy] cannot apprehend the king of that country, in despair he goes into that place, and destroys the city."

Ma'mun, the Prince of the Faithful, when he heard this speech, was pleased by it, and it seemed wonderful.

The Gizistag Abālish compares the human body to a city in which dwells a king. The soul is the king of the body, and when Carrion storms the body, the soul of the unbeliever is still within the body. The demon of dead matter, like an invader, arrests the soul and drags it to his own king, presumably the Evil Spirit. At death, the soul of the righteous person is immediately taken to the abode of Ahura Mazdā, leaving the body. In rage and frustration, Carrion occupies and ravages the soulless body. The Videvdad does not explain its reasons, but it is likely that the concept was similar even then.

Death in the Avesta was not only a personal tragedy. It was a crisis for the community because it allowed the powerful death demon entrance via the corpse of a human or a dog. The passage from the Gizistag Abālish quoted above implies that the more advanced the departed soul was, the more rage the demon of dead matter feels when entering the body. Following this logic, the corpse of the highest priest would be possessed by the most powerful demon, and this made corpses particularly frightening. There was no idea of a "final resting place" of the body, for the body became "alive" with demons, and the *dakhma*s were the places where they partied.

NATURAL DISASTERS

Natural disasters such as floods and droughts still plague the areas where the Avestan people settled. Of all the calamities humans suffer, those we call "acts of God" can be the most horrendous. Typhoons, hurricanes, floods, volcano eruptions, etc., kill more people every year than human crimes. Considering the dualistic stance of the authors of the Avesta, these catastrophes could not have been "acts of God," rather they were "acts of the demons." The intervention of gods was essential for the relief from these miseries. Most of these natural disasters were created by the Evil Spirit against the lands made by Ahura Mazdā, as related in Videvdad 1. Many of the words denoting them are incomprehensible, but we still get a good idea of the types of "counter-creation" against the good creations of Ahura Mazdā. As the good god created beautiful things, the Evil Spirit countered them with evil things, as we saw in Chapter 2.

In this description we can follow Ahura Mazdā's creation of what was good and what the Evil Spirit created to oppose those good things. This list is ranked by the degree of goodness, but, to match the goodness, the evil must be as serious. Therefore, we have an idea of what the Avestan people dreaded the most. Although the dragon, the representative of the Evil Spirit, was the principal evil, it was followed directly by the cold winter. The winter with its frozen waters, frozen plants, and frozen earth brought excessive hardship and death to people and their flocks in this area. After the harsh winters, floods from the melting snow and ice plagued them. Then as spring came, the locusts appeared to glut themselves on tender crops, which were finally destroyed by the heat and drought of summer. We find here both climatic disasters— excessive heat and floods—and blights on the crops.

Among other natural disasters, drought and bad crops (bad seasons) were the most important. All of these were blamed on the forces of evil. This evil could only be countered by good ritual acts and verbal spells meant to repel or drive it off. Thus, although the Evil Spirit caused the original natural disasters in the beginning of the creation, sorcery and witchcraft could intensify the evil of calamities at a given time.

Natural scourges (*vōignā*), perhaps floods, are dreaded in the Avesta, and several deities are asked to protect against them, for example, Sraosha, principal fighter of the powers of darkness:

YASNA 57.14

Let evil, fearful scourges go
far from his house, far from his town,
far from his tribe, far from his land,
in whose house obstruction-smashing Sraosha of the Rewards
is satisfied [and] recognized.

Tishtriya, god of the rainy season, complains that these conditions are the result of people not sacrificing to him.

Insect attacks, such as by lice, corn-eating bugs, and wool moths, are other annoyances of the natural sort, but they came from the failure of people to avoid certain apotropaic rituals designed to keep evil away. These insects were thought to arise from the improper disposal of the hair and nails (Videvdad 17.3).[18]

DROUGHT AND THE MYTH OF TISHTRIYA[19]

The myth of the star god Tishtriya, Sirius, as related in his hymn in Yasht 8, is about the natural cycles of drought and rainy seasons. It features two super-natural beings who affect this cycle: the "demon of drought" (Apaosha) and "witches" identified as "falling stars," presumably meteors, perhaps also comets, but foremost among whom is the "Witch of Bad Seasons" (*pairikā yā duzhyāriyā*). Tishtriya is closely associated with the star Satawaēsa, a rain-producing deity, and, as the overseer of the stars, "which contain the seed of water," he is closely involved in the production of rain and is invoked by all beings suffering from drought.[20] When he approaches the Vourukasha Sea, the great ocean in the sky, in the shape of a horse, his presence makes the waters swell and become agitated (Yasht 8.8), and then the star Satawaēsa is able to gather the rain clouds (Yasht 8.9), which eventually assemble on the peak of the mountain Us-hindawa, in the middle of the sea (Yasht 8.32).

Tishtriya is especially repellent to sorcerers and witches. Even cattle and sheep recall him as they face attacks from violent men (Yasht 8.5). His relationship with grazing animals is probably related to his role in bringing rain to the pastures.

Thus, Tishtriya's shape shifts as he moves through the starlit sky, wondering who will sacrifice to him. For ten nights, he appears as a splendidly radiant and strong fifteen-year-old, which is the age when a man first receives his *kusti*, a sacred elaborately woven cord Zoroastrians tie around their waists.[21] For another ten days, Tishtriya takes on the form of a bull with golden hooves. For still another ten days, he comes in the form of a wonderful white horse with tawny ears and a golden bridle. It is at this point that the fight for the sake of Order begins. In this form of a beautiful horse, he is confronted by the demon Apaosha in the form of a horrid black horse, mangy and scruffy, with bald spots. His tail and ears are dingy colored, and his demeanor is frightening (Yasht 8.21). They struggle for three days and three nights, and at first Tishtriya wins, keeping the demon away from the Vourukasha Sea, which the demon intends to disrupt in order to ruin the seasons.

Tishtriya offers purification for the soul of the one who would offer to him, as well as a herd of horses, and even a herd of men. Tishtriya, however, seeing the strength of the demon, cries in distress to Ahura Mazdā, warning him that without the proper sacrifice he will not have the capacity to destroy the demon. He laments that because people are not sacrificing to him, he is weak. If people did sacrifice to him, his strength would increase greatly (Yasht 8.24).

Ahura Mazdā then decides to worship Tishtriya himself, declaring that by this worship he will bring Tishtriya the power of "ten horses, camels, bulls, mountains, and flooded rivers" (Yasht 8.25). Vitalized, Tishtriya comes down to face the demon again, this time overcoming him. Again Tishtriya approaches Ahura Mazdā and extols himself, and he promises boons of plenty of grains in return for worship. He then again comes down to the Vourukasha Sea in the horse shape. In response, the sea swells and surges as the entire ocean convulses with power (Yasht 8.31). To support Tishtriya, Satawaēsa assembles the fog-making clouds and the wind blows them to the settlements, and *haoma* grows for the sacrifice. The demon of drought is again thwarted in his efforts to dry the world up (Yasht 8.27–29).

In the second part of the myth, the Evil Spirit tosses "witches" up into the sky to hold back the stars and so disrupt the rains, causing bad seasons and drought (Yasht 8.39). Among these "witches," the "Witch of Bad Seasons" is Tishtriya's main opponent, and he attacks her in response to her attempts to produce bad weather and thus cut off the life of all beings. Tishtriya chains her up with powerful chains that could hold a thousand men:

YASHT 8.50–51

I set in place, O Zarathustra of the Spitāmas, yonder star, Tishtriya,
as great in sacrifice-worthiness, as great in hymning-worthiness,
as great in satisfaction-worthiness, as great in glorification-worthiness
as even me, Ahura Mazdā,
to stand against and mount defenses against [them],
to overcome [them] in turn and to answer the hostilities
of that witch, the one of bad seasons,
whom people of evil speech call by name the one of good seasons.

YASHT 8.52–54

For if I had not made, O Zarathustra of the Spitāmas, yonder star, Tishtriya,
as great in sacrifice-worthiness, as great in hymning-worthiness,
as great in satisfaction-worthiness, as great in glorification-worthiness

as even me, Ahura Mazdā,
to stand against and mount defenses against [them],
to overcome [them] in turn and to answer the hostilities
of that witch, the one of bad seasons,
whom people of evil speech call by name the one of good seasons,—
[then] indeed here in one and the same day or in one and the same night,
that witch, the one of bad seasons,
would have cut off the thread of life [?], before its passing,
of the entire existence with bones.
[But now], back and forth it runs.

YASHT 8.55

For Tishtriya, wealthy and munificent,
chains that witch with chains for two feet and for four feet,
invincible ones, and for all feet,
just as if he were to chain one man among a thousand men
who were the strongest in bone-strength.

YASHT 8.56

For if, O Spitāma Zarathustra,
the Aryan lands had prepared for Tishtriya, wealthy and munificent,
a sacrifice and a hymn according to the established rules,
as is the sacrifice and hymn to him
most according to the established rules, according to best Order,
here no army or scourge would reach the Aryan lands,
neither swooning [?] nor falling sickness [?]
nor an army chariot nor one with an uplifted banner.

Although I will discuss the dry, infertile nature of witches in later chapters, they already appear as important evil beings. In this case, they are clearly nonhuman or demonic beings. This will not always be the case. Another fascinating detail found in this myth is that Ahura Mazdā, the high god, must sacrifice to other gods to bolster their power. In the discussion on the Gathic poet-sacrificer and his struggle to maintain cosmic order, the act of sacrifice is to some extent mechanical. That is, it aids the gods if performed properly. It is not performed as an act of worship in the sense of appeasing the gods, although they are satisfied when they receive libations, but for other reasons. The gods derive strength from the sacrifice, and in turn they can maintain the order of the cosmos. Humans benefit from this directly, as they can live in an ordered world. It is not a surprise, then, that a god may perform a sacrifice to strengthen another god when they have common goals.

The continued dread of enemy armies and bad seasons mentioned in the hymn to Tishtriya are both caused by adherence to the Lie, as is seen in the prayer of Darius I to Ahura Mazdā:

DARIUS AT PERSEPOLIS (DPD[22] 12–20)

King Darius announces:
Let Ahura Mazdā bring me support together with all the gods!
And let Ahura Mazdā protect this land
from the enemy army, from bad seasons, from the Lie!
May no enemy army, bad seasons, or Lie demon come against this land!

CONCLUSIONS

In the Avestan worldview, the Good Spirit, Ahura Mazdā, and the Evil Spirit, Angra Mainyu, are permanent features of the world. These spirits are found in a less explicit form in the Gāthās, being more like opposing forces; however, in the Young Avesta, the two opposing parties are very well elaborated. The persistent presence of these two opposing forces leads to a conflict that must be dealt with on all levels, from the level of the gods to the level of humans.

The organization of the world depends on acts performed by both men and gods, rather than appeals to the gods in the way of prayer and supplication alone. From the Gāthās we already see that the powers of the gods are increased by sacrifice. It is a meticulous and precise process, with the utterance of formulas accompanied by sacrifice. The forces of evil, likewise, can be augmented by evil sacrifice and evil spells, as we see in the Young Avestan texts. The Gāthās present a picture of "good-doers" and "evildoers" who are very much alike except that, according to the poets who produced them, their acts have opposite goals.

The Avestan system of good and evil does not allow the gods to be the source of evil. Therefore, humans, as the creatures of Ahura Mazdā, can become evil only by means of cooperation with—or contamination by—evil. Evil, being externalized, can thus be exorcised from the good creation. The evils mentioned in the Avesta are a window into the Avestan worldview. Defiling evils such as anal intercourse, corpses, stillbirths, diseases, and menses, especially untimely menses, are important in this regard and will be discussed in the following chapters.

Good is manifested in order, life, and growth, whereas evil is manifested in disorder, death, destruction, and infertility. Thus, the evils in the Avesta are things that represent lack of life and growth. Anal intercourse produces no offspring. Therefore, infertility is what makes it evil. Similarly, untimely menses is often a symptom of a disordered and infertile reproductive system in females. Stillbirth represents death as well as a failure of the act of reproduction. Disease and old age are processes of deterioration and disorder that lead to the final disordering of the body, which is death.

Lack of rain affects the fertility of the earth and is caused by witches, who are the agents of the Evil Spirit, and who cause infertility by their dry nature. Locust swarms, winters, and floods also disturb the fertility of the earth. Evil is thus whatever causes disorder as the Avestan people understood it. This is anything that decreases life and prosperity. Evil is unrelated to morality in these cases, for even accidental or unintentional acts or conditions can be its source. Thus, disease, menstruation, old age, and other natural occurrences are classed as evil.

CHAPTER 6

SORCERERS, WITCHES, WHORES,
AND MENSTRUATING WOMEN

HARMFUL BEINGS AGAINST WHICH humans need protection are of different kinds. Some are active agents of evil and the enemies of Ahura Mazdā's ordered cosmos. This kind of evildoer is intrinsically evil. Then there are also beings that are by nature good, but may become harmful at certain times or under certain conditions. We should also distinguish between humans and nonhumans—that is, supernatural beings in the other world, what the ancient Zoroastrians called "the world of thought."[1]

Most gods are depicted as fighting the forces of evil, be those forces supernatural or human, cosmic natural disturbances, or ailments befalling humans. Usually the explanation for these disturbances is lack of sacrifice to—and worship of—the deity on the part of humans, as we have just seen in Chapter 5. As soon as the gods receive their sacrifice, they will fight the evil and provide blessings for their worshippers. On occasion, however, the gods can also pose a threat to humans who ignore ritual or perform bad acts.[2]

There is a problem with defining the evil agents mentioned in the Avesta, because their specific actions are hardly ever described. The traditional translations are based upon the translations of the modern descendants of the words or on those of related words in other Iranian or cognate languages. We must therefore take care that we do not imbue an Avestan term with all the content of the modern English equivalent.

Evil agents are frequently arranged in lists and often in male-female pairs. An example of such a list is the following from Yasna 9.18:

YASNA 9.18

[I call] down [all] so that I may overcome the hostilities of all hostile
  ones,

of *daēwa*s and men, of sorcerers and witches,
of false teachers [*sāstar*], poetasters [*kawi*], and mumblers [*karpan*],[3]
of villains on two feet, of those who darken Order[4] on two feet,
of wolves on four feet,
and of [their] army with wide front, deceiving and falling [all over].[5]

SORCERERS AND WITCHES

The exact nature of the male "sorcerer" (Avestan *yātu*, Middle Persian *jādūg*) and his female counterpart, the "witch" (Avestan *pairikā*, Middle Persian *parīg*) is not known. In the Achaemenid inscriptions, the word *yātu* occurs once, coupled with *kayada* (see below), in an apotropaic utterance in a building inscription of Artaxerxes II at Susa: "This which I have made—let no *yātu* and no *kayada* destroy it!"[6] The Accadian versions of this inscription use two verbs only (no nouns), the first with the basic meaning of destroying with physical blows and the second to harm in a moral sense.[7]

However, the later Zoroastrian literature mentions some famous "sorcerers" (*jādūg*) who are described in some detail. In the Book of Yōisht ī Friyān, the sorcerer Axt went to the city of "riddle-solvers," slaying anybody who could not answer his riddles. Finally, they mentioned Yōisht ī Friyān to him as a person who could solve his riddles. Axt invited him, but Yōisht ī Friyān refused to enter his house because the sorcerer had hidden dead matter in various places to pollute his guest. After Axt had asked Yōisht ī Friyān a number of riddles, all of which he could answer, Yōisht ī Friyān asked Axt three riddles which he could not answer. He sought the help of Ahriman in hell, but to no avail, and he was ultimately slain by means of the knife used to cut the *barsom* and a spell taken from the Avesta.[8] In the Memorial of Zarēr, in the battle over the religion brought by Zarathustra, the sorcerer Widrafsh killed Zarēr with a spear on which the demons in hell had cast a spell and that was made with the poison of Wrath (*heshm*) and the sin of Lust (*āz*).[9]

Sorcery is "defined" in several places in the third book of the Dēnkard.[10] For example, in chapter 169 the sorcerer (*jādūg*) and the *mar* (Avestan *mairya*, see below) are associated with corpses; in chapter 295 sorcery is characterized by the use of the evil eye (*dush-chashmīh*); in chapter 340 the naked sorcerer is said to be more powerful than the clothed one; in chapter 369 demons, sorcerers and *mar*s are said to have the ability to change into different shapes. In the Pahlavi Rivāyat, one of the characteristics of sorcery is the ability to slay inordinately large numbers of sheep and cattle at the same time and sacrificing to the demons. One way of destroying huge numbers of sorcerers and witches is by having intercourse with one's closest relatives[11] (*khwēdōdah*) or lighting fires at night.[12]

The Rigveda contains some intriguing curses against sorcerers, which give a better idea of what activities these evil beings were thought to engage in:

RIGVEDA 7.104.20[13]

There they go! The dog-sorcerers[14] are flying away.
Viciously they wish to harm Indra, who cannot be harmed.
Indra sharpens his weapon against the slanderers.
Now let him loose his bolt at the sorcerers.

RIGVEDA 7.104.22

Kill the owl-sorcerer, the owlet-sorcerer,
the dog-sorcerer, the cuckoo-sorcerer, the eagle-sorcerer, the vulture-sorcerer.
Indra, crush the demon to powder as if with a millstone.

RIGVEDA 7.104.24

Indra, kill the male sorcerer and the female who deceives by the power of
    illusion.
Let the idol-worshippers sink down with broken necks;
Let them never see the rising sun.

The sorcerers of the Rigveda appear as shape-shifters able to take various forms, such as dogs, wolves, owls, and other birds. They are also able to use the power of illusion for deceiving people. In the Avesta, sorcerers appear in lists, such as that in Yasna 9.18 cited above. However, there is little information besides their frequent mention. Yasht 11.6 (to Haoma) depicts them in their get-togethers, reveling and perhaps plotting their evil:

YASHT 11.6

[H]e, O Zarathustra, should pronounce this word to be spoken
when there come . . . and deceiving get-togethers.
Then [those] of the *daēwa*-worshipping ones possessed by the Lie,
and the sorcerers among those possessed by sorcerers
and the witches among those possessed by witches
will fear the hostilities. Forth they will run.

Down with the *daēwa*s!
Down with the *daēwa*-worshippers!
Let them seize [them by] the mouth!

We know even less about the actions of the *pairikā*, "witch." In Manichean Middle Persian texts, the *parīg* is routinely mentioned together with demons, wrath-demons, and other denizens of the realm of evil, and the same connections are found in Pahlavi texts.[15]

A much more recognizable female evil agent was the "whore" or "prostitute" (Avestan *jahī*, *jahikā*; Middle Persian *jeh*).[16] Of all women, she was the most evil and dangerous. The whore was not a simple prostitute for the authors of the Avesta. Rather, she was a sorceress intent on using her powers to harm any "man who sustains Order," a faithful Mazdayasnian, as described in the hymn to Haoma:

YASNA 9.32

Against the whore possessed by sorcerers,
whose activities are for pleasure, who offers her lap,
whose thought flutters away like a cloud pushed by the wind,
for the benefit of the Orderly one who wishes to obtain [his] body,
strike [your] weapon, O tawny Haoma!

Her actions and their results are described in greater detail in Chapter 18 of the Videvdad, to which I shall return in a moment. Again, the Rigveda has instances of descriptions of witches, who seem to be sensitive to the sounds of the priest pounding the plant soma ("haoma" in Avestan), during the ritual. Soma is used as a weapon against witches and other demons. Witches, like sorcerers in the Rigveda, are shape-shifters:

RIGVEDA 7.104.17

She who ranges about at night like an owl,
hiding her body in a hateful disguise,
let her fall into the endless pits.
Let the pressing-stones slay the demons with their rumblings.[17]

The *kawi*s and *karpan*s are set figures of the Gāthās, where they are presumably the poet-sacrificer's rivals. The term *kawi* is the same as Old Indic *kavi*, "poet," and is used in the Young Avesta as the title of a series of sacrificers, whom the later tradition refers to as the Kayanids. The exact meaning of *kar-pan* is not known. The term *kawi* is pejorative only in the plural, which is how it survives into the later texts (Pahlavi *kayg* and *karb*). They are generic evil-doers, but throughout Dēnkard 7 they are especially presented as the opponents of Zarathustra. The intrinsic evil of these rivals may have been similar to that of the "obscurantist" (see below).

The "villain" (*mairya-*) must originally have denoted a "young man," as in Old Indic *marya* and in the Achaemenid inscriptions, where *marīka* seems to mean simply "young man,"[18] but in the Young Avesta he is invariably represented as maleficent.

The "obscurantist" (Avestan *ashamaogha*, Pahlavi *ahlomōgh*) is traditionally rendered as "heretic." However, there is no evidence in the Avesta or the later Zoroastrian books that it was a technical term for someone who had left the orthodox faith. Literally, the word must have meant someone who obscures or darkens (*maogha*) the cosmic Order (*asha*) and probably referred to people who performed bad sacrifices, destined to bring darkness and death rather than light and life.[19] In book 3 of the Dēnkard, he is "defined" in several places. In chapter 189 the "heretic" is characterized by thinking that god does not exist; in chapter 307 he is said to say that the Evil Spirit is equal to the gods; in chapter 331 he is characterized by a natural tendency to dissimulation (*nihān-khēmīh*), inspired by Akōman ("Evil Thought"); in chapter 338 (similarly chapter 410) he is characterized as not believing in Ohrmazd and not professing the religion.[20]

Another list of maleficent beings is the following:

YASNA 61.2–4

for the discomfiture and removal of the Evil Spirit, with [his] creations,
he of bad creations, full of destruction,
for the discomfiture and removal of male and female ghosts[?],
for the discomfiture and removal of the male and female ghost[?],
for the discomfiture and removal of male and female wizards[?],
for the discomfiture and removal of the male and female wizard[?],
for the discomfiture and removal of thieves and violators,
for the discomfiture and removal of the *zanda*s and those possessed by
    sorcerers[?],
for the discomfiture and removal of the contract-destroyers and the one
    whose contract is deception,
for the discomfiture and removal of those who smash the sustainers of Order
    and those who are hostile to the sustainers of Order,

for the discomfiture and removal of the un-Orderly one who darkens Order
and the commander who causes much destruction,
for the discomfiture and removal of each and every one of those possessed by
    the Lie,
whose thoughts are not according to the models,
whose words are not according to the models,
whose acts are not according to the models,
O Zarathustra of the Spitāmas!

Additional terms in this list are "sorcerers and sorceresses" (*kakhwarda*;
fem. *kakhwardī*), the exact meaning of which is not known. The word *kakhwarda* was borrowed into Sanskrit as *kākhorda*, where it denotes evil spirits
often associated with *vetāḍas* ("ghouls"),[21] and into Armenian as *kaxard* (with
derivatives), which is used in the New Testament mainly to render *pharmakós*
(and derivatives) "sorcerer,"[22] originally someone practicing sorcery by means
of potions. The actual meaning of "male and female magicians" (*kayada*; fem.
kāidyā or *kayadī*) is likewise unknown, but the *kayada* was included with the
yātu in Artaxerxes II's inscription, as we just saw. It is commonly thought
that the term has to do with astrology or similar practices, since the first part
of the word (*kay-*) seems to be that of *kaēta*, as well, found in various Iranian
languages in such meanings. For instance, Middle Persian *kēd* is found in the
Kār-nāmag ī Ardashīr ī Pābagān, where an Indian *kēd* is consulted whether
such and such a procedure should be adopted.[23] In Manichean Parthian we
find the expression *kēdīgān ud mārīgarān*, "the *kēdīg*s and the spell-makers,"
whose presence is one of five things that ruin a land.[24] In its only occurrence
in the hymn to Tishtriya, the *kaēta* is described as "lying," but that does not go
very far toward identifying them as astrologers.

Finally, we have here the earliest mention of the *zanda*, the meaning of
which is unknown, but in the third century the term *zandīg* was applied to
non-Zoroastrians, particularly, probably, to the Manicheans.[25] The earliest
attestation of Middle Persian *zandīg* is in the inscription of the high priest
Kerdīr, who began his career under Shāpūr I the Great (240–271), as *ēhrbed*
(*hērbed*), "Zoroastrian teacher," and rose under Ohrmazd I, Wahrām I, and
Wahrām II, via priest (*mowbed*), to the honorary title of "priest of Ohrmazd."
In his inscription he tells us how he persecuted foreign religions; it is worth
quoting the passage, which is quite reminiscent of the Avestan passages:

And in land after land, place after place, in the entire empire, the services for
Ohrmazd and the gods were made more prominent, and the Mazdayasnian
tradition and the priests [*mowmard*] were held in great honor in the land.

And the gods, the water, the fire, and cattle [gōspand] received great satisfaction. And Ahriman and the demons [dēwān] received great harm, but the teaching of Ahriman and the demons left the land and nobody believed it any more.

And Jews, Buddhists [shaman], Hindus [braman], Nazoreans [nāzarā?], Christians, Baptists [magdag?], and Manicheans [zandīg?] were struck down in the land, and their idols were destroyed.

The dens of the demons were demolished, and thrones and seats for the gods were made.[26]

A famous zandīg in Pahlavi literature is the "accursed" Abālish, whose fictitious debate at the court of the Caliph al-Ma'mun with the Mazdayasnian leader Ādurfarnbay, son of Farrokhzād, is reported in a small Pahlavi text. Abālish was a god-fearing zandīg originally, well-versed in the religion of Ohrmazd, "but the demon of wrath scrambled his thoughts and scuttled into his body. He withheld his hand from the doing of good deeds [and] worshipping the gods, and made him dispute with all the learned people of the Mazdayasnian religion, the Arabs [Muslims], Jews, and Christians of Pars."[27] The zandīg was therefore not necessarily evil, unless he actively opposed the good religion.

Thus, although it is impossible to determine the exact nature of the evil acts of these various sorcerers, etc., they clearly belong in the category of beings employing magic for destructive purposes. Since we do not know exactly how the Avestan terms yātu, ashamaogha, kaēta and kayada, and kakhwarda differed in the time of the Young Avesta, we shall refer to them in the following simply as sorcerers or evil agents.

There is no justification for denying, as some do, that there were sorcerers who actually practiced magic for harming others.[28] Most feared were their curses and spells, which had to be opposed by counter-curses. The potency of words was indisputable, whether they were manthra, the sacred words for the Mazdayasnian, or (Pahlavi) nifrīn,[29] curses of the sorcerer. Just as the Zoroastrian priest was thought to exert a tremendous amount of control by his use of words, so could the sorcerer.

It seems then, that in the case of the Avesta, although "outsiders" may have accounted for some of the people accused of being sorcerers and witches, there may have been, more specifically, people involved in the practice of rites thought to be harmful. Thus, while it would be safe to say that the "outsiders" of the religion were denounced as sorcerers, this does not account for the vituperation against them. The Iranian people knew that other people worshipped in different manners, and while they may have considered them

deceived, or even demon-worshippers, there was a special anger and fear reserved for sorcerers. This can only be explained by the assertion that there
were indeed people who practiced magic with the aim of killing or harming
others.

The sorcerer in the Avesta was one of the most evil of beings, but he or
she was probably human, and so a creature of Ahura Mazdā's who, however,
had allied himself or herself with evil. They therefore differ from demons,
who were evil by nature,[30] being created by the Evil Spirit. In the Yasna, the
sorcerer was repudiated along with the worst of demons, because it was his
choice to be evil, and his actions were against the gods, the earth, and God's
creatures. Sorcery was considered particularly insidious because it could be
concealed. A sorcerer could have any external appearance, maybe even be
wolves in the form of humans:

YASHT 3.11

He smashes the brood of snakes.
He smashes the brood of wolves.
He smashes the brood of two-footed [wolves].
He smashes the despisers.
He smashes the ones of distraught minds.
He smashes the fevers.
He smashes the slanderers.
He smashes the sowers of discord.
He smashes the ones with the evil eye.

Old Iranian sorcerers are portrayed as always trying to trick the righteous
into being polluted by dead matter or catch him by word juggling and so make
him lose his faith, as in the case of Yōisht ī Friyān. In this, they emulate the
cosmic Lie herself, whose principal weapon is deception and delusion. It was
by this means that the *daēwa*s were originally turned bad, and it was for the
same reason that the opponents of Darius' accession to the throne turned away
from him, Ahura Mazdā's chosen king. The way to combat evildoers was by
the word of Ahura Mazdā; only if the evildoers are punished will the land remain healthy:[31]

YASNA 30.6

Especially the *daēwa*s did not discriminate correctly between these two,
    because deception

would come over them as they were discussing, because they would prefer the
worst thought.
Thus, they would scramble together to wrath, with which mortals would
sicken this state.

YASNA 30.8–9

Thus, also, when the retribution comes for these sins, then, O Mazdā, he
shall constantly present the command to you by [his] good thought for [you]
to announce it to these, O Ahura, who shall be placing the Lie in the hands of
Order.
Thus, also: may *we* be [the men (of those?)] who shall make it Perfect, this
state of existence, O Mazdā and you, the Ahuras . . .

With this compare the Bisotun inscription of Darius:

DB 4.33–40

These lands which became rebellious, the Lie made them rebellious, so that
these [men] lied to the people.
Then Ahura Mazdā delivered them into my hands; as was my wish thus I
treated them . . .
You who will be king in the future, guard strongly against the Lie.
The man who lies, him punish well if you think as follows: May my country
be healthy!

FEMALE AGENTS OF EVIL

In the Gāthās, the only female evil we find is the Lie, which is merely grammatically feminine. It is unlikely that the pollution taboos we see later on were
present at this time. Looking at the Rigveda, we can see that the situation was
the same at that time in India. In the Yasna, although the pollution element is
not as evident, there is much concern for female agents of evil. Granted, evil
seems to be quite well distributed at this point, because there are many male
demons with their female counterparts. The Videvdad, being a text concerned
with issues of pollution, had much to say on the subject of female pollution.
The stigma of pollution women had to bear barred them from participation
in many religious rites.
Women, because of the periodic nature of their pollution, were possessed,
as it were, by the pollution-causing demon on a regular basis. Blood itself, as

a ritual pollutant, was not, therefore, the main factor in the theological and social segregation of women. It was more the notion that women had a special connection with evil that was behind the severe sanctions against them.

The pollution rules of the Videvdad make it clear that its authors had an intense fear of menstrual and other feminine blood. Blood from wounds represented the risk of death, a condition of pollution and decay. If it were simply the fear of death behind blood pollution, then why is it that the Videvdad had no restrictions against injured men that resembled those set forth for menstruating women? Why were they not vegetarians? Slaughtering animals creates blood, pain, and a dead body, yet this was accepted as something good, as long as the proper rituals were observed.

Feminine blood could be logically called "creative blood," because it springs from natural causes, not from disease or injury, and it has to do with procreation. In a system where creative forces, especially fertility, are seen as godly and positive, it seems at first glance illogical that creative blood was considered to be demon-given.

The association of blood with disease and death certainly is a factor. However, the idea that blood, given its negative connections, issues from a woman's body on a regular basis without a cause, such as a wound, may have been a source for the connection between women and demonic contamination. Added to this, during pregnancy, considered a very beneficial state, the monthly blood ceased to flow. Infertility, or at least the state of not being pregnant, was thus tied to blood and its connection with demons, specifically Carrion, the demon of dead matter. Uli Linke notes that blood "was attractive to certain powers, but only those associated with unpleasantness, war, and death"[32] for Indo-Europeans, and so women's bleeding bodies were thus linked with the pollution of the corpse among other dangers.

In later texts, such as the Bundahishn, we find some myths that explain how the pollutions described so vividly in the Videvdad came to be. They cannot be dismissed completely as later additions because of the Videvdad's descriptions of the menstruating woman as being akin to a demon. During the menstrual period, a woman can harm all good things of the world, including men, simply by her glance. There is no other pollution that allows its sufferer this sort of power. It is very close to the idea of death, when the body becomes possessed by a demon, but in this case the soul remains in the body. It would naturally follow that the pollution of the demon, along with the close association with it, might cause the soul to also be affected. It is true that during the course of a disease, particularly a severe disease, a human was thought to be possessed by a disease-causing demon. If we examine the Bundahishn mythology, it seems that it is the periodic and frequent nature of the possession during menstruation, coupled with the particular demon who causes it, that are ultimately responsible for the concept that women are by nature associated with the demonic.

In the beginning of creation, according to the Bundahishn, the god Ahura Mazdā created good things, while the Evil Spirit created evil. Women are Ahura Mazdā's creation, but, in a myth of the Bundahishn, the Evil Spirit gave women menstruation by kissing the demon called "the Whore." Women were created by Ahura Mazdā, but as the Evil Spirit blighted every good creation, he was able to inject some evil into the process of human reproduction. This view might offer some insight as we try to understand female agents of evil.

We saw above that Avestan *pairikā*, traditionally rendered as "witch," represented mainly a supernatural or mythical being, but she was also the archetypical whore. The Whore is a demonic creature in the Avesta, but it is not until the Pahlavi texts that we have a clear explanation of the myths involved in her genesis. It was the powerful demon, in Avestan called Jahī (or Pahlavi Jeh), the archetypical whore, who thwarted Ahura Mazdā's defeat of the Evil Spirit as they battled in the beginning of time, according to the Bundahishn.

BUNDAHISHN 4.1–9

It says in the Tradition that, when the Foul Spirit saw that both he and the demons would be undone by the Righteous Man, he had been stunned. For three thousand years he lay stunned.

During that stupor, the [animal-?]headed demons one by one lied: "Rise up, our father, for we will fight such a battle that Ohrmazd and the Amahrspands will be in dire straits!"

One by one they enumerated their evil deeds in detail.

It did not pacify the wicked Foul Spirit, and he did not rise from his stupor for fear of the Righteous Man until the wicked Whore came at the completion of the three thousand years and lied: "Rise up, our father, for in that battle I shall let loose so much harm upon the Righteous Man and the toiling Bull that their lives will not be worth living. I shall steal their Fortune, I shall harm the water, the earth, the fire, the plant, and the entire creation established by Ohrmazd!"

She enumerated her evildoings in such detail that the Foul Spirit was pacified. He jumped out of his stupor and placed a kiss on the Whore's head. The pollution now called "menses" appeared on the Whore then.

The Foul Spirit lied to the Whore: "Ask for whatever you want, and I will give it to you!"

Then Ohrmazd knew in his omniscience that, at that time, the Foul Spirit was able to give the Whore what she wanted and that she would acquire much profit thereby.

The Foul Spirit's body was like a frog to look at, but he showed a man like a fifteen-year-old youth to the Whore and bound the Whore's mind to him.

The Whore lied to the Foul Spirit: "Give me the desire for man, so that I can sit down as his ward in his house!"

The Foul Spirit lied to her: "I shall not tell you to ask for anything again, for you only know how to ask for profitless, bad things." But the time had passed, and if she had asked for it, he would not have been able to give it to her.

This myth is of great importance for the understanding of the pollutions of women. There is an interesting switch from the demonic woman created by the Evil Spirit to the earthly woman, who was created by Ahura Mazdā. Woman as a category here becomes merged with the Whore, Jeh, whose origin is unknown. First, Jeh claims that she can do a better job of polluting the creation than can the other demons. She can make life unbearable, for she can pollute the water, the earth, the fire, and plants. We may note here that these are the very same items that a menstruating woman must avoid at all costs, because she can destroy them with only a glance. Secondly, menses is the gift the Evil Spirit gives her, and thus to all women, for the act of Ahriman's kissing Jeh is the cause of menstruation in women. When she asks for an additional gift, Ahura Mazdā is alarmed. He realizes that he must do something to influence her. She is looking at the Evil Spirit in the form of an ugly toad. Ahura Mazdā sends her the vision of a handsome fifteen-year-old boy, so that her mind would latch onto it, and presumably not be attracted to the form of the Evil Spirit. This works, and Jeh the Whore asks that she may have lust for man and that she may become the mistress of his house. It is difficult to separate Jeh the Whore from the human woman; after all, this is an etiological myth that tells us that a woman was the cause of evil's revival, that menstruation is demon-given, and that women desire to be wives to men because god managed to trick the Whore into having lust for men.

While, as Zaehner explains, the above passage from the Bundahishn does not explicitly equate human women with the whore Jeh,[33] the fact that women were believed to cause the same harm as Jeh makes the connection inevitable. Another passage from the Bundahishn seems to confirm the connection in the minds of some followers. In it, the good god Ohrmazd (Ahura Mazdā) addresses human women:

BUNDAHISHN 14.1

Ohrmazd said, when he had fashioned the woman: I made you too, whose adversary is the Whore species.

And I gave you a mouth near the anus, so that intercourse would seem to you like the taste of the sweetest foods to your mouth. And you will be my helper because man will be born from you. Still, you hurt me, Ohrmazd. But if I had found a vessel from which to make man, then I would never have made you, whose adversary is the Whore species. But I sought in the earth, in the plants, and in the cattle, on the highest of mountains and in the deep river valleys, but I did not find a vessel from which to produce the Righteous Man, except for woman, whose adversary is the Whore.[34]

Although this passage describes woman as a creature reluctantly created, because god had no other choice, it does not imply that sex itself was considered impure or sinful. It instead points to the notion that finding a mate for Righteous Man was essential, so that he might have sex and reproduce. Woman's association with the Whore seems to be the problem here. All good things created by Ahura Mazdā have their "adversaries," or things created by the Evil Spirit to harm and harass them. I know of no other good creations that actually take on the powers associated with their demonic counterparts as women do when menstruating. Another interesting feature of this myth is that it is *man* who must be reproduced, and woman is his vessel. Woman, in this case, appears to be not the female of the human species, but the "vessel of man."

It is also striking that while the charges of whoredom are varied, they tend to center around menstrual blood. The whore can also be a woman who has multiple partners. The authors of the Avesta feared the mixing of their semen with that of unbelievers (Videvdad 18.62 below). Another way to become a "whore" was to expose men to menstrual blood, which would contaminate them. The passage already quoted above (Yasna 9.32), in which Haoma is invoked for the protection from the "prostitute" who wants sex for pleasure, not for procreation, is then followed by one in which the theme of pollution is introduced. In a rather explicit manner, the author renounces sex with the woman who has not undergone purification:

YASNA 10.15

I relinquish the aperture of the woman, the villainess, whose dirt has not been removed,

who thinks she is deceiving the priest and the *haoma*,
she who [herself, however,] deceived goes to perdition,
she who sits down devouring the sacrificial cake that belongs to Haoma.
[Haoma] does not give her priests as sons, nor indeed any good sons.

The deception of the priest mentioned here almost certainly refers to the concealment of menstruation, a sin that damns both the woman and the unwitting man who had sex with her in this condition. The "whore" is also accused of devouring the *draonah*[35] offering meant for Haoma, an act attributed to the witch in the Avesta; for example:

YASHT 8.57–58

Zarathustra asked in turn:
What are indeed, Ahura Mazdā, the sacrifice and hymn to him,
Tishtriya, wealthy and munificent,
according to best Order, most according to the established rules?
Then Ahura Mazdā said:
The Aryan lands should bring him libations.
The Aryan lands should spread out the *barsom* for him.
The Aryan lands should cook a sheep for him,
white or of good color or whichever color it resembles.

YASHT 8.60 [SAME AS YASHT 14.52]

For if a villain should seize it, or a witch or a . . .
who has not performed the Gāthās, then Tishtriya,
wealthy and munificent, will go away taking the healing with him.

In this way, the "whore" enters again into the realm of the supernatural, performing acts of the "witch." If a woman wanted to work her sorcery on a man, she could do so by having sex with him while she was menstruating, thus causing him to be defiled. The Videvdad explains the seriousness of this act:

VIDEVDAD 15.7

Fourthly of these acts that mortals perform, he who releases his semen in a woman . . . in menses, bleeding—for the perpetration of this deed [their] bodies then become forfeit.

A woman did not have to be a prostitute or a sorceress to be unclean and dangerous. Indeed, all women were suspected to be allies of the Evil Spirit during their polluted periods. During menstruation, all women were considered as "impure as a harlot, and as blighting to the creation."[36] Although women took part in the ritual of the tradition through their husbands, sons, and other male family members, religious acts for women were limited. During menstruation, they were reduced to striving to contain their demonic possession and avoiding the spread of their pollution.

The prostitute has already been mentioned in the general discussion of women above. Some of the textual evidence specific to the Avesta will clarify her role as an evildoer. Of all women, the prostitute (Avestan *jahī, jahikā*, Middle Persian *jahī, jeh*) is the most evil and dangerous in the Avesta. In this sense, although the name Jahī is used, it means "Whore" in a more general sense. The Whore, for the authors of the Avesta, was a sorceress who was intent on using her powers to harm an "Orderly man," a Mazdayasnian, as we saw above in Yasna 9.32.

The accusation of sorcery is partially dependent on the threat of menstrual contamination, as previously mentioned, but the Avesta gives other reasons for equating prostitution with evildoing. Again, it is wise to remember that the Avestan concept of whore was not equal to our modern usage of the word "whore." It might have corresponded loosely, but as I have mentioned, the charges of whoring could be applied to a woman in a ritually polluted state who had sex with a man. The whore could also be a demonic character, as we see in chapter 18 of the Videvdad, where the Lie (the female demon Druj) tells Sraosha which males—that is, figuratively, which human actions—make her pregnant with evil brood. The fourth of these are actions of the whore, which are the only ones of the three that cannot be atoned for by religious observances. In the case mentioned in Videvdad 18.54–55, the "whore" refers to a fifteen-year-old girl who has become eligible to be initiated into the religion, but does not perform the ritual of tying the sacred *kusti*.

VIDEVDAD 18.54–55

Then the deceiving Lie said to him in turn:
O beautiful Sraosha of the Rewards, this is the fourth of these "males" of mine: a whore who, after her fifteenth year, goes about without tying the sacred girdle. . . .
After she has taken the fourth step, immediately afterward, we the *daēwa*s at once gobble [?] up tongue and fat.

We being thenceforth in command, the bony living beings of Order are destroyed; like *zandas*, possessed sorcerers destroy the living beings of Order.

This is one example that shows the varied use of the accusation of whore-dom, but more importantly, as in the case of a witch, such a girl is accused of stealing the offerings meant for the gods, or causing them to be stolen. The girl who does not follow the ritual of *kusti* tying is accused of consorting with sor-cerers to destroy the good creation, and has committed a sin for which there is no expiation.

Curiously, it seems that if the crime really had to do only with failing to fol-low a ritual meant for both sexes, then the Videvdad would mention both men and women as offenders. The Avesta links the witch and whore with the steal-ing of the offerings meant for the gods most frequently. Unlike the other three evil acts the Videvdad mentions in this chapter, this is the only one that is inex-piable. Similarly, when Zarathustra consulted Ahura Mazdā about these mat-ters, the transgressions that bothered the god the most had to do with women. In the case of the first, the indignation of having one man's sperm mixed with another's harms the same items that a menstruating woman harms:

VIDEVDAD 18.61–64

Zarathustra asked Ahura Mazdā:
O Ahura Mazdā, most Life-giving Spirit, sustainer of Order,
who upsets you with the greatest upset[?], Ahura Mazdā,
who harms you with the greatest harm?

Then Ahura Mazdā said:
The whore, O Zarathustra, sustainer of Order,
who mingles the semen of the [ritually] qualified and unqualified,
of those who sacrifice to the *daēwa*s and those who do not,
of those who have forfeited their body and those who have not.

She causes to stand still one-third
of the rushing waters flowing in rivers
by her looking at them, O Zarathustra.

She takes away the growth of one-third
of the plants growing up, beautiful, green,
by her looking at them, O Zarathustra.

She takes away one-third
of the wool of Life-giving Ārmaiti [the earth]
by her looking at them, O Zarathustra.

She takes away one-third
of the good thoughts that the man who sustains Order has thought more
    [than others],
the good speech he has spoken more,
the good deeds he has performed more,
his obstruction-smashing strength and his support of Order
by her looking at him, O Zarathustra.

The crime of being a prostitute deserved severe punishment, according to
the Videvdad. The prostitute deserved to die more than gliding snakes, howling wolves, or she-frogs, all of which were *khrafstar*s, demon-created animals,
and hence deserved to die. Since the killing of *khrafstar*s was an act of great
merit, the comparison suggests that the same was true for killing a prostitute,
although there is no evidence suggesting that this took place:[37]

VIDEVDAD 18.65

And those [females] I say to you, O Zarathustra of the Spitāmas,
are more worthy of smashing
than the winding snakes or than the wolves with . . .
or than the female wolf . . . who falls upon the flock
or than the frog of a thousand spawns, which falls upon the water.

In the hymn to Ardwahisht, Best Order, we have a curse embracing most evil
things in existence, including the evil women:

YASHT 3.9

You most lying, with lying speech, run away!
O whore possessed by sorcerers, run away!
O whore, female magician, run away!
[In the?] southerly [and] northerly wind, run away!
[In the?] southerly [and] northerly wind, get lost!
And these ones: the ones from the seed of snakes!

He smashes the most lying, the one with lying speech.
He smashes the whore possessed by sorcerers.
He smashes the whore, female magician.
He smashes the southerly [and] northerly wind.
[In the?] southerly [and] northerly wind, get lost!
And the one of these of mine: the ones with the appearance of snakes!

MENSTRUATION

We have seen that according to the authors of the Avesta, menstrual blood was caused by demon-possession. During the menstrual period, a woman was considered a possessed creature who was capable of inflicting the same harm that her possessing spirit, Carrion, the demon of dead matter, could inflict. Videvdad 16 sets out the rules for dealing with the problem of the pollution of menstruation. A hut must be built some distance away from the good things of the earth that might be blighted by the woman. In other words, it was to be set away from the village, bodies of water, vegetation, etc. A menstruating woman had to avoid seeing other humans and animals, plants, fire, water, and even the sun, so as not to give them the evil eye. She could have no fire for heat, food was brought to her in a metal dish, and the rations had to be meager, so as not to strengthen the demon within her (Videvdad 16.6). The food was held out to her on the end of a long spoon, because the person who brought it had to be careful to remain three paces from the woman. If a child touched the woman, as might happen if the child was an infant, and no wet nurses were available, the child would have to be purified after the contact (Videvdad 16.7).

After five nights had passed, the flow should have stopped, otherwise she should stay in the hut for a longer period.[38] If, after nine nights had passed, she still had a flow, it was "a work of the demons, which they have performed for the worship and glorification of the *daēwa*s" (Videvdad 16.11). A longer-than-normal menstrual period was an evil, because it produced such a prolonged contamination.

After the flow of menses stopped, a period of a minimum of three to nine or more days, the woman was allowed to begin the purification process (Videvdad 16.12).[39] This process was similar to the "purification of the nine nights," the *barshnūm*.[40] A woman undergoing the purification had to be washed with bull's urine three times and, finally, with water. If, after the purification, the flow began again, the woman had to undergo the full three days of confinement and begin the purification once again. The Videvdad advised the family to kill *khrafstar*s such as insects, especially ants, and other noxious animals such as crabs and frogs as part of the atonement and purification for the woman. In the summer, two hundred grain-carrying ants could be killed, and, in winter, any other kind of *khrafstar* (Videvdad 16.12). These acts were generally connected with the expiation of sin.

Touching a menstruating woman or having sex with a woman who was menstruating was a sin that carried a heavy penalty, from two hundred lashes for touching, to being accused of committing an inexpiable sin equal to cooking the corpse of one's own son and dropping its fat into the fire, thus contaminating the holy fire.

VIDEVDAD 16.17

He who releases his semen
in a woman having the signs, having the marks, and bleeding,
he performs a deed no better than he who might cook
the corpse of his own son on a spit and carry the fat onto the fire.

It is important in this discussion to remember that the Avestan authors were by no means unique in these views, which are found in many traditions all over the world. However, the complex injunctions aimed at female pollution in the Videvdad were taken to a degree that was unsurpassed in other traditions.

Perhaps because women were excluded from Zoroastrian ritual for the most part, some of them might have engaged in practices that came to be known as witchcraft. Women were excluded not only from the priesthood, but also at certain times of impurity, from society. Priests performed healing exorcisms, provided medicine for the sick, and performed purifications. Because of contamination concerns, a man could not treat female problems or needs, including childbirth. Women as herbal healers (witches, as opposed to priests), health providers for other women, and perhaps women with knowledge of magical ritual practices may have been present on the periphery of the Zoroastrian society, given their frequent mention.

ABORTION

As was the case in most premodern societies, seeing to women's health was a job other women performed for their sisters. The severe sanctions against menstruating and other bloody women as suggested by the Avestan evidence seem to preclude the existence of males in women's health areas, especially when it concerned reproductive health. The woman dealing with the polluting "afflictions" of the female body might be suspected of being in league with the demons who were supposed to be the cause of them in the first place.

The Avesta mentions that women performed abortions with the use of herbs. These women were considered evil, perhaps even witches, and were condemned in the Videvdad (15.13). Abortions were performed with herbal drugs to expel the fetus. The abortion provider was called "an old woman," which suggests that the woman was menopausal. While she was no longer polluted by periodic blood, in many societies a menopausal woman was believed to have magical powers. These powers brought her respect to some extent, but they also exposed her to the risk of being branded a witch.

According to the Videvdad, a woman wishing to have an abortion must approach the old woman, who then would give her instructions and drugs. The passage concerns the sin of a man who impregnates a young woman and, not wishing to take responsibility for the child, sends her to an old woman for an abortion. The man demands: "seek out and consult the old woman about these things!" Due to the pollution generally thought to surround women, their only recourse during times of health crises must have been other women, but there was a risk for such a healer. Although the man was charged with committing a sinful act by ordering the young woman to get an abortion, the old woman was also considered an offender:

VIDEVDAD 15.13

He who approaches a young woman . . . whether she is given [in marriage] or not, and gives her a child, and if this young woman says: the child was made by this man, and if this man says: seek out and consult the old woman about these things!
If, then, this young woman seeks out and consults the old woman about these things, [and] this old woman brings some bang[41] or . . . or killing drug or casting out drug, or any other of the abortive plants, [saying:] Rid yourself of this child!
If, then, this young woman rids herself of this child, [then] they should perform equal [penalties] for this action, both the man, the woman, and the old woman.

The Avesta considered abortion a depravity for several reasons that are not connected with the moral issues of killing an unborn child. The most serious was producing dead matter, and again, it is pollution that produces evil. The woman would be a vessel of death after giving birth to a dead fetus. Secondly, procreation was valued as a small victory for the side of the gods, whereas infertility was a victory for the demons.

Female agents of evil—at least those about whom we have some information—were all somehow connected to feminine blood. The whore, the witch who sought to pollute, the menstruating woman, and the old woman who performed abortions were all polluted by blood. The oft-mentioned sorceresses were not described, so we really do not know much about their actions. We do know that they were accused of stealing, or trying to steal, the sacrificial offerings, an act also connected with the "whore" and a menstruating woman who failed to follow pollution rules. They were believed to consort with demons and perform sorcery. Women in general were seen as having potential tendencies toward the demonic because of the idea that bleeding connected with female procreative functions invited demonic possession. What makes blood-polluted women so unique is that their "crimes" are hardly demonic if one does not take into consideration the notion that they succumb voluntarily or involuntarily to the influence of the demon Carrion.

CHAPTER 7

THE EVIL EYE, CORPSE-ABUSING CRIMINALS, DEMON WORSHIPPERS, AND FRIENDS

THE EVIL EYE

Sight is one of the most important senses when perceiving the world around us, and in many cultures eyes were closely tied to the soul. Sight can also be the transmitter of the evil thought to dwell in the heart; thus, simply by looking at someone or something, an evildoer can destroy. In the Avesta, the Evil Spirit was the first to use the evil eye to cause disease, and Ahura Mazdā was the first to respond by using a spell to counter it. Videvdad 22 tells how the Evil Spirit sickened the creation of Ahura Mazdā by his envious glance.

Thus, by giving the "evil eye" to the creation of Ahura Mazdā, the Evil Spirit was able to afflict it with diseases, just as an envious person can destroy someone's child or animal by giving it the evil eye. Belief in the power of the evil eye is one of the most widespread of superstitions. The power of the eye to touch something, so to speak, simply by a glance from any distance, is the root of this fear. If the person producing the vision is evil, then contact with that evil is established by a glance. The power of the eye also is seen in the gods. In Indian mythology the god Shiva brings destruction with his third eye, which he uses in anger. Mithra, a god we will meet at the end of this chapter, has ten thousand eyes to see the offenders, and he destroys those who offend him. He is associated with the sun, which in Indo-European myth is linked with the eye. In Yasna 1.11 the sun is the eye of Ahura Mazdā as well.

In Videvdad 22.2 the Evil Spirit casts his evil glance at Ahura Mazdā, and creates disease and destruction for his creation. The belief that a person can cast the evil eye out of envy is widespread among Indo-European and Semitic cultures,[1] and this is an early reference to it. People generally believe that the evil eye is provoked by envy of prosperity, beauty, or health. In modern Iran, belief in the evil eye is still common. Popular notions are very similar to those of classical authors who wrote on the subject.[2] The eyes were believed to emanate rays that could harm people or things. As early as Yasna 9, there are references to the evil eye in spells. Yasna 9.29 seeks to ward off the evil eye from the property of the person who recites it:

YASNA 9.29

May you not be able [to walk] forth with the legs,
may you not at all be able [to grasp] with the hands!
May he not see the earth with his eyes,
may he not see the cow with his eyes,
he who does sinful things to our thought,
he who does sinful things to our body!

In the Videvdad the evil eye is mentioned in an exorcistic spell against illnesses. Again, the source of the power of the evil eye is the Evil Spirit:

VIDEVDAD 20.9

May I conquer and chase [various diseases]!
May I conquer and chase the woman with the evil eye, who is rot and filth,
[diseases] which the Evil Spirit whittled forth
against this body, that of mortal men.

Recall from the previous discussion on menstruating women that they were not allowed to look at fire, water, plants, the sun, men, and other creations of Ahura Mazdā. Their glance alone was thought to pollute these things. Therefore, this is an example of the evil eye as well. Even if a woman were righteous and good, the possessing demon could use her eyes to do great harm. In the Yashts, the evil eye is mentioned on several occasions. In Yasht 3.8 it appears in an exorcistic passage in which evil is ordered to depart:

YASHT 3.8

Brood of snakes, run away!
Brood of wolves, run away!
Brood of two-footed [wolves], run away!
Despisers, run away!
You of distraught mind, run away!
Fever, run away!

Slanderer, run away!
Sowers of discord, run away!
You with the evil eye, run away!

The eyes of the demons and evil or envious people have so far been mentioned in connection with the Avesta, but even the eyes of the gods could be dangerous. This is not to say that the eyes of the gods are evil, but they could bring misfortune to evil people and to the demons. The important issue is that the eyes can be powerful and dangerous. Yasht 1.29 points to this:

YASHT 1.29

Then Zarathustra said:
I shake [?] you down back into the earth!
By the eyes of Life-giving Ārmaiti [the earth]
the villain was struck down senseless.

The gods Mithra, Tishtriya, and Sraosha, in particular, were powerful against the demons. Mithra is a solar deity who was described as having ten thousand eyes:

YASHT 6.5

I will sacrifice to Mithra who provides wide grazing grounds,
with a thousand ears, ten thousand eyes.
I will sacrifice to [his] cudgel well swung down
upon the head[s] of the *daēwa*s.
Mithra who provides wide grazing grounds.
I will sacrifice to the companionship, as well,
which is the best of all companionships:
that between the moon and the sun.

Mithra used these eyes to spy any evildoer—even those who sought to conceal themselves.

YASHT 10.82

whose thousand crafts [?] Ahura Mazdā brought forth,
a thousand eyes for the one who looks far and wide.

So with these eyes and with these crafts [?]
he espies both the contract-hurter and the contract-breaker.
So with these eyes and with these crafts
Mithra cannot be deceived,
who has ten thousand spies,
the one rich in life-giving strength
the all-knowing, undeceivable one.

Being a star, Tishtriya was similarly charged with seeing the demons with his bright eyes, and destroying them. The eyes of the gods presiding over or personifying celestial bodies can be understood to be the bright bodies themselves:

YASHT 8.4

We sacrifice to the star Tishtriya, wealthy and munificent,
who contains the seed of water, lofty and rich in vitalizing strength,
forceful, whose eyesight reaches into the distance,
lofty and whose work is above,
the lofty one from whom [comes] good fame.
From the Scion of the Waters [is its] seed.

The god Sraosha, however, presided over the night. He was charged with warding off the evil eye of those evil people and demons who used the cover of night for their activities. In Yasht 11.4–5, we find a spell that was meant to protect one from frightening places where there was some inauspicious influence, or darkness. In these places, the evil one might cast the evil eye on a person:

YASHT 11.4–5

And whoever, O Zarathustra, may pronounce this word to be uttered,
a man or a woman,
with a mind allied with Order,
with speech allied with Order,
with action allied with Order,
[when] in deep water or exposed to great hostility
or in a dark, cloudy night,
at the crossings of rivers in spate
or at the crossroads,

in the gatherings of Orderly men
or in the get-togethers of *daēwa*-sacrificing ones possessed by the Lie,
wherever in back alleys [?],
or wherever in roadless places,
fearing fear,
not ever shall on this day, in this night
the one possessed by the Lie, irritated, angered, irate,
espy him with [his] evil eyes by any espying whatever,
nor may the hostility of a cattle-rustling robber
reach [him] by any reaching whatever!

Thus, the eyes of the gods were powerful against the demons, even as much as the demons had the power to cause evil by their malevolent glances.[3] The many eyes of the gods were also used for their obvious effects in controlling evildoers who thought they might not be observed, yet the predominant idea in these passages is that the eye has power, and that this power is determined by the strength of its owner. The demons had the power to give the evil eye. On the other hand, the gods could likewise protect themselves and the good world with their powerful eyes. As in the case of the gods as the source of disease, the results caused by the evil eye were negative, but they were meant for the ultimate purpose of benefit for the universe by punishing transgressors.

A Pahlavi text, the Selections of Zādspram, contains a fascinating passage in its hagiography of Zarathustra that tells the following story: One day a wizard came to visit Pourushaspa, the father of Zarathustra, who gave his guest a bowl of mare's milk. Young Zarathustra must have known that the man was a sorcerer, because he angrily kicked the bowl of milk, spilling it. The wizard was furious and threatened to destroy the family with his evil eye. Zarathustra countered that he would stare at the wizard with both eyes and destroy *him*. They began a staring duel: the wizard staring with his evil eye, and Zarathustra with his good eyes. After a while, the wizard was unnerved and got on his horse to leave. He had only gone a short distance when he fell down dead. Since then, all of his descendants have also died on the same spot.[4]

It is not surprising that Zarathustra, although a good man, was capable of destroying with his glance. The gods, as we have seen, had powerful eyes that acted against demons and other evil entities, so why would not the same be true for a good man who was versed in good magic? The expression "to fight fire with fire" is apt here. It was not that the gods or the good man used the evil eye, but that the powerful eye of the doer of good acts can be just as deadly. The power of Avestan magicians will be discussed in following chapters.

After describing the installation of Thrita as the first human healer, the priest pronounces the following spell:

VIDEVDAD 20.7

Disease, I tell you to go back!
Destruction, I tell you to go back!
Burning, I tell you to go back!
Fever, I tell you to go back!
etc.
Evil eye [*aghashi*], I tell you to go back!

We already saw an earlier reference to the evil eye in the Gāthās and echoed in Yasna 9.29.

In the hymn to Best Order, it is explained how the Ashem Vohū prayer has the power to smash, among others, the ones with the evil eye:

YASHT 3.11

He smashes the sowers of discord.
He smashes the ones with the evil eye.

YASHT 3.15

He shall smash the one most sower of discord with respect to discord.
He shall be the enemy of the one most sower of discord with respect to
    discord.
He shall smash the one with the evilest eye with respect to the evil eye.
He shall be the enemy of the one with the evilest eye with respect to the evil
    eye.

Cursing the one with the evil eye also occurs in the Rigveda where both Indra and Soma are called upon in a similar manner:

RIGVEDA 7.104.2

Indra and Soma, let evil heat boil up around him who plots evil, like a pot set
on a fire.
Set unrelenting hatred against the fiend, the flesh-eating Brahmin-hater with
the evil eye.

We will shortly discuss carrion-eaters as another category of evildoers. Here we see the flesh-eater classed with the one with the evil eye.

In the Avestan and Pahlavi compositions, the eye was powerful. Sometimes the evil eye belonged to someone who was envious, hateful, and demonic. In the case of a menstruating woman, the demon who possessed her could in effect peer through her eyes and give the evil eye to the good creation. This idea is confirmed in Dēnkard 8.31.21 where the evil eye is paired with the glance of the menstruating woman, which are both harmful. The Bundahishn mentions a king who could kill with the power of the evil eye:

BUNDAHISHN 33.9

There was one whom they call Zēnīgāw, who had poison in his eyes. He had come from the Tāzīgs [Arabs] to be king over Iran. Whomever he looked at with his evil eye was killed.

The power was not limited to evil, however, and, as we just saw, the gods as well as righteous people such as Zarathustra could possess it for the chastisement of the evildoers or demons. Again, this is a case where we can see that the means of carrying out protective measures against evil may be performed using the same deeds and similar formulas. Like the situation in the Gāthās, there seemed to be a rivalry among camps that were more alike than different.

CORPSE-ABUSING CRIMINALS

Death and the demonic were closely connected in the Avestan worldview. All activities associated with dead matter were dangerous because of the possibility of inexpiable pollution. The power of the demon-infested corpse was thought to be so great that only qualified priests and qualified dogs were allowed to carry out the important parts of the rituals meant to disperse the carrion demon. The priest, however, did not come into direct contact with the dead body. Those persons directly connected with disposing of dead bodies were thought likely to become polluted themselves. The corpse carriers moved corpses to the *dakhma*s so that carrion-eating birds could dispose of the bodies.

Even then, dogs had to dispel the demon of death before even they could touch the body. Other people were named in the Avesta as people who had something to do with the dead. Among them are the *nasukesha*, which seems to mean "corpse cutter," though his exact function is not known. This did not appear to be a legal function, whatever it was, unlike the profession of the corpse carrier, because of the penalties prescribed for the punishment of the *nasukesha*. If one looks at examples from other cultures, it seems likely that a person might use parts of a human corpse for sorcery, but this is improbable in the case of the corpse cutter of the Avesta. The sin of corpse cutting was punished severely, yet the sinner was maintained by the community until his death, indicating the possibility that the crime might be accidental. Accidental crimes were punished severely, as we have seen in the case of a woman who unknowingly had sex with her husband during her menses. In later interpretations, corpse cutting has all the signs of sorcery, as we will see.

The Videvdad contains precise information on the degree of corpse cutters' sin and what must be done about it. It was believed that a corpse cutter was the cause of the increase of spiders, locusts, and drought, and that they increased the fury of the winter season produced by demons, which killed cattle and produced too much snow:

VIDEVDAD 7.25–27

How will those men be purified, O Ahura Mazdā, sustainer of Order, who, impure, carry dead matter with feces onto the water or the fire?

Then Ahura Mazdā said:
They will not be purified, O Orderly Zarathustra.
They will give most strength to dogs and locusts,
those corpse cutters possessed by the Lie.
They will give most strength to the waterlogged earth without pasture
those corpse cutters possessed by the Lie.

They will give most strength to the *daēwa*-created winter with deep snow . . .
those corpse-cutters possessed by the Lie.
This lie-demon, the Carrion, will then rush upon their nails,
and afterward they become impure forever and eternity.

If we are to understand that Videvdad 7.25 is answered by Videvdad 7.26, as it should be answered, then it seems to indicate that the crime of corpse cutting had to do with the introduction of dead matter into water and fire, the two most sacred elements. Thus, burning corpses or dumping corpses into bodies of water were crimes a corpse cutter might have been accused of perpetrating.

Videvdad 3.18–21 explains that a corpse cutter should be confined to an enclosure built in a place far away from the community and from all life. He should be brought meager food and rags until the time that he becomes old and senile and his semen dries. At this time he may have been killed, and his dead body was exposed to vultures. If he had committed no other sins, such a punishment was believed to redeem his soul, but if he had been otherwise sinful, he would be punished in the afterlife as well (Videvdad 3.21).

When we consider Videvdad 3.14–21, the idea that a corpse cutter was a person contaminated by a dead body seems more likely. While becoming contaminated unknowingly was serious, it could be rectified. If a person unknowingly touched a dead body, for example if he was hunting and came upon a dead person or dog, that person was expected to approach a village, keeping a safe distance, and to call out for help (Videvdad 8.100).[5] Qualified persons could decontaminate him or her. However, if the person described as a corpse cutter knowingly approached the water or fire after becoming contaminated, this sin would become a permanent pollution. The person may have otherwise been sinless, and for that reason immediate execution was not prescribed.

In later interpretations, as I have mentioned, corpse cutting may have referred to a form of sorcery. The Pahlavi Rivāyat (47.5) relates that Zarathustra was falsely accused of "corpse cutting/bearing" (nasā-kesh) when they found a human skull and other bones in his pocket that had been put there by the agency of the Evil Spirit.[6] Williams, in his commentary, interprets nasā-kesh as "corpse-bearer" in the Pahlavi text. This interpretation would not work according to what we find in the Videvdad. Although corpse bearers were contaminated as a class, there was no evidence that this was a crime. If each corpse carrier were subject to this kind of punishment, nobody would be left to do the work. One could interpret the word to mean an illegal carrier of corpses, which is the meaning in the Videvdad. Such a person carried a corpse without observing the precautions of being bound to another man to increase their power, and of course a dog had to be present.

The Pahlavi Rivāyat myth was most likely modeled after the myth of Yōisht ī Friyān and the sorcerer Axt, in which the sorcerer tried to conceal bones where they might contaminate the righteous Yōisht ī Friyān.[7] The accusation of sorcery by the use of human bones was common in most of the ancient and preliterate world. A sorcerer could, for example, point a bone at his victim, causing him to die.[8]

Another such activity was that of the nasuspā ("corpse thrower"), mentioned in the following series of evildoers in Yasna 65.8. This is closely related to the above offender. It was probably a person who disposed of dead bodies without observing the required care and regulations. This sin appears to be more serious because no expiation was recommended. While a person who was exposed to a dead body and then went on to contaminate the fire and water might be saved after having been punished, a corpse thrower would never be spared. The inexpiable sin of "throwing corpses" is listed in Videvdad 1 as the Evil Spirit's counter-creation for Arachosia (Videvdad 1.12).

Other sins concerning the dead were to dump a corpse into a body of water, or into running water, and to burn a body (Videvdad 7.25). This may be why the corpse thrower was cursed in Yasna 65.8, dedicated to the waters.

If a Mazdayasnian found a dead body in water, he had to remove it, even if there was a risk of contamination, because the deed was of great merit. Leaving a body in water, on the other hand, was sinful because the water was grieved, and people and animals could not drink it (Videvdad 6.30-31).[9]

So dire was the sin of contaminating water that a believer was not only allowed to handle a corpse in this situation, but he was required to do so. The pollution from such an act was expiable. However, atonement was not possible for other instances of corpse carrying without the proper preparations.

Even in a situation such as when a man found a corpse in the wilderness and had to dispose of it or accidentally touched it, there were ways to become purified, but it took help from another. It was a sin to refuse a man the help of purification if one saw him running on the road declaring that he had touched a corpse. Anyone who ignored the plea of a man in need of purification had to take on a third of that man's sin.

CANNIBALISM

Among the more gruesome practices mentioned in the Avesta is the eating of human or dog flesh. Videvdad 7.23-24 deals with the eater of the corpse of a man or dog, who both contain the seed of "man." Such a person can never be purified:

VIDEVDAD 7.23–24

How will those men be purified, O Orderly Ahura Mazdā,
who have eaten from carrion of a dead dog or man?

Then Ahura Mazdā said:
they will not be purified, O Orderly Zarathustra.
Those men should be cut to the grist [?], be cut to the heart,
those men remove the white of the eye from the eye.
This lie-demon, Carrion, will then rush upon their nails.
Afterward they become impure forever and eternity.

One of the worst sins, therefore, was the cooking and eating of the dead bodies of humans, and their kin, dogs. Dog bodies were considered on a par with human bodies as far as contamination was concerned, so this crime might not have been altogether rare. Eating a dog was also cannibalism because dogs were considered one-third human as stated in Bundahishn 8.28. This sin was so serious that the Videvdad recommended that if one came upon a corpse-cooking person, one should kill him or her at once. The cauldron with the cooking dead body had to be taken off, and the fire dispersed, so that it could go out sooner. Sweet-scented wood needed to be brought to appease the fire, which had been so desecrated (Videvdad 8.74–75).[10]

It seems contradictory that first one put out the fire, and then offered it sweet smelling wood. It is possible that some of the fire was retained for bringing to the place of the fire sacrifice, to be combined with other wronged fires. The final result of the combination of fires was the great Ātakhsh ī Wahrām (modern Ātash-e Bahrām).[11]

If we look at the Indian tradition, cannibalism was usually connected with myths of overpopulation, where famine caused people to eat each other.[12] The other case in the Hindu tradition was the Rākshasas, man-eating demons, who were produced from evil. They were thought to eat human flesh, yet were always hungry. Rākshasas were believed to live in crematoria and other places where flesh was readily available. In this case, cannibalism was connected with the practice of sorcery and witchcraft. The cooking of human or dog flesh in the Avesta was believed to strengthen, or even create, demons, sorcerers, and witches, and therefore the magical rite described above sought to destroy the demons by the power of the scented fire.

Sorcery and the improper use of dead bodies were frequently linked in the Avesta, as we have seen. Failure to take action against the evildoer, especially in connection with the evil use of dead bodies, was tantamount to assisting the Evil Spirit. The person who performed the ritual appeasement of the fire was promised a reward in the next world. However, the failure to make amends to the fire resulted in punishment.

DEMON-WORSHIPPERS AND FRIENDS

HOMOSEXUALS

More interestingly, the demon-worshipper did not have to perform an actual sacrifice to qualify as such. The following text shows that homosexual intercourse counted as sacrifice to demons, because it did not produce the desired result of renewal and furthering of life, but instead caused the progress of mankind to come to an end (see *Dādestān ī dēnīg*, questions 71–76). This has to be seen in the light of the fact that natural intercourse with the proper aim of promoting fertility was considered a virtual sacrifice, repeating and imitating the primordial sexual act between Ahura Mazdā and his daughter Ārmaiti, the earth.[13] Just as women could become allied with demons, and at times demonic; so the homosexual actually became a demon. The passive homosexual was thus described as a "she-male" of the demons and the active partner as one who "mounts demons."

VIDEVDAD 8.31–32

Who is a *daēwa*? Who sacrifices to *daēwa*s?
Who mounts *daēwa*s? Who is the vessel of *daēwa*s?
Who is the she-male of *daēwa*s?
Who is as much as a *daēwa*? Who is every *daēwa*?
Who is a *daēwa* before death?
Who becomes a *daēwa* in the other world after death?

Then Ahura Mazdā said:
the male who is sodomized, the male who sodomizes, O Zarathustra of the
    Spitāmas,
he is a *daēwa*, he sacrifices to *daēwa*s.
he mounts *daēwa*s, he is the vessel of *daēwa*s.
he is the she-male of *daēwa*s.
he is as much as a *daēwa*, he is every *daēwa*.
he is a *daēwa* before death,
he becomes a *daēwa* in the other world after death
when a man releases semen in a man
or a man receives semen of men.

Homosexuality was sometimes contrasted with the practice of *khwēdōdah*, next-of-kin marriage, or incest. One of the highly unusual customs of ancient Zoroastrianism, *khwēdōdah* was considered the highest act of worship. A man could marry his mother, sister, or daughter in this system—the closer the relation, the better. The Pahlavi Rivāyat 8.a1–c1 explains that the first pair of humans was brother and sister, so they naturally performed *khwēdōdah*. It cites the importance of the family bond: that families would never have to see their daughters being married off to other tribes, as well as the detrimental effects of marrying foreigners. *Khwēdōdah* was considered particularly effective against sorcery. Why it was contrasted with homosexuality is the interesting issue. Homosexuality was believed to generate demons, whereas *khwēdōdah* destroyed them by producing the best of men. The most excellent sort of *khwēdōdah* was when a man had sex with his mother, because that is closer than any other relationship. The worst intercourse was when the Evil Spirit had anal intercourse with himself, as we will see in the Pahlavi Rivāyat below. In a way, that is the closest sort of "incest," but because he is the Evil Spirit, he used the incorrect orifice. His offspring were the great demons. The Pahlavi Rivāyat presents this interesting view:

PAHLAVI RIVĀYAT 8C.1–6, D.1–2

It says in a place that Ohrmazd said to Zarathustra:
The four best things are the following: sacrificing to Ohrmazd, the lord [of the world]; giving firewood, incense, libations to the fire; propitiating the righteous man; and he who performs *khwēdōdah* with one's birth mother, daughter, or sister. And the greatest, best, and foremost of those four is he who performs *khwēdōdah*. So wonderful is *khwēdōdah*.

In order to make evil among mankind and to harm Ohrmazd, the lord, and all the [other] gods, Ahriman and the *dēw*s practice anal intercourse with all the [other] *dēw*s all the time.

Hunger, peril, thirst, old age, sickness, diseases, desolation, the oppression coming from harmful animals, and all the other evil in the world—anal intercourse is the more [harmful].

It is well known that, if all the harmful animals in the world were to die and [be piled up] to the height of a mountain and all the poison, rot, and filth were to come to one place, the stench would not reach Ohrmazd and paradise.

But when people practice anal intercourse, the stench from the anal intercourse goes all the way to the realm of the Adversary.

Today most evil comes from the anal intercourse, but, in the same way, when Sōshāns comes, all mankind will practice *khwēdōdah*, and all the lie-demons will be destroyed by the wonder and power of *khwēdōdah*.

It is also well known that, when one man [performs] a *khwēdōdah* [with] his birth mother and another with his female child, then he who does it with his birth mother takes precedence over the other, because the one from whose body he came is closer [to him].

For it is well known that, when the accursed Ahriman performed anal intercourse with himself, it was a heavier [sin] than when he did it with the *dēw*s.

The vituperation against anal intercourse is comparable to that against intercourse with a menstruating woman. Menstrual blood was equated with death, thus the woman was possessed by a demon. The pollution produced by coming into contact with menstrual blood in any other situation is expiable, but a person who knowingly had sex with a menstruating woman similarly caused the birth of demons and therefore committed an inexpiable act. The seriousness of this offense arises from the contact of semen, which is considered the life-giving seed, with dead matter.

The real concern seems to be the contact of the sperm with menstrual blood *or* fecal matter, because they both represent death and are appropriate for demons. The Yashts tell a snippet of the myth of Taxma Urupi, a warrior who wore a cape of fox hides, and was known for his ability to defeat witches, sorcerers, and wizards (Yasht 19.28). In this Avestan text, we find a story about how he was able to control the Evil Spirit and ride him like a horse:

YASHT 19.28–29, TO THE DIVINE FORTUNE [*KHWARNAH*][14]

. . . which followed Taxma Urupi with the fox hide,
so that he ruled on the sevenfold earth
over *daēwa*s and men, sorcerers and witches,
false teachers, poetasters, and mumblers,
so that he was able to subdue
all *daēwa*s and men, all sorcerers and witches,
so that he rode the Evil Spirit changed into the form of a horse
for three hundred years around both borders of the earth.

Exactly who Taxma Urupi was in the earlier myths is unknown. Besides the above, we only get fragments consisting of name lists for the most part. Later myths may or may not shed information on earlier beliefs, but we know that he was a character in the mythical beginnings of history. Taxma Urupi is mentioned in the Persian Rivāyats, which tell this fascinating story in some detail.[15] There it is said that Taxma Urupi was known as the "Binder of Demons" because he was able to control even the great Ahriman and force him to take the form of a horse so that he could ride him. This was greatly vexing for the Evil Spirit, who wanted to find a way out of his predicament. Ahriman thought that he would seduce Taxma Urupi's wife to find out his possible weakness. He promised her silk and honey as presents, and, unknown to her at the time, he also decided to reward her with menstruation, the most contaminated condition besides death. The gifts of honey and silk are significant because these two things are produced by insects; therefore, they are part of the evil creation.

Ahriman wanted to know why Taxma Urupi always stopped on Mount Alburz at a certain spot before reaching the Bridge of Judgment. Ahriman in his horse form would lower his head and try to continue, even though Taxma Urupi beat him furiously. The text does not tell us why this made Ahriman happy, but it is commonly understood that hell itself lies below the bridge, a convenient spot so that the sinners who fail to cross the bridge fall into its depths.

The next night Ahriman went to that spot, bucked until he threw Taxma Urupi, and then he swallowed him whole. To become part of the Evil Spirit was just too horrible a fate, and Yima, the first king and Taxma Urupi's brother, asked the god Sraosha to think of some way to recover the body. Sraosha told him that Ahriman was most fond of two things, music and anal intercourse. He advised him to attract the Evil Spirit by singing and then to propose anal intercourse, with the stipulation that Yima be the active partner first. The plan worked, and as soon as Ahriman got into position for the deed, Yima snatched away the body of Taxma Urupi and ran for his life. Yima washed the body and made a *dakhma* for it. By sticking his hand into a polluted place, however, Yima contracted leprosy. Sraosha advised him to wash with the urine of a bull to cure it. From this myth are found several etiologies: the cause of leprosy, the construction of the first *dakhma* (where corpses are exposed), the cause of menstruation, the efficacy of a bull's urine for decontamination, the sin of anal intercourse, and the untrustworthiness of women.

Again, the pollution of menstruation is paired with the pollution of anal intercourse. The fact that Yima contracted a disease from entering the anus of the Evil Spirit makes the connection with death and disease quite obvious. The reason for the wickedness of anal intercourse has more to do with pollution than the "moral" idea that it is somehow unnatural. Like sex with a menstruating woman, anal sex is considered polluted. It is an affront to the male seed, which produces new life, to put it into contact with death-related matter such as menstrual blood and feces.

DEMON-WORSHIPPERS

While the Avestan priests offered the sacrifice to Ahura Mazdā and the other Zoroastrian divinities just before dawn or during the day, they claimed that the demon-worshippers offered sacrifices to the Evil Spirit and the demons during the night (see Yasht 5.94, cited below). The priests believed that their sacrifices would further the prosperity and fertility of the good world, while any sacrifice offered during the night would produce the opposite result and fortify evil in the forms of infertility, disease, and death. Unlike other evildoers, the activities of the demon-worshippers, as well as their sacrificial offerings, are described in some detail in the Avesta. The most fascinating but at the same time most tantalizing description is that of the sacrifices of the Viyāmburas found in the hymn to Verthragna, a deity closely associated with magical practices:

YASHT 14.54–56[16]

Then he drove forth from there [on his chariot],
Verthragna, set in place by Ahura Mazdā, [saying]:
[Am I?] not, O men, worthy of sacrifice and hymns,
as well as the breath-soul of the cow, set in place by the web-holder [?],
as long as now the Viyāmburas,
daēwa-sacrificing men and daēwas,
make the blood flow and pour forth the pouring;
as long as now the Viyāmburas,
daēwa-sacrificing men and daēwas,
bring unto the fire [twigs] of this plant called Juniper,
[and] this [thing] called Salt;
as long as now the Viyāmburas,
daēwa-sacrificing men and daēwas,
bend forth the back,
comb aside the middle,
stretch out all the limbs.
They appear to smash, [but] do not smash.
They appear to crush, [but] do not crush.
As long as now the Viyāmburas,
daēwa-sacrificing men and daēwas,
They obstruct [their] perception.
They turn [their] eyes away.

The vivid description in this passage certainly seems to point to the existence of rival magicians, or what the Avesta called sorcerers. The use of salt
in sacrifices was common among the Egyptians and Greeks, and the crack-
ling sound salt makes when it hits a fire may be meaningful. The demon sacrifice included a blood offering, as did the Mazdayasnian ritual performed
for Verthragna, but it was considered destructive (in the Avesta), unlike the
Mazdayasnian ritual. The demon sacrifice was believed to generate power that
was used to uphold the strength of the Evil Spirit, whereas the Avestan sacrifice was performed to aid the gods. Even given the spare evidence we have
from the Gāthās, there is some evidence that points to rivalry among sacrificers.[17] Later, it is conceivable that these rituals developed in various directions.
The use of similar rites for different gods, or in this case to generate a different
sort of power, seems to be supported by the evidence in the Videvdad.

Martin Schwartz has discovered some very interesting parallels between
the practices described here and those of the Kafirs of Kafiristan (presently
Nuristan) in northeastern Afghanistan. He finds that the Kafirs still use ju-

niper for attaining trance and they perform bloody sacrifices as described in the verses above. The apparent evidence of a possible survival of such a cult indicates that these passages were aimed at real people rather than imaginary demon cults. Whether or not they were truly demonic was in the eyes of the authors of the texts. However, judging from the evidence from other cultures (Egyptian, Babylonian, etc.), there is no doubt that these sorts of rituals were used for good *and* for bad purposes.

Part of the fear of rival sacrificers in the Gāthās was the concern that they might gain valuable resources from the gods. In the Vedas too, demons sacrificed and performed penances. The authors of the Vedas were convinced that the demons could gain powers by their sacrifices. As in the case of the Avesta, they could ask for boons from the gods, and because of the mechanical nature of sacrifice as a magical rite, they could obtain their desired boons. However, the authors of the Avesta declared that the gods would not accept the sacrifices of demon-worshippers, even when aimed at them. The many examples of "demonic sacrifices" point to the existence of rival groups vying for the favor of the gods. That the demons failed to obtain the desired result is indicated in the following:

YASHT 5.94–95

Zarathustra asked her in turn, Ardwī Sūrā Anāhitā:
O Ardwī Sūrā Anāhitā!
How do the libations of yours become here
which demon-worshippers possessed by the Lie offer as yours
after the sun has set?

Thus she spoke, Ardwī Sūrā Anāhitā:
O upright, Orderly Spitāma [Zarathustra]!
to be woe'd down, to be [ground] under the heels,
to be laughed back, to be howled back,
this they are in for, these [libations] that fly after me
by hundreds and a thousand,
. . . at the sacrifice to the *daēwa*s.

The details in the above passages are important hints for forming a picture of what demons were thought to do. As is expected, they sacrificed after the setting of the sun, a common demonic practice, but the goddess Ardwī Sūrā Anāhitā assured Zarathustra that although the demons offered thousands of sacrifices to her as were offered to her by the Gathic rival poet-sacrificer, the demons were laughed at and booed.

Much like the *Rākshasas*, the demons of Hindu myth, the demon-worshippers congregated in evil, polluted places such as the *dakhma*s, described in Videvdad 7.55. The demon-worshippers were described as eating human flesh in the same manner that people cook and eat sanctioned food. The demons and their worshippers congregated in the most polluted places and seemed to have a good time. The places of worship of the followers of demons were predictably associated with night and death, as told in the Videvdad.

The demon-worshippers had their usefulness, however, as they were apparently experimented upon by surgeons-in-training, probably as "outsiders" and so expendable humans:

VIDEVDAD 7.36–37

When these Mazdayasnians drive forth to perform healing,
which should they first experiment on:
on Mazdayasnians or on *daēwa*-worshippers?

Then Ahura Mazdā said:
They should experiment on *daēwa*-worshippers prior to Mazdayasnians.[18]

BAD SACRIFICERS AND GREEDY PRIESTS

One did not have to be a demon-worshipper to ruin the effect of the sacrifice. Bad sacrificers could do just as bad a job. The quality being in the eye of the beholder, however, the bad sacrificer in the Avesta was most often to be equated with the rival sacrificer. This is the case in the Gāthās, where the rival sacrificers were denigrated and even cursed, as in the following passages:

YASNA 31.18

But let no one among you keep listening to the formulas and the ordinances
of the one possessed by the Lie! For he has placed the home or house or
settlement or land in bad settling and destruction. Teach them, you all, a
lesson thus: with a blow![19]

According to the Old Avesta, evil probably got into the Ordered Cosmos of Ahura Mazdā by a wrong ritual, a ritual using bad announcements and so inviting the wrong gods, and based on wrong choices informed by bad *manyu* ("spirit, inspiration"):

YASNA 45.1

May the one of bad announcing not destroy a second time this state of
existence with his bad choice, the one possessed by the Lie, impeded by [? the
utterances of his] tongue.

This first bad ritual was probably performed by the *daēwa*s:

YASNA 30.6

Especially the *daēwa*s did not discriminate correctly between these two,
because deception
would come over them as they were discussing, because they would prefer the
worst thought.
Thus, they would scramble together to Wrath, with which mortals would
sicken this state.

In the Old Avesta, the bad poet-sacrificers are the *kawi*s ("false poets" or
"bad poets") and the *karapan*s ("mumblers") and others, who in later literature
became the mythical opponents of Zarathustra and his revelation:

YASNA 46.11

The "mumblers" and "poets" have harnessed by [their bad] commands
mortal man to evil actions in order for the [present] state of existence to keep
being destroyed, they whom their *own* breath-soul and their *own* vision-soul
will make shudder in anger when they have come to where the Ford of the
Accountant is and become, for their entire lifespan, guests in the house of
the Lie.

The bad priest was a dangerous person because he was considered to have
magical powers, and these could be abused. Knowing the formulas and being
able to call the gods was to be in possession of power ordinary people did not
have. The fact that rewards (goods and resources) were limited was a concern for the authors of the Gāthās. The opposing sacrificer gradually became
a demon or sorcerer in the later texts of the Avesta. The good priest was the
agent of the gods and was vital to maintaining order with his sacrifices and
other rituals, while the bad priest was at the opposite pole. The bad priest was
an evil character because he was a specialist in magic, and therefore he was
sometimes suspected of misusing his power.

A bad sacrificer was often also a greedy sacrificer, who did not give the gods their due and as such was the victim of a curse by the god Haoma. The greedy sacrificer took for himself the foodstuffs and *haoma* that were meant for the gods and for distribution to the community. The curse that Haoma casts on the one who would steal his share of the sacrifice is one of the few curses directly from the mouth of a god upon a human offender. There are many threats in the Avesta, but few in the voice of the god:

YASNA 11.3, 5–6

The *haoma* curses the eater:
May you have no offspring and be followed by bad fame,
who keep me for yourself when pressed,
as [if I were] a thief whose head is forfeit.
But my head is not forfeit,
I, the Orderly, death-averting Haoma.

He who robs me of that *draonah*—[20]
the cheeks together with the tongue, as well as the left eye,—
which Ahura Mazdā, sustainer of Order, gave me,
or steals it or withholds it,
in his home no priest, charioteer, or husbandman will be born.
In his home only stinging and crawling [? things] will be born.

And already in the Old Avesta:

YASNA 32.13

. . . the command by which the glutton seeks a seat in the abode of worst thought,
as do the [other] destroyers of this state and those who, O Mazdā, ever complain—to [my] pleasure—about [*my*] messenger-smoke [?], that of *your* poet, which shall keep them from the sight of Order.

The Gathic instances are unclear, except for the apparent gluttony of the priests and the abuse of the *haoma* and cow. However, the curse of the god Haoma against a greedy priest in Yasna 11 presented the plant/deity as angry and possessive of his share of the sacrifice. A person who dared to deny Haoma his sacrificial portion or to keep the pressed *haoma* for himself would not have fertility in his household. Instead, a reverse fertility would occur: noxious creatures, the miscreation of the Evil Spirit, would flourish.[21]

Miserly and envious people were often suspected of witchcraft. If a person was envious, he or she might wish to destroy the possessions or happiness of the person who was the object of the envy. Envy was often associated with the evil eye, because looking upon the goods or happiness of others with a heart filled with envy was believed to cause harm, as we saw above. The authors of the Avesta composed curses to counteract the envy and hatred of the envious and miserly. Sraosha was invoked to dispel stinginess.

YASNA 60.5

In this house may Readiness to Listen [Sraosha] overcome lack of listening,
concord [overcome] discord,
generosity [overcome] lack of generosity,
humility [overcome] scorn,
the correctly spoken word [overcome] the deviously spoken word
[and] with Order [overcome] the Lie!

Ardwī Surā Anāhitā is invoked in a curse against, among others, the miserly, the ungenerous, and the envious. Envy is indeed said to be "*daēwa*-made" in Yasna 9.5.

The power wielded by a priest was tremendous for the believer. The priest could entreat the gods to protect the community, and he could appease the more dangerous gods to keep them at bay. He could, by the use of mantric formulas, defeat the demons who brought disease, pestilence, bad weather, and famine. If a priest secretly became allied with evil, however, he could bring disaster and death to the community. Instead of appealing to the gods, he could appeal to the demons. These threatening passages were meant to keep priests in check. Another "crime" they could commit was to be covetous of the offerings meant for the gods and the community. The offerings could be considerable, and a greedy priest might take advantage of this to gain riches. Envy and covetousness were wicked emotions that might well invite demons and the use of the evil eye.

Above all was the fear that a person possessing the magical power inherent in the ancient mantras might choose to use that power to call upon the demons for boons of a demonic sort. This again demonstrates the idea that god worship might not have been as different from demon worship as we might imagine.

ROBBERS AND WOLVES

For people who lived a seminomadic or nomadic lifestyle, robbers, perhaps
cattle rustlers, and wolves were great evils. These evildoers were all guilty of
the same offense: robbery. The wolf was a thief because it stole livestock at
night. These thieves had to be stealthy and silent, so they were cursed to become visible to the performer of the ritual. In a spell with a similar purpose
as that in Yasht 4, which uses magical lines to render the priest invisible to his
foe, he tries to conceal himself:[22]

YASNA 9.21

This I ask you as my fifth request, O death-averting Haoma:
May we be the first to notice the thief and the robber,
the first to notice the wolf!
May no one first notice us!
May we notice all first!

Both Haoma and Sraosha were invoked for the protection against robbers
and wolves. The thief and the robber were also the object of a spell in Yasna
9.21 and 30. It was Sraosha, the protector of the world during the hours of
darkness, who, with his familiars, the rooster and the sharp-sensed dog, made
known the presence of the thief and the wolf. The wolf represented not only
a thief who stole livestock, but also a *khrafstar*, a creation of the Evil Spirit.
The dog was a creation of Ahura Mazdā endowed with a great deal of spiritual power. Its ability to see the Carrion demon also translated into the ability
to see evil things at night. The barking of a dog could also frighten demons,
wolves, and thieves.

The story of the creation of the wolf illustrates the theme of duality we so
often see. In the Bundahishn, the Evil Spirit was a stupid and not very creative fellow. Each creature that the good Ohrmazd created has an opponent
created by Ahriman. Thus, the dog was created by Ohrmazd, and Ahriman's
counterpart was the wolf, a creature very much like a dog, but harmful.[23] The
Bundahishn tells the story that Ahriman had planned at first to create the wolf
species as disembodied, unseen evil spirits. Being among the most powerful
of his spirits, they could sneak up on unsuspecting humans. Ohrmazd became
aware of his plan and created several monstrous forms such as the wolf, the
elephant, and the lion. He showed them to Ahriman, who was delighted, and
he attached the evil spirits to these forms saying, "Ohrmazd did what I was
going to do."[24] It was thought that he was taking these for himself, not guess-

ing Ohrmazd's plan. The Bundahishn explains away the similarity between the wolf and the dog in this way.

The dog served, along with the rooster, as opposition to demons and sorcerers.[25] This they did by cooperating with the god Sraosha, whose job it was to see evil in the darkness of the night. It is probable that the dog's ability to sense danger, especially at night, when demons were believed to roam, was what made it a prime candidate for the position it came to hold. The crowing of a rooster is called *kukkut* in Sanskrit, while a dog is called *kukkura*. Both of these animals tend to make a ruckus at dawn, which was the time when it was believed that the gods took back the world from the demons. The barking of a dog at night was taken as a sign that danger in the form of wolves, thieves, or demons was threatening the household. Dogs were credited with having special vision capable of seeing otherwise invisible demons. As Sraosha was the protector of the night, the dog also was charged with this task. Thus, Yasna 61.3 invokes Sraosha "[f]or the discomfiture and removal of thieves and violators."

Goddesses were also called upon for protection, especially for the home, land, and cattle, which were domains often protected by goddesses. Thus, Ardwī Surā Anāhitā, a goddess presiding over the (heavenly) waters, was invoked in a curse designed to make backfire the wicked curses planned by the evil ones who preyed on the author and his community.

Grouping the robber with the wolf was a common occurrence, as we see in the Avesta. Both were considered villainous personalities who took advantage of the cover of the night to take from people. The Rigveda also groups these two evildoers:

RIGVEDA 2.28.10

If someone I have met, O king, or a friend has spoken of danger to me in a dream
to frighten me, or a thief should waylay us, or a wolf—protect us from that, Varuna.[26]

RIGVEDA 10.127.6

Ward off the she-wolf and the wolf; ward off the thief.
O night full of waves, be easy for us to cross over.[27]

RIGVEDA 1.42.2–3

The evil, vicious wolf who threatens us, Pūshan, chase him away from the
path.
The notorious highwayman, the robber who plots in ambush,
drive him far away from the track.[28]

THE GODS WHO HELP AGAINST HUMAN EVILDOERS

All the gods helped support the ordered cosmos of Ahura Mazdā and therefore helped the god-fearing humans. In addition to Haoma, whose importance we have seen above, three gods were especially often invoked for assistance against supernatural and other evil: Mithra, Verthragna, and Sraosha.
They had similarities in that they were all very early martial gods and they
demanded offerings for their services.

MITHRA

Mithra was the personified contract and protector of all the agreements between gods and humans, which maintain orderly social and political conditions. He was the dispeller and punisher of demons. Among his opponents
were "witches" and "sorcerers," as well as *kawi*s and *karapan*s (see above).
The Evil Spirit and his minions, Wrath, Sloth, and all kinds of other demons,
feared him and his thunderbolt (*vazra*)[29] when he drove forth in the company
of the other gods: Verthragna in the shape of a raging boar (Yasht 10.70),
Sraosha, Rashnu, and the *frawashi*s (Yasht 10.96–97). They were wise to fear
him, because the consequences of Mithra's anger were tremendous according
to these texts.

Mithra exacted his revenge primarily on the battlefield, where he punished
anyone who had broken a contract or had failed to honor him. Armies called
upon Mithra in apotropaic spells aimed at enhancing their strengths and
giving them vision to see the otherwise unseen enemies. Charioteers begged
endurance for their teams in battle, while the horses of the opposing party re-
belled and refused to move, or ran where they should not go (Yasht 10.20).
Even the most skilled warrior found himself frustrated because, by his divine
magic, Mithra reversed anything the warrior tried to do. The offending warrior found that his arrows flew backward, away from their intended goal.
The spears he flung fell harmlessly to the ground, and axes failed to find the
heads of his enemies (Yasht 10.40). Mithra made the offenders blind and deaf,
and bound their hands so that they could not even defend themselves (Yasht

10.48). They were thrust into fear and terror, and then he would finally behead them, flinging away their heads (Yasht 10.37).

Mithra, like other gods, could be summoned by sacrifice and libations. Therefore, if two armies asked for his help, whom did he choose? Wars are generally started by breaking agreements or contracts. According to the Avesta, Mithra would destroy whichever army was the contract breaker, even if it attempted to offer him worship. This may be why there is a stress on the contract in the Yasht dedicated to him. Yet, aside from the offense of "contract-breaking," Yasht 10.39–40 points to Mithra's rage at being ignored and not being offered a share of the sacrifice. We see once again that the gods responded to the sacrifice without the necessity of any element of human devotion. There is, instead, a right and wrong side. The breaker of the contract was on the wrong side:

YASHT 10.19

Mithra angered and enraged will come up [upon him] to that side
where the contract-belier is not at all watching in his mind.

Yasht 10 is presented in both curses against the enemies and apotropaic spells for the protection of the people who think they are the wronged party. We will see that the martial gods were themselves quite dangerous, and steps had to be taken to ensure that they did not attack the people who were trying to appeal to them for help. Once the gods were enraged, they might have found it difficult to distinguish between the right and wrong parties. This may have given the "right side" a means of remaining "right" if they lost a battle after appealing to the god, for they could have blamed their loss on the god's anger.

Although Mithra was usually called at times of war, he was also an enemy of witches, demons, and other evil creatures, as was the case with most of the martial gods.

YASHT 10.34

so that, with good thought and optimistic,
joyous and thinking good thoughts,
we may overcome all opponents;—
so that, with good thought and optimistic,
joyous and thinking good thoughts,

we may overcome all enemies; —
so that, with good thought and optimistic,
joyous and thinking good thoughts,
we may overcome all hostilities,
conquer the hostilities of all those hostile
*daēwa*s and men, sorcerers and witches,
false teachers, poetasters, and mumblers.

Ahura Mazdā even offered sacrifices to Mithra (Yasht 10.56),[30] to increase his strength as he did with several other demon-opposing gods, as we saw in the case of Tishtriya. Another characteristic of the gods deputed to fight witches and sorcerers was that they were very jealous of their offerings. Libations had to be kept from evildoers, and could not be consumed by an inappropriate person. In this case, it is spelled out very clearly, demanding that the person receiving the libations must perform austerities and ritual purification. As in the case of a person authorized to use mantric spells, such a candidate for receiving the libations had to be well-versed in the sacred liturgy.

YASHT 10.122

Then Ahura Mazdā said:
For three days and nights they should wash [their] bodies,
they should undergo austerities amounting to thirty whiplashes
for the sacrifice and hymn to Mithra who provides wide grazing grounds.
[Then] for two days and nights they should wash [their] bodies,
they should undergo austerities amounting to twenty whiplashes
for the sacrifice and hymn to Mithra who provides wide grazing grounds.
Let no one consume these libations of mine
who is not well-versed in all the ritual models of the Texts of Praise and
    Sacrifice.

In the Vedic pantheon, Mithra is Mitra, the keeper of contracts, but there he is associated with Varuna. They are often invoked together for the maintenance of order. In the Rigveda, Mitra's function was similar to that of Mithra, and he was also a solar deity. He did not exhibit the fierce aspect that characterizes Mithra in the Avesta, instead he appears to be rather mild-natured.

VERTHRAGNA: THE SMASHER OF OBSTRUCTIONS AND DEFENSES

Like Tishtriya, Verthragna was a magical shape-shifter who assumed the forms of the noblest males of the most splendid creation. First was the forceful Wind, a male entity with healing potential. He was deadly in this form to hostile demons and men, sorcerers, witches, and tyrants (Yasht 14.4). In his second form, he appeared as a beautiful bull with golden hooves and well-fashioned horns. In his third form, he was a white stallion with tawny ears and a golden bridle. In the fourth, he was a rutting camel, who was dangerous in his passion when released for mating. In the fifth, he was the magnificent boar already described. In the sixth form, he was a fifteen-year-old man in the bloom of youth and vitality. In the seventh, he was the magical Vāregna bird, created by Ahura Mazdā. In the eighth, he appeared as a wild ram with curled horns. The ninth was a buck with sharp horns; and in the tenth, he was a warrior, carrying a golden sword. All of these forms were male, and represented what these early people considered the perfection of masculinity among creatures.

The hymn to Verthragna contains a unique Avestan example of the use of feather magic (see Chapter 8). Verthragna, like Mithra, was especially opposed to sorcerers and witches, who were never allowed to take the sacrifice that was meant for him, and it was the responsibility of his worshippers to see that these particular evildoers did not approach Verthragna's sacrificial offerings. Yasht 14.49–53 gives the details of the sacrifice he requires:

YASHT 14.49–50

In turn Zarathustra asked him:
What is indeed, O Ahura Mazdā,
the sacrifice and hymn to Verthragna, set in place by Ahura Mazdā,
according to best Order, most according to the established rules?
Thus said Ahura Mazdā:
The Aryan lands should bring him libations.
The Aryan lands should spread out *barsom* for him.
The Aryan lands should cook a sheep for him,
white or of good color or whichever color it resembles.

YASHT 14.51–53

May not a villain seize it or a witch or a . . .
who has not performed the Gāthās,
who destroys the existence, who opposes this *daēnā*,
that of Ahura Mazdā, that of Zarathustra,
For if a villain should seize it or a witch or a . . .
who has not performed the Gāthās,
who destroys the existence, who opposes this *daēnā*,
that of Ahura Mazdā, that of Zarathustra,
then Verthragna, set in place by Ahura Mazdā,
will go away, taking the healing with him.
Straightaway scourges will come upon the Aryan lands.
Straightaway armies will fall upon the Aryan lands.
Straightaway the Aryan lands will be smashed
for the striking of fifty by striking a hundred,
for the striking of a hundred by striking a thousand,
for the striking of a thousand by striking ten thousand,
for the striking of ten and by striking countless ones.

SRAOSHA: THE GUARDIAN OF THE NIGHT

The god Sraosha was the "night watchman" of the gods, being most active at night, a time thought to increase demonic power. While Mithra could dispel the night after it had run its course, Sraosha was the god who protected the world at night. Mithra stayed in his state of all light and did not venture into the darkness. Sraosha was the most powerful in obstruction smashing, and he was called "the crusher of the Lie."[31] He was described as one "who unsleeping in wakefulness protects the creatures of Mazdā . . . who protects the entire corporeal being with raised weapon after sunset." Indeed, the Avesta proclaims that he has not slept since the two spirits created their creatures, but has watched over the creatures of Ahura Mazdā, while battling demons day and night.

All of the demons would become frightened before him and they "run into their darkness" to escape a confrontation with him (Yasna 57.18). His principal opponent was "Lieful Wrath," and he was described as a mighty smasher of all kinds of demons.

The rooster and the dog were familiars of Sraosha because they would frighten the demons who came to attack the good of the world at night. By its own magic, the rooster was able to see the invisible demons, and its voice dispelled them. The dog's anti-demon abilities served to repel the Demon of Death, as well as other demons.

One was advised to pray to Sraosha at night at the most frightening places: crossroads and the confluence of deep rivers, because these places were filled with magical potency and could be used by the agents of evil, notably demon-worshippers (Yasht 11.4). The association of crossroads with evil magic is well known from other traditions. Virgil says that the name of Hekate, the goddess associated with darkness and death, "is howled by night at the city crossroads" (*Aeneid* 4.609). A corpse of a criminal buried at the crossroads could placate her.[32] In the Shatapatha Brāhmana (2.6–2.8), Rudra's realm is said to be the crossroads, where he can either help or hurt the traveler. From modern times, S. J. Tambiah says of the north central African people, the Azande, that when they feel they may be victims of a sorcerer, they go to well-used crossroads to disperse the spell.[33] In the Avesta, crossroads are mentioned again as the places where priests carry out the powerful feather ritual connected with Verthragna.

There were other places and times these ancient people considered dangerous at night, and thus under the protection of Sraosha. These were back alleys, roadless places, and cloudless nights. His worshippers sought the protection of this god from the robbers and evil spirits who would spy on them at night.

Sraosha was said to break up the get-togethers of sorcerers and witches at night. According to the Avesta, fearing his hostilities, witches, sorcerers, and demon-worshippers would run for their lives (Yasht 11.6).[34]

Sraosha was benevolent for the most part when it concerned humans, and he was a source of comfort at night. His function as a special enemy of the night demons, witches, and sorcerers made him an important god in the realm of Avestan magic because he was most powerful at the times and places where evil magic was performed the most. He was the god who protected the places prone to the influence of magic, such as crossroads and river crossings (Yasht 11.5).[35] In the Yasna, Sraosha was only involved in activities having to do with protection from the dark elements, but in the Yashts, he became part of the Mithraic entourage, without losing his original functions.

Sraosha was also invoked to keep the afflictions of diseases away, presumably because the Avestan people believed that disease was caused by the unseen demons who entered the body. Death, the "Dismemberer," a demon we cannot see, was an associate of "Wrath, with the Bloody Banner," and a special foe of Sraosha (Yasna 57.25).

CONCLUSION

Few of the evildoers described in this and the previous chapter were the supernatural or invisible demons that we will encounter later in the curses and spells of the Avesta. Rather, they were humans who the authors of the Avesta thought had joined the side of evil by their own choice. In many cases, notably those of sorcerers and witches, these evildoers had significant powers similar to those of the spiritual demons created by the Evil Spirit. In other cases, such as the greedy priest and prostitute, they may seem to us to be relatively benign. This was not the case for the composers of the Avestan texts, who had other criteria for judging evils. The prostitute, for example, was accused of sorcery. However, the Avestan definition of "prostitute" is imprecise, and, as in our culture, the word can be used as a derogatory term for any "improper" woman.

Women were the targets of considerable attention as potential evildoers because of natural functions. Menstruation is a major pollution in many cultures, but the Avesta saw it as a state of temporary demon possession, and indeed a woman had to undergo a shortened exorcistic ritual following menstruation. A mother who had suffered a stillbirth had to undergo a major exorcism. In these cases, it was not a volitional state of evil for the human subject; nor can we say that the person was innately evil, for, as we have noted, humans were created by Ahura Mazdā, who is incapable of creating evil. The mythic association of women with the Evil Spirit complicates the problem. Women came to be seen as dangerous, and because of their central place in the home and as wives and mothers of the believers, they were thought to be in an advantageous position if they wished to pollute their husbands and families. They were controlled by segregation at times of pollution, and by the many warnings in the Avesta.

Aside from the cases where the evildoer made a choice to be evil, such as is the case with sorcerers and corpse-throwers, the person involved, namely a woman in menses or a person polluted by contact with the dead, was actually considered possessed by a demon. This did not excuse the crime, however, and the person was just as dangerous and had to atone for "crimes" committed while possessed.

In the other cases, human evildoers were seen as people who needed to be cursed or otherwise controlled by mantras and rites. For this end, we will see in the two following chapters how the Avesta attempts to keep them under control by the use of spells, curses, and exorcisms.

CHAPTER 8

EXORCISTIC AND APOTROPAIC RITUALS

HEALING OF DISEASES

In comparison with the Indian treatment of disease, we know very little about early Iranian cures. The āyurvedic medicine of the Indians was based on the balance of three "humors" in the body: wind, bile, and phlegm. The āyurvedic literature featured three primary texts, which date from roughly 300–700 CE.[1] With the exception of later texts, and those dealing with mental illness, they tried to avoid the idea of demon possession.[2] The Atharvaveda (c. 900 BCE), on the other hand, was a treasure trove of exorcistic spells and rituals. Magico-ritual treatment of disease was not supplanted by the āyurveda. Rather, each still tends to be used for certain needs. There are fewer texts for the Iranian tradition, but a mixed use of treatments seems to also be the case for them. However, they had no equivalent to the āyurvedic system; rather, much like the composers of the Atharvaveda, they believed that all diseases were the result of demonic possession or the result of demon-induced disorders.

The Avesta tells how the villainous Evil Spirit looked upon the creation of Ahura Mazdā and "sickened" it. All of the creation became sick, not just living entities but the earth itself. Exorcising the demons that attacked the good creation was a constant occupation for the authors of the Avesta. The sacrifice was important as it removed demonic influence on a cosmic scale. Each person performed purification rituals on a daily basis for removing demonic influences caused by pollutions. Women had to contain the threat of the blood pollution caused by demons, and everyone's body ultimately falls to the Demon of Death.

In view of all the diseases and ailments of both living beings and nature itself, various remedies were needed, and healing is indeed a concern that runs like a red thread through the Avesta. People could ask gods to help cure diseases or other evils that befell them and nature, or, more commonly, they performed the proper ritual to obtain the desired result. There were three basic methods of healing or treatments for diseases, depending on the nature of the disease: surgery,[3] herbal medicine, and spells and incantations, as stated in the Videvdad (7.44).[4]

Healing by the Sacred Word (*manthra*) involved healing spells and the more drastic spells and curses of exorcism. Combinations of the methods were probably also practiced, but the healing by spell was considered the most effective in the Videvdad. It is conceivable that diseases that did not respond to herbal medicines and surgery would be considered the work of stronger demons, in which case exorcism would be the only remaining option.

Surgery is described at length in Videvdad 7, notably the training of surgeons. This training involved experimental surgery on humans, and the specimens used for this purpose were demon-worshippers, as mentioned above. At this time surgery was a risky procedure at best, and needed to be practiced on people who were "outsiders" and so expendable.

For such an early mention of medicine, the above is quite amazing and very practical. The "surgeon" was absolved from the equivalent of malpractice suits after three successful surgeries, an interesting detail. The use of magic in the form of exorcism was necessary after herbal healing and surgery failed to solve the problem.

VIDEVDAD 7.36

O Orderly creator . . .
When these Mazdayasnians move forth to perform healing,
which should they first experiment on:
on Mazdayasnians or on *daēwa*-worshippers?

VIDEVDAD 7.37

Then Ahura Mazdā said:
They should experiment on *daēwa*-worshippers prior to Mazdayasnians.
If one cuts a *daēwa*-worshipper a first time and he dies,
if one cuts a *daēwa*-worshipper a second time and he dies,
if one cuts a *daēwa*-worshipper a third time and he dies,
then this one will be considered as inexperienced for ever and eternity.

The healing methods are represented as having been initiated by Ahura Mazdā to heal the diseases brought upon the world by the Evil Spirit and first practiced by primordial healers among gods and men. Thus in the Gāthās, the poet-sacrificer addresses Ahura Mazdā as the "healer of the existence" through his utterances:

YASNA 31.19

He who first thought Order has now listened [to my words?], namely, you, the knowing one, the healer of this existence, O Ahura, being in command of your tongue at will for the correct uttering of the words, you who, through *your* glowing fire,[5] O Mazdā, provide a firm stance to [my] legs in the race for good [renown].

YASNA 44.16

I am asking you this: tell me straight, O Ahura!
Who is the smasher of obstructions[6] fit to protect all who *are* by *your* announcement?
Let brilliant [assistances/gifts?] be given to *me*! Assign, O healer of this existence, [me as?] a model [winner?]!
Thus, let readiness to listen [= Sraosha] come to *him* on account of [my/his] good thought,
O Mazdā, to *him*, to whomever you wish![7]

The world was in need of healing, since it had been sickened by demons and mortals.

In a sense, healing for the Avestan people was not reserved for disease alone. Disease was a powerful indication of demonic influence, but it was only part of the cosmic scheme. According to the Bundahishn, the Evil Spirit fell upon the newly created and perfect world like a ravenous wolf. He attacked the stars, the sky, and the earth before falling upon living things. He introduced pain, hunger, sloth, disease, and death. The gods helping Ohrmazd (Ahura Mazdā) produced herbs to fight disease. They created an herb to serve as a cure for every disease the Evil Spirit introduced. This indicates that the Avestan people believed that there was an herbal cure for all diseases, if it could be found. Thus, herbal cures might have been the first step in curing a disease, if the priest had the proper herb.

The use of surgery was no doubt trickier. The injunctions to practice surgery on the "demon-worshippers" demonstrate that they recognized the need for expertise in the art of surgery. This did not mean that they believed that some diseases were disorders that were not demon-induced. As with herbal remedies, the cure depended on counteracting the demonic principle that caused the disorder. Surgery could remove the demon-damaged part from the body, or in the case of broken bones or injuries from sharp things and weapons, the cause might obviously be accidental. A sorcerer or witch might have caused the "accident," but it would be foolish to cure such an injury with mantric spells alone. The Atharvaveda treats surgery in this manner as well— it is necessary in certain obvious cases.[8] As was the case for the healers of the Atharvaveda, mantras were most likely used for every cure, but full exorcisms were not routine.

Exorcism was reserved for the most difficult cases, and for routine major pollutions caused by demons. I have already mentioned several of these cases: the pollution of touching a dead body, the pollution of a woman who has had a stillbirth, and at least once during a person's life to remove the pollution of having been in the womb. This third pollution was the result of the belief that menstrual blood nourishes the fetus—the same blood that is produced by demon-possession.[9]

Emile Benveniste,[10] Jean Puhvel,[11] and more recently Bruce Lincoln[12] have suggested that these three methods of healing correspond with the three social classes, healing by mantra being a priestly form, surgery a form for the warriors, and herbs a form for the commoners. Since the Avesta states that Ahura Mazdā created herbs to cure every disease, this would indicate that herbs are the first line of defense for all people. If herbs did not work or could not be found, then mantras might be used, or, if appropriate for the case, surgery might be used. I doubt that the healers came from different classes based on their techniques. The priests were most likely skilled in at least the methods of herbal healing and mantric healing. Surgery produced contaminating blood, but the Avesta makes no mention of the risk for the surgeon. Therefore, its use by the priests will have to remain a conjecture.

MYTHS OF FIRST HEALERS, FIRST EXORCISTS

Mircea Eliade noted that it is common for healing myths to be linked with the creation myth.[13] The power of the first healing may be regained by recalling three myths together: those of creation, the origin of disease, and the first cure.

Bronislaw Malinowski noted that the act of recalling the myth is a reenactment of the original magical act. More recently, Lincoln noted the relationship between the myth of the original use of magical healing and the healing ritual.[14] Most important in the success of healing by exorcism is the belief on the part of the patient that the magic will work. Retelling the myth of the original magic reminds the hearers that the magic was originally successful, and that, by following this same prescription, a qualified practitioner can succeed too. The original myth has information about the successful ritual, and by reciting the myth, the gods and even the mythical magician are called upon to lend their assistance. The Avesta contains the myth of Airyaman, the first healer god, and Thrita, the first human healer, and this myth recalls the power of the god.

After the Evil Spirit had created his 99,999 diseases, the corruption was so great that Ahura Mazdā called upon the sacred ancient spell, the "Life-giving Sacred Thought," Manthra Spenta, to heal the world. He promised to offer a sacrifice to Saokā[15] of a thousand fleet horses, a thousand fleet and high-humped camels, a thousand brown cattle, and a thousand pregnant females,[16] all very fertile animals (Videvdad 22.3–4).[17] The spell in question was the powerful Old Avestan prayer, the Ā Airyēmā Ishiyō (Young Avestan: Airya-man Ishiya), the final and concluding strophe of the entire Gāthā collection, which sums up the beneficial effects of the sacrifice performed in the manner of Zarathustra.[18]

Ahura Mazdā ordered his messenger, Nairyasangha, to go to the mansion of Airyaman and ask for the assistance of the Airyaman Ishiya (Videvdad 22.7), and Airyaman came with the animals required for the sacrifice and with the nine channels and furrows required for the exorcistic purification ritual. Airyaman was thus able to show humans how to become purified and so ward off diseases.[19] His role here is therefore that of the primordial physician god. However, the mention of the nine furrows leads one to believe that his healing was by exorcism, whereby a demon is ordered to leave a person's body.

The first human healer, on the other hand, was Thrita, the son of Sāiuzhdri and brother of Ashawazdah,[20] and first mentioned in Yasht 5.72, where he is asking Anāhitā for a boon that he may overcome his enemies. We know very little about Thrita and his connection with healing other than what is said in Videvdad 20.

Thrita's name corresponds to Old Indic Trita, a Vedic water deity who became connected with the expiation of sin and purification, especially during the sacrifice. In the Yashts, Thraētaona is depicted as responsible for healing; thus, in Yasht 13.131 it is recommended that his *frawashi*[21] be worshipped to ease the suffering from "itches, fevers and the terror dragged forth by dragons." Georges Dumézil explained that the name Thrita is "the exact onomastic equivalent of Trita,"[22] but he shows that Thraētaona is the one who corresponds functionally to Trita. Both characters were the third of brothers,[23] and they both battled three-headed demons. In fact, in the hymn to Haoma (Yasna 9.7),[24] Thraētaona's father is said to have been Āthviya, a name that corresponds almost exactly to the common epithet Āptya of Trita.[25] It is possible that Thrita and Thraētaona were different mythical personalities but with similar functions, which caused their myths to be conflated over time.

In the Videvdad, the myth of Thrita, the first healer, introduces a series of spells used for exorcism and healing.[26] The myth also tells how Ahura Mazdā created herbs to counteract the diseases created by the Evil Spirit.

VIDEVDAD 20.4

Then I, Ahura Mazdā, brought up healing plants,
numerous—many hundreds,
numerous—many thousands,
numerous—many ten thousands,
among them, the *one*: Gaokarna.[27]

The Videvdad 21.2 goes on to describe how Zarathustra employed the purifying waters to heal illnesses. Here the worshippers invoked the clouds to bring rain and then asked Zarathustra to drive away illnesses, including diseases afflicting women.

The importance of the waters as healing agents is ubiquitous in the Avesta as it was throughout the Atharvaveda.[28] We have seen that, at the supernatural level, the god Tishtriya makes the heavenly Vourukasha Sea release its water, and so heal the Aryan lands from drought and bad seasons (Videvdad 21.4). In the world of the living, the sacrificers performed the ritual in the manner of Zarathustra and pronounced healing apotropaic spells to achieve the same result. Rain is cleansing and it is necessary for the growth of medicinal herbs.

These spells are then punctuated by curses to drive away the demons, calling them by name.[29] This spell invokes elements in a logical manner, as per the Avestan rain mythology, which involves the clouds and the Vourukasha Sea, as we have seen. Thus, after the clouds are invoked to produce rain, the Vourukasha Sea is invoked.

After the waters are invoked, the sun is summoned for help. The rain and sun are both purifying elements, and thus they are invoked for keeping away disease. Then the exorcising priest would recite his intentions to wash away the impurity and to grant offspring to those who did not have them.

This leads to the invocation of the moon, who was the keeper of the fertility created by Ahura Mazdā after the Evil Spirit first made his attack on the world. After the first man and the first bull fell ill and died because of the Evil Spirit's diseases, the sun and the moon took up and cleansed the seed of the two: the moon cleansed the seed of the bull, and the Sun that of the first man, Gayōmard (Bundahishn 6.44 and 14.5). This part of the myth explains why infertility is a disease caused by demons and explains how it can be healed. Both the sun and the moon are invoked for fertility, as they have the seed of all fertility in the world. Finally, the stars, which were thought to contain the seed of water, are invoked.

After this, the exorcism begins. The priest calls the demons by name to expel them. As S. J. Tambiah explains, the summoning of the demons responsible for disease uses the language of command along with allusions to myths to "prepare the ground for the next sequence,"[30] which in the case of the Avestan ritual is the cleansing with bull's urine and the removal of the demon from each part of the body or thing to be cleansed:

VIDEVDAD 21.17

Rise at your rising [O sun]!
You are constrained[31] in *kakhwazhi*!
You are constrained in iron![32]
You are constrained, whore possessed by sorcerers.
May I conquer and chase *ashire* . . .
May you not destroy the bony living beings of Order!

EXORCISM

Just as the world of the gods and demons was divided on a cosmic battlefield, with good forces opposed by evil forces, so in the world of the living humans found themselves arrayed on opposite sides. Thus, the divided other world was a model for this world peopled by both the good priests and the Mazdayasnian community of believers, and on the other side sorcerers, witches, bad magicians, and a host of demons.

To defend themselves against magical forces, the authors of the Avesta used magic. As on the battlefield, where both sides take up similar weapons, so, in the struggle against evil, the good people used magic to defeat their enemies. The Gāthās provided them with the ancient and venerable language they required for the most powerful magic, and the Avesta, with its rich fund of curses and spells, was a source of magical formulas. In choosing sides, the believers had to identify themselves and those who were their enemies. In some cases, it was clear: as we have seen, any person who threatened the safety and prosperity of the community was evil. However, in other cases, the threat was intangible.

The function of exorcism for such a community was all-important in confronting and expelling the evil that they feared, especially when it came in the form of a mysterious disease. Tambiah sums up the function of exorcism succinctly, noting that evil must be personified so that the patient can understand the nature of the illness.[33] Exorcism is the identification of and the driving away of evil spirits by ordering them to leave a person's body or to leave a place.

Disease was not the only condition needing the ritual of exorcism. In the Avesta, other situations call for exorcism, such as the need to cleanse someone who has been contaminated by contact with a dead body, and other similar occasions that require serious ritual cleansing. The latter cases could be cured by exorcism if the necessary criteria were met. In contrast, a disease could persist even after exorcism. This pointed to a very powerful demon. This would allow the believer to have faith in the efficacy of the cure despite the lack of a positive result.

For the authors of the Avesta, a demon could be more powerful than the gods. The demons and the gods possessed similar powers, although acts of sacrifice by humans aided the gods and renewed their strength. Thus, rituals took on cosmic proportions and could affect the outcome of the bigger battle fought by the spirits of good and evil. Demon worshippers were believed to similarly strengthen the demons by their sacrifice, and this is why they are so vilified in the Avesta.

The Avesta advises the use of a combination of exorcistic spells and rituals using water and the urine of a bull to command demons to leave the body. Houses could be exorcised as well, not because they were believed to be haunted by the ghost of a dead person, but because they were possessed by demons. A house in which a person died was considered polluted by the demon that caused the death, or by the Carrion demon, not by the spirit of the one who had died.

Exorcisms in the Avesta appear to be separate from the healing rituals performed by the herbalist or the surgeon, but because the source of all illnesses was demon possession, exorcism may have been reserved for the worst cases or for cases where the cause of the disease was unknown. However, many herbs themselves were thought to have powers to incapacitate a demon-created illness and, as we saw above, were created by Ahura Mazdā at the same time as the Evil Spirit was creating diseases. These herbs were meant to directly counteract the diseases created by demons. It appears, however, that exorcism was still favored as a more powerful magic than the herbs alone.

The Avestan people's need for the exorcistic ritual is ultimately tied to the dualistic cosmology, which requires a belief in demons as the cause of all misfortunes. While some conditions could not be avoided, certainly disease could often be fought by various means. Although in the later Pahlavi texts there was often the suggestion that unrighteous acts could bring on a disease, it was so only because the body would be open to attack by demons.[34] Therefore, demons, rather than bad acts, were the direct cause of disease. In the Avesta, there is no suggestion that evil acts alone cause disease, or that diseases have their source in the gods as punishments for moral transgressions. Again, we see that it is possible to incur the wrath of a god and thus become diseased, if, for example, a witch were allowed to steal the offerings meant for the god. Tzvi Abusch has investigated a similar phenomenon in Mesopotamian views on witchcraft. He shows that there is a relationship between witchcraft and the anger of the gods, who then send bad luck and illness.[35]

Exorcisms served to identify the disease and its cause, as well as to cure it. Diseases could be caused by sorcery, the intrusion of a disease-causing demon, or by breaking a taboo (even inadvertently), such as touching a corpse or a menstruating woman. The belief that any of the above could cause illnesses and that they could be cured by exorcism played a significant role in the recovery of a sick person.

Tambiah comments that exorcism provides a kind of "shock therapy" that can possibly help effect a real cure because the patient is made to "confront, formulate and give objective form to his illness in terms of a demonic agent which is culturally defined."[36] Thus, Tambiah feels that some physical illnesses can be alleviated by exorcism as well. In their study of modern Iranian "illnesses by fright" and "heart distress," Byron J. Good and Mary-Jo Delvecchio Good argue that this kind of classification may be equivalent to real disease categories.[37] They note that sickness in one culture may be the work of spirits, but a physiological disorder in another: "Illness realities are thus biologically constrained and culturally constructed."[38] For understanding exorcisms in the Avesta, it is important to understand what disease meant to its authors.

MAGICAL LINES

We know very little about specific ritual acts that accompanied spells, but we do have some tantalizing details, mostly from the Yashts and the Videvdad, which contain some of the most specific instructions for the performance of magical rites, including line and feather magic. The use of lines is described in Yasht 4 in a spell to make oneself invisible, in Videvdad 9 as part of the *barshnūm* ceremony, and in Videvdad 17 for the disposal of hair and nail trimmings. Jamsheed K. Choksy comments that the lines can only be opened and closed by ritual specialists.[39] The lines are drawn in multiples of three, up to nine, and the act is accompanied by the recitation of the spells. According to Choksy, the circles around the object of the spell act as barriers to keep out impurities, and perhaps were meant to protect the practitioner of the rite, as is the case in other cultures. Late Byzantine magic, for example, uses these circles to protect a sorcerer while he performs magic.[40]

In Yasht 4.6[41] the lines to be drawn around the performer of the ritual while reciting the spell cited below are circles, but could conceivably also be squares. After the body has been hidden by the power of the lines, the priest recites a binding incantation to disable the demon or enemy (Yasht 4.5). Finally the demons are cursed:

YASHT 4.7[42]

He shall smash at the names of these Lies, cutters of corpses.
Smash the brood[?] of the *karapan*s, and burn the scorched dead—
[you] Zarathustra the libationer—"from the terrible hell,"[43]
"each according to his own wish, howsoever his pleasure."[44]

THE BARSHNŪM PURIFICATION RITUAL

Much of what we have been discussing has to do with purification. In the Zoroastrian way of thinking, as pollution was caused by one or more demons, any purification ritual was also an exorcism. This, then, had to be performed by a qualified priest, and if someone unqualified were to pose as qualified, he would cause damage to the person(s) undergoing the purification. Videvdad 9 sternly warns that if a man offers to perform the cleansing ritual but is unfit, then, instead of helping, he increases the strength of the demon Druj. If someone was found to be such an offender, the penalty was that he should be tied up, stripped of his clothing, and then perhaps have his head removed.[45] The penalty appears to be very strict because the text associates this illicit action with the increase of illnesses.[46]

The text makes it clear that the power to perform the ritual must remain in the hands of the priests, for they are ultimately the ones who will decide whether or not a person is qualified. As we will see later, the priests believed that they were the heirs to Zarathustra's legacy. Warnings that spells should not fall into the hands of persons not of Zarathustra's lineage are repeated after the instructions for "line magic" (Yasht 4.9) and "feather magic" (Yasht 14.46). These are two of the rare cases where we find actual directions for magical rituals. The belief that these spells could be misused by witches, sorcerers, and, generally, the unqualified, points to the magical power they contained. Such power could be misused, which makes these formulas very different from the idea we have of "prayer."

According to Videvdad 9, the *barshnūm* exorcistic ritual, the most powerful of cleansing rituals, was carried out over a period of nine days. It was only called for in the case of severe contamination, such as improper contact with a dead body. The ritual had to take place in a dry, infertile place: "Whatever is of this earth most devoid of water, most devoid of plants" (Videvdad 9.3).

Six holes were dug three feet apart, and a furrow was drawn around these holes with a special metal instrument (Videvdad 9.10). The specialist who performed the cleansing stood outside of the furrow at all times, while the candidate for purification stayed within the defined lines (Videvdad 9.12). The priest took a stick that had nine knots from branches on it, and tied a ladle to its end. With this he could reach over to the person in need of purification, and pour the *gōmēz*, or bull's urine, then water, over the body of the person as he passed from one of nine trenches (*magha*, see above, Chapter 6) to the next (Videvdad 9.14). In other words, he was purified nine times, using the urine of an ungelded bull (Videvdad 19.21).[47]

The use of *gōmēz* for purification is an Indo-Iranian custom that survives even today. The word *gōmēz* does not give us any indication as to whether this urine is taken from a cow or a bull. In India, cow urine is used, but it seems that bull's urine was preferred in Iran:

VIDEVDAD 19.21

Then Ahura Mazdā said:
You should take bull's urine, O Zarathustra, around a bull.
A spade made according to the law, purified, you should carry [it] out upon the earth set in place by Ahura [Mazdā].
This man who is to be purified should dig an encircling furrow all around.

However, this was not so strict a requirement, as urine from sheep or cattle could be used. Moreover, even the urine of a man or woman in a next-of-kin union (*khwēdōdah*) was a possible substitute:

VIDEVDAD 8.13

Then Ahura Mazdā said:
Of small or of large domestic animals, but not of men and women, except those two who are men and women in next-of-kin unions. These should make urine with which these corpse-cutters can wash their hair and bodies.

The contaminated person had first to be exposed to the glance of a dog (the *sagdīd*), which might be lifted up and carried over to see the person (Videvdad 8.36). If the person had been exposed to the dead body after it was seen (or nibbled on?) by a dog, the person could be purified with a shorter ablution that did not include the entire ritual with the pits. Washing with urine and water would be sufficient. This is because the Carrion demon flees during the *sagdīd* ritual, when seen by a dog. If the corpse had not been seen by a dog or flesh-eating bird, then the carrion demon had to be exorcised with the full *barshnūm* ritual.

The exorcistic spell was said to "stun" the demon, so that it could be removed:

VIDEVDAD 9.13

Then that Lie is stunned at each of these words [uttered]
for the striking of the Evil Spirit possessed by the Lie,
for the striking of Wrath with the bloody mace,
for the striking of the giant demons,
for the striking of all the demons.

During this ritual with its mantric words and rites, the Carrion demon rushes from the person's body in degrees, from the nostrils to the tips of his toes (Videvdad 9.13–26). This took place as the person moved from one pit to the other, cleansing himself or herself with urine and spells. Thus, the demon was driven out, and the person was finally purified enough to be exposed to water and fragrant herbs, this being the last substance used to thoroughly cleanse the person (Videvdad 9.32). Nevertheless, the now purified person had to go to his or her house and remain secluded, away from contact with other people and other living things for nine days, after which he or she needed to be cleansed again (Videvdad 9.34). Paying the priest who did the cleansing was an important part of the ritual. Otherwise, the demon might have had a right to return (Videvdad 9.39):

VIDEVDAD 9.39

If these Mazdayasnians are capable, they should offer to this man [the purifier] these small and large animals.
If these Mazdayasnians are not capable [to offer] these small and large animals, they should offer to this man other offerings, until this man who is to be purified goes away from those houses satisfied and without grievance.

PURIFICATION AFTER A STILLBIRTH

In Chapter 5, I touched upon the contamination of death visited upon a woman who had suffered a miscarriage. The presence of a dead body, that of her unborn child, rendered the mother a walking *dakhma*, or place of death, and for a time she was as contaminated as a corpse. Before she could be integrated into the community again, she had to undergo an exorcism to remove the Demon of Death from her body. This was a dangerous process, and if it failed—that is, if the woman died—then it was a victory for the demons.

In the Videvdad (5.45–54 and 7.60–69) it is advised that an enclosure should be built for the woman who had suffered a stillbirth, to isolate her from people and other living things for at least nine nights. She had to be kept a certain distance from living entities and from items she might contaminate, such as fire, water, plants, animals, etc. Her body and clothes had to be washed with cow's urine for purification. First, she was made to drink bull's urine, so that she could be cleansed from the inside. Then she was to be given food that would barely maintain her life, because any extra food might give strength to the corpse demon within her. If she became feverish and was in danger of dying herself, then, in order to save her, she could be given some water. The reason she was denied water normally was that water is a pure element and should not ever touch contamination. Thus, if the demon Carrion infected a woman, offering her water would offend the gods and strengthen the demons.

The Videvdad warns, however, that although saving the woman's life is a priority, if she had to be given water, then someone would have to pay the penalty of a severe whipping (Videvdad 7.70–72). It does not specify if it is the woman who must be whipped, or someone else who could take her place, such as her husband.[48]

VIDEVDAD 7.70–72

And if fever comes upon her shuddering body, and if the two ills of the worst kind come upon her, namely hunger and thirst, should this woman drink water?
Then Ahura Mazdā said: Let her drink! That is her greater concern, that she should save her life breath.
Before each of these learned men: the learned men, the knowledgeable men, learned and Orderly, this woman should drink water with her hands [?].
Then you, the Mazdayasnians, must make a penalty.
The spoken model, the spoken punishment makes the penalty.
What is the penalty for it?
Then Ahura Mazdā said: In return for this, upon him who is guilty of this capital crime
one should apply two hundred strokes with the horse whip, two hundred with the bastinado.

DISPOSAL OF HAIR AND NAILS

Hair and nails have magical significance in many cultures, and this was true for the authors of the Avesta. Hair and nail parings, when detached from the body, are objects that still have connection with the person whose body produced them. Therefore, they were thought to be a source of danger if they got into the wrong hands. Magical transference from the detached body leavings to the body itself was linked to the hair and nails. The symbolism of hair and nail paring is clear: a part of a person that represents the whole. The belief that these materials could be used by sorcerers was widespread in the ancient world.[49]

For the ancient Iranians, hair and nail parings presented similar dangers, although the Avesta does not mention their use by human sorcerers. Rather, the supernatural powers of evil are strengthened by them, and they can transform such bodily refuse into weapons to be used against the world of good. Improper disposal of nails and hair, for example burial, was said to produce evil beings. These effects were identical to those produced by sacrifice to the demons. On the other hand, nails could be put to good use if disposed of properly. Thus, we find that both good and evil powers contended for this human waste product.

The Videvdad (17.1–2)[50] warns that when a man, while combing or shaving, or paring his nails, drops them into a hole or crack, this act is actually equal to demon-worship. The comparison of irreligious practice to demon sacrifice is significant because it illustrates the Zoroastrian concept that as the Yasna gives strength to the gods, depraved acts are the same as offering a sacrifice to the demons, that is, the demons would be strengthened.

Demons and *khrafstar*s, noxious creatures, were believed to be born on earth from improper disposal of the hair and nails. Lice, corn-eating bugs, and wool moths were especially produced (Videvdad 17.3).[51] Hair was most dangerous, so it was to be taken at least ten paces from the faithful, twenty from the fire, thirty from water, and fifty from the sacred *barsom* of the sacrifice. A hole ten to twelve fingers deep had to be dug, and the faithful person was required to recite the following spell from the Spentāmanyū Gāthā (Yasna 48.6): "Thus, for *her* [= Ārmaiti, the earth], Mazdā through Order shall now make plants grow" (Videvdad 17.5). Lincoln notes, "[I]n its new setting the Gathic quotation has become a spell, a ritual by which the proper disposal of hair and nails leads to the production of vegetation."[52]

It is an old Indo-Iranian motif that hair represents the plants on the earth, an idea that also appears later in the Bundahishn:

BUNDAHISHN 34.5

Similarly, when I set in place the earth, which carries the entire existence with bones, it had no support in the world of the living. When I led the sun, moon, and stars into the intermediate space in the form of light; when I gave men grain for them to cast into the ground and it grows up again and becomes manifold, and also when I gave the plants colors of many kinds; when I gave the plants and other things fire so that it does not burn; when I established sons in the wombs of their mothers and protected them, and gave them individually hair, skin, nails, blood, sinews, eyes, ears, and the . . . limbs; when I gave the water fattiness so that it flows; when I set in place the cloud in the world of thought to carry the water of the world of the living and to rain it down wherever it pleases; when I set in place the wind, which blows up and down as it pleases, as is plain to see by the power of the wind, and it is impossible to seize it with one's hands—every single one of these it was more difficult to set in place than performing the Resurrection, for in the Resurrection I have the assistance of those who were not [alive] when I did those other things.

Since I made that which was not, why should it not be possible to make that which was? For at that time I shall call the bones from the earth in the world of thought, the blood from the water, the hair from the plants, the soul from the wind, as they received them at the original creation.

Clearly, the Avestan spell for binding the power of hair is uttered in order to return the hair to plants, thus strengthening the order of the universe, rather than letting it become a source of strength for the demons. The above passage further states that at the time of resurrection, people's bodies will be renewed by calling forth from the creation the various parts of the body. The bones will be restored from the earth, the blood from the water, and the hair from the plants.

After "planting" the hair, three magical circles were to be drawn around the hole, although multiples of three were also recommended, while chanting the Ahuna Vairiya (Videvdad 17.6), whose power to strike the demons is discussed below.

Nail parings were disposed of using a separate spell and a slightly different ritual. It is possible that they were thought to be somewhat less dangerous, because they were planted outside of the house, one finger deep, and the magical circles were drawn as above. The spell for disposing of nail parings was similar to that of hair disposal, because it sought to transform the material into a weapon for good, rather than for evil. It is interesting to note that both hair and nail parings seemed to have such potential power that they would inevitably be used for something by the gods or demons. They were by no means a neutral material. As part of the spell ritual, the nails had to be exposed to the vision of a holy bird.[53] The Vāregna bird was able to use them as weapons to kill the giant demons. The nails were transformed into spears, knives, bows and arrows, and stones and slings to be used by the good bird, but, if the giant demons got hold of the nails, they would use them against humans and conceivably the gods themselves:

VIDEVDAD 17.9–10

To you, O bird, favored by Order,
I exhibit these nails, I make known these nails.
May these nails be for you, O bird,
favored by Order, spears and knives,
bows and arrows with eagle feathers,
sling and sling-stones against the giant *daēwa*s.
If they do not exhibit [them],
those nails will afterward be for the giant *daēwa*s spears and knives,
bow and arrows with eagle feathers, sling and sling-stones.

VIDEVDAD 17.11 AND 16.18

All those who are possessed by the Lie and have the Lie in their bodies
are people who do not hold the teaching.
All those who will not listen are people who do not hold the teaching.
All those who sustain no Order are people who will not listen.
All those who have forfeited their bodies are people who sustain no Order.

FEATHER MAGIC

The use of the feathers of a magical bird in the spell ritual is one of the most interesting of the magical rituals found in the Yashts. Not surprisingly, it comes from the Yasht dedicated to the great god of war Verthragna. The feathers used in this ritual had to come from the Vāregna bird, which is one of the forms of the shape-shifting Verthragna. Therefore, their use was connected to casting spells for victory in battle. The formulas were directed to the attention of Verthragna, and the ritual was performed at the time when the two armies were arrayed against each other in battle lines. This was one of the longest and most important spell passages in the Yashts and has many of the components that Malinowski, Tambiah, and others have recognized as essential spell language. It will be helpful to look at this magical procedure and analyze its parts, although it is lengthy:

YASHT 14.32–33

We sacrifice to Verthragna, set in place by Ahura [Mazdā].
Orderly Zarathustra sacrificed to him . . .
Verthragna, set in place by Ahura [Mazdā], gave him that sight which the vulture has,
who from nine lands away sees a piece of bloody meat the size of a fist,
as much as the glimmer of a glimmer, of a needle, as much as the tip of a needle.

YASHT 14.34

We sacrifice to Verthragna, established by Ahura [Mazdā].
Zarathustra asked Ahura Mazdā: O Ahura Mazdā . . .
If I become the target of the blame and insult of many hostile men,
what is the healing for this?

This spell does not break down as easily as other spells we have seen, although each part clearly has similar functions. Yasht 14.32–33 is an introduction to the god whose power is the basis of this spell. Yasht 14.34 introduces the myth of when the magic was first used. We find Zarathustra asking Ahura Mazdā for a remedy against his enemies, and probably healing for himself. Yasht 14.35 provides the mythic instructions for the ritual, as told by Ahura Mazdā to Zarathustra, the original magician. He is to perform the ritual of brushing the body with the feather in an apotropaic rite, and then utter a curse against the enemy. This is at once a spell to protect the body from injury and a curse against one's enemies.

The feather symbolism is quite intriguing. The Vāregna bird is described as being like an eagle or falcon, soaring and gliding in search of prey.[54] The eagle, for the Iranians and many other peoples, was a symbol of royal sovereignty as well as a solar symbol. Verthragna, a companion of the solar god Mithra, was a warrior god who brought victory to those favored by Mithra on the battlefield. Often, however, he was more of an enforcer for Mithra, punishing those who crossed him. Yasht 14.36 is an assurance that the magic will work because of the magical potencies of the Vāregna bird. This is a reference to the etiological myth of the first use of magic. Zarathustra, the first user of this magic, asked Ahura Mazdā for medicine to make him praised and safe from his enemies. Ahura Mazdā, the lord and instructor in the ritual, told him how to proceed:

YASHT 14.35–36

Then Ahura Mazdā said: Take, Zarathustra of the Spitāmas,
the feather of the Vāregna bird, whose feathers are speckled [?].
With this feather you should brush the body!
With this feather you should speak against the opponent!
When praised it brings the boons of the firm bird . . .
Nobody can strike it down nor . . .

The next strophe, Yasht 14.37, is apparently a binding spell to incapacitate the enemies that are the victims of the spell.

YASHT 14.37

Those the lord, land-lord of commanders [?],
[can]not smash a hundred [times, although] a smasher of men,
[can]not strike [even] once [although] . . .
He strikes one [and?] goes forth.

Yasht 14.38, on the other hand, is a declaration of the power gained and a curse:

YASHT 14.38

All the other feathered ones fear me. . . . Let all foes fear me!
Let all enemies fear the force and obstruction-smashing strength laid down in
    my body!

Yasht 14.39 and 40 are again references to ancient myths in cryptic language.

Verthragna, embodiment of the "obstruction-smashing strength," is a god concerned with masculinity, which he embodies perfectly in his ten forms as superb male creatures: the healing, anti-sorcerer wind, a bull, a stallion, a rutting camel, a boar, a fifteen-year-old male human, the Vāregna bird, a wild ram, a horned buck, and a warrior. Yasht 14.39 refers to some of these forms:

YASHT 14.39

The divine lords and ladies shall ride on him.
The divine ladies shall ride on him.
Those of good fame shall ride on him.
Kawi Usan rode on him,[55]
he whom a stallion carries,
he whom a rutting camel carries,
he whom the river in spate carries.

Another important function connected with Verthragna and his form as the Vāregna bird is his connection with the *khwarnah*, Fortune, a divine entity associated with heroes. When Fortune flees an unworthy person, it takes the form of the Vāregna bird. The spell found in Yasht 14 is specific to the battle-field. Those invested with Fortune will win the battle, so we see the importance of the Vāregna bird as the bringer of victory, as well as that of Verthragna, who destroys armies.

Yasht 19 describes Fortune and the persons associated with it in mythic times. Fortune flies to the leader it chooses, and that person gains victory. If it leaves that person, disaster follows. Yasht 19.31 describes the myth of Yima, the first mythic king. When he reigned, everyone lived forever, and looked as young as fifteen-year-olds. Then Yima lied and Fortune flew away as a Vāregna bird. It happened three times before Fortune left Yima forever. It then went to the hero Thraētaona, who slew the three-headed dragon so important in Indo-European lore:[56]

YASHT 14.40

That which firm Thraētaona carried,[57]
who smashed the giant dragon with three mouths, three heads,
six eyes, a thousand tricks, the mighty strong, deceiving Lie,
that evil one possessed by Lie, the mighty strong Lie
that the Evil Spirit whittled forth [against] living beings:
against the bony world of the living,
for the destruction of the living beings of Order.

This myth is also significant in that it was another story of the first use of magic to defeat evil, and it is also remembered because it was Verthragna who aided Thraētaona in slaying the three-headed dragon.[58]

Fortune in the form of the Vāregna bird then went to a hero named Kersāspa. Like Thraētaona, Kersāspa was a dragon killer. Yasht 19.40 tells the story of his adventures with a horned, man-eating, horse-devouring dragon. One day Kersāspa decided to cook his afternoon meal in an iron pot. He chose a hill and lit his fire. Unbeknownst to him, the hill was actually a sleeping dragon. Naturally, the dragon got hot and began to sweat until he woke up startled. Kersāspa ran away, but he must have later slain the dragon.

After leaving Kersāspa, the Evil Spirit sent his minions, which included another three-headed dragon, to steal Fortune. Ahura Mazdā responded by sending his own forces, which included the Holy Fire, who threatened to burn the dragon's buttocks, thus saving Fortune. Other demons and villains tried to steal Fortune after it fled to the Vourukasha Sea, the place connected with healing and fertility. Finally, in Yasht 19.71, Fortune reached Zarathustra, who was the most powerful user of mantras. The heroes Yasht 19 mentions form a line of succession culminating in the most powerful man, Zarathustra. It also chronicles the demons, wizards, and tyrants who tried to seize Fortune to achieve their own power.

The reference in Yasht 14.39 to Kawi Usan also merits discussion. He was apparently a user of magic[59] who petitioned the goddess Ardwī Sūrā Anāhitā for boons. He asked to be given the greatest power over men and demons. He is listed as one of the boon-seekers, including the heroes mentioned in Yasht 19 as being blessed with Fortune, as well as the demons who tried to take Fortune by force, including the three-headed dragon, who sacrificed to Ardwī Sūrā Anāhitā.

Yasht 14.41 again invokes the god Verthragna in one of his shape-shifting forms as a great bird. There is a declaration of the intent to perform a sacrifice to the god and then instructions on how to invoke the god whose power is the strength of the spell.

YASHT 14.41

We sacrifice to Verthragna, established by Ahura [Mazdā].
Verthragna surrounds and covers this house . . .
like yon great bird the eagle,
like those clouds filled with water settle on the large mountains.

Yasht 14.43–44 gives instructions on when and where to perform the sacrifice and ritual. The ritual was performed on the battlefield when two forces were arrayed and prepared for combat.

YASHT 14.43

Thus Ahura Mazdā said:

When two armies come together, Spitāma Zarathustra, each in ordered battle line,

[then although] captured they shall not be captured,

[although] smitten, they shall not be smitten.

The place of the ritual, more specifically, was at a crossroads:

YASHT 14.44

You should hold out four feathers [?] to each of the roads.

On whichever side he is first sacrificed to,

the well-fashioned, well-shaped strong one,

Verthragna, established by Ahura [Mazdā],

on that side Resistance/Valor follows.

The crossroads is a dangerous place in many traditions, while in others it can be a sacred place. In this case, it appears that there was a sacred power at the crossroads, as well as danger. The god Sraosha was invoked in spells to ease the terror of crossroads and the confluence of deep bodies of water, which were dangerously infused with evil (Yasht 11.4).

The feather ritual of Yasht 14 was performed by holding out the four feathers of the Vāregna bird to each of the four roads that intersect at the crossroads. The following are some of the few instructions we have on the performance of the rituals that accompanied the spells of the Avesta:

YASHT 14.45

I invite hither the force and the obstruction-smashing Strength,

the two protectors, the two guardians, the two overseers,

the two [who] bend[60] [the enemy?] hither, the two [who] bend [them] to the sides, the two who bend [them] forward,

the two [who] sweep [them] hither, the two [who] sweep [them] to the sides,
the two [who] sweep [them] forward.

The army protected by the spell cast with the feathers of the Vāregna bird
was promised that "[although] captured they shall not be captured, [although]
struck down, they shall not be struck down" (Yasht 14.43). Verthragna, a
capable war god, was well suited to preside over this sort of spell. We see that,
again, the warning against teaching this magic to anyone not closely related
to Zarathustra was considered dangerous. Zarathustra was warned that this
formula must never be taught to anyone but select family members or priests:

YASHT 14.46

O Zarathustra, do not teach this Sacred Word
other than to [your] father or son, brother or sibling,
or the priest who guards the roads[?].
And these words of yours,
which were strong and solid,
were strong and eloquent,
were strong and obstruction-smashing,
were strong and healing,
and these words of yours,
which save a head even when forfeited,[61]
turn back by their sound[?] even a weapon that is raised.

Yasht 14.46–58 concludes this spell. This is a series of warnings and instructions on how to placate the god.

YASHT 14.51

A villain should not seize it, nor a witch or a . . .
who has not proclaimed the Gāthās, who destroys [this] existence,
who opposes this religion, that of Ahura Mazdā and Zarathustra.

The consequence of ignoring the warnings was the wrath of the war gods,
Mithra, Rashnu, and Verthragna. The method of sacrifice is explained, includ-
ing the sacrifice of a sheep of any color. The dire warning is given that should
a villain or a witch seize the sacrifice, scourges will destroy the Aryan lands.
This is a clear confirmation of the magical nature of the rituals and spells in
Yasht 14, for neither is there discourse with the gods nor are there prayers that

can change the course of a ritual gone bad. The mechanical nature of the ritual is evident in that any imperfection in the performance can result in disaster. As for the concluding strophes 54–56, see the discussion on demon worship in Chapter 7.

The use of a feather to make a man invincible is also found in the Shāh-nāmah, the great Iranian epic of the kings, put into writing in Persian by Firdausi, a Muslim, in 1000 CE. In the Shāh-nāmah, Zāl, the father of Rustam, the great warrior-hero of the epic, was abandoned by his father, the king, because he was born with white hair, a sign of witchcraft. The newborn Zāl was taken in and raised by the preternatural Sīmurgh bird, whose feathers could be used for magic. When Zāl was grown up, the Sīmurgh brought him back to the palace, saying, "Take with you a single feather from my wing and with it you will continue to be under the protection of my influence. If ever a difficulty overtakes you or any dispute arises over your actions, good or ill, then cast this feather of mine into the flames and you will at once experience the blessing of my authority. I will come as a black cloud, with speed, and transport you unharmed to this place."[62]

Zāl called the bird for help on several occasions, including at the time of the difficult birth of Rustam, a strange man whose matrilineal lines were traced directly to Zahhāk, the demon-dragon Azhi Dahāka of the Avesta. Zāl became desperate when his beloved wife was apparently unable to give birth to the large baby she was carrying. The Sīmurgh bird told Zāl to have a man expert in spells to cut her belly open and remove the child. Then she instructed Zāl to brush one of its feathers over the wound and it would heal magically. Later, when his son grew up and was wounded in a battle, Zāl used the feather to save the fallen son, Rustam. It is likely that part of the myth of the Vāregna bird survived among those of the Sīmurgh. Thus, in Yasht 19.35, when Yima lost Fortune, it was taken by the Vāregna bird, but when Rustam's *farr*, the Persian equivalent of Avestan *khwarnah*, was lost, it was returned to him by the Sīmurgh.[63]

CONCLUSION

This chapter has reviewed Avestan rites and *manthra*s with practical applications including healing by exorcism, dispelling pollution-causing demons, and disposing of bodily waste in a safe manner. The authors of the Avesta thought of disease as an invasion of a spirit or demon into the body. Thus, although surgery and herbal medicine were options, the most effective method of curing was exorcism by spells and curses.

For a patient who is convinced that his or her disease is caused by demons, the exorcistic rite is a battle between the forces of good and evil. With the community and the good magician on his or her side, there is hope for a cure. The patient believes illness is caused by the evil magic of demons. Therefore, it is reasonable to expect that it will be cured by good magic. In the case that the ritual is unsuccessful, as long as the practitioner of the rites has a record of knowledge and success, the failure can be attributed to the evil magic of the demons and their cohorts—the sorcerers and witches.

CHAPTER 9

STRUCTURE OF AVESTAN INCANTATIONS

SPELLS AND CURSES IN THE YOUNG AVESTA

The preceding chapters have introduced both real and invisible demons feared by the society that gave birth to the Avesta. The incantations we find in the Avesta were composed for the protection of that community as a response to this perceived threat. In other words, their magic was defensive, rather than offensive. There is no instance in the Avesta of anyone targeting someone in particular while casting a spell or uttering a curse, with the exception of those cast against named supernatural beings, but, again, this kind of protective magic was meant to counteract evil magical spells. If the bad magician is harmed, it is justice, because the good magic simply deflects the bad magic, causing the evil magician to suffer the fate he or she intended for others. Thus, the good magic is believed to "find" the evil magician, and innocent persons are not usually affected, as in the following text:

YASNA 8.3

O Life-giving Immortals!
O *daēnā* of the Mazdayasnians!
O good [men/gods] and good [women/goddesses]!
O libations!
Whoever declares himself a Mazdayasnian among these Mazdayasnians
[but actually] while seeking victory by a [?] composition [?] of Order
destroys by sorcery the living beings of Order.
Do point him out, O waters, O plants, O libations!

As a result, incantations tend to be very general, and unlike the spells found in the Atharvaveda, there are very few that target specific illnesses or other conditions. There are no serious rituals or spells meant for use by laypeople. Although disposing of nail clippings and the like had their protective spells meant for general use, major incantations and rituals such as feather magic were strictly forbidden to non-priests. Furthermore, the priest had to be in the line of Zarathustra. Spells and curses played a more prominent role in the Avesta than descriptions of the magical acts or material magic that accompanied the words, or vice versa.[1] This is natural, considering that the Avesta is an oral composition. In what follows, I will discuss the meaning of the terms "spell" and "curse" and then analyze their forms in the Avesta.

Malinowski described magical incantations as coercive: a "means to a definite and expected end."[2] Max Weber, while recognizing that religion can contain elements that may seem magical, distinguishes religion from actual magic by calling the latter sorcery. He defines sorcery as "magical coercion."[3] However, this coercion does not always work. The Yasht passages such as Yashts 5 and 15 act as warnings that sacrifices and other such rites with their accompanying spells will not always produce the desired result. The Indian Purānas contain many stories about demons who sacrificed or practiced austerities that forced the gods to give them their requested boon. For example, the demon Hiranyakashipu wanted eternal life. He performed severe austerities until Brahma was forced to come down from heaven to see him. Although Brahma could not give him eternal life, for he himself was unable to achieve it, he was able to satisfy the demon with other boons. In all of these cases, the gods have to find a way to undo the damage the demons did. The Yashts that contain lists of people who appealed to the gods always include several demons, including even the three-headed, six-eyed dragon who represents the Evil Spirit. Unlike the Hindu gods, the Avestan divinities of the Yashts refuse to give boons to demons.

YASHT 5.29–31

The three-headed Giant Dragon sacrificed to her in the land of the Beaver[?] a hundred stallions, a thousand bulls, ten thousand rams.
Thus he asked her: Give me that prize,
O good Ardwī Sūrā Anāhitā, you most rich in life-giving strength,
that I may make [everything] devoid of men all over the seven continents!
She gave him not that prize, Ardwī Sūrā Anāhitā.

In Yasht 15 in particular, we see that even though the dragon was an expert poet-sacrificer, and even though he offered proper libations and gifts, he was rejected. He prayed to Vayu that he might have the power to depopulate the earth. By making his intentions quite clear, perhaps the composers of this text sought to answer the question of why he was rejected even though his offering was quite generous. Neither the expertise of the priest nor the grand offerings bring the result. Instead, the god or goddess seems to choose not to reward the demonic petitioner based on his or her discretion.

In the Gāthās, the poet-sacrificer had to plead his case so that the rival poet did not achieve his boons. The composers of the Yashts appeared conscious of this dilemma and made it clear that the gods can choose to whom they will respond. Based on the Hindu material, one wonders if these texts were at some time altered so that the demons were denied their rewards. All of the demons who tried to obtain blessings were successful to some degree in their evil plans, despite having been rejected by the gods.

The above cases aside, warnings for major incantations in the Avesta advise that if an unqualified person uses the spells, the result will be disastrous. As in the feather magic above, only a close relative of Zarathustra was allowed to use the spell. The coercive nature of magic is tempered by these examples. The purpose of incantations and rites is still rather practical. They are aimed at achieving health and protection from invaders, diseases, demonic spells, and curses aimed at the community.

Malinowski held that spells were different from ordinary speech, because they were believed (by the Trobriand Islanders) to produce supernatural effects. He asserted that the power of verbal magic was that "the repetitive statement of certain words is believed to produce the reality stated."[4]

The rhetorical aspects of magic are obviously crucial in a belief system depending on orally transmitted "texts." Malinowski concluded that the spell was the most important aspect of the magical ritual. This is substantiated by the evidence of the Avesta, as we shall see. There is no ritual evident in the Avesta that is not accompanied by the recitation of sacred words. Malinowski's three spell components are made up of the phonetic elements that express emotional states, the use of commanding language especially with repetition, and mythical allusions recalling the origin of the magic.[5]

All three elements are found in the Avestan ritual texts:

1. The emotionally charged character of the words as evidenced by repetitions and parallelism, especially in curses, for instance in: "Perish, O deceiving Druj! . . . Rush away, O Druj!" (Videvdad 8.21)
2. The explicit statements of the desired end, for instance in: "the one does not sustain Order, who darkens Order . . . let the hostilities go back against

him! . . . let the dangers [go back against him] who made them!"
(Yasna 65.8)

3. The mythological allusions, of which we shall see examples presently

Spells and curses in the Avesta employ a specific language pattern, and they often invoke the gods who were most effective for combating a particular evil. Not only are certain rhetorical ingredients required to insure the efficacy of a spell, but certain conditions must also be met. The Avesta specifies the occasion, the place where the spell may be performed, and the qualifications of the performer. If these conditions were met and then the *manthra*, the holy utterance or spell, was recited, the composers of the Avesta expected a result. They took their magic quite seriously, so much so that if they did not see the expected result, they feared a backlash of some sort. There are warnings to this effect after most of the powerful spells in the Avesta. The authors feared most that the spell might be heard or used by witches and sorcerers. Likewise, unqualified performers could cause the good spell to destroy the community.

Tambiah agrees that spells are the most important part of the magical ritual, although he finds that the spell is usually effective in conjunction with ritual action. He also notes that the repetition of certain words and constructs was an important feature of spells. Another element is important in spells, according to Tambiah: the use of imperatives and verbs that act upon a list of enumerated parts or items that "undergo an event or process by which it acquires the desired attribute or quality.[6]

The forms of spells and curses bear certain similarities even when compared cross-culturally. Many spells employ repetitions and similar verbal forms. In "The Magical Power of Words," Tambiah uses Malinowski's Trobriand spells to illustrate the patterns that he finds in spells in general. However, most of the Trobriand examples Tambiah uses are examples of good magic not used against evil, but to assist in gardening or fishing, etc.[7] All of the Avestan examples that we will see have to do with preventative magic or exorcism, but we will focus on the verbal patterns.

Another point is that, for now, we are using examples of spells, curses, and exorcistic passages without distinction, because in the Avesta all of these forms have a similar verbal pattern. Later, the individual types of incantations will be discussed separately. Both Tambiah and Malinowski identify the important elements of spells as imperative language, the use of verbs, and lists of words in particular patterns. Tambiah's observations are also helpful when considering the magic of the Avesta when he notes that the utterance of a word is an action in magic and has the power to influence a change. He uses Austin's well-studied "performative" model,[8] which Tambiah interprets to mean that thinking and action are closely connected. Uttering a command or a promise is an action in itself, which has the power to effect a change. When the Avestan priest declares: "Block their perception! Tie down their hands! Grind together their jaws!" (Yasht 1.27), his utterances have a "performative" quality, as Tambiah puts it.

In the realm of exorcism, which plays an important role in the Avesta, the declaration is the act. For example, when the priest demands after the ritual, "Diseases, run away! Demons, run away! Fevers, run away!" (Yasht 3.7–8), it is expected that those demons have fled and that the person undergoing the exorcism is ritually clean.

Apotropaic or exorcistic Avestan spells against evil have their own logical patterns. The important part of these spells is the verb: a hostile action directed at the offender, and, in some cases, the actual name of the offender against which the incantation is meant to act. This type of spell accomplishes its goal by declaring the action and by naming what will be acted upon. Very important is the name of the offending being, because it is necessary to cover all the known demonic beings, or else there may be a means for an unmentioned demon to attack. The Avesta takes great care to mention all of the conceivable evils in this kind of spell.

STRUCTURE OF AVESTAN SPELLS AND CURSES[9]

Avestan spells and curses typically contain verbs expressing the ongoing or desired action. The nouns in the spell will denote the person who will perform the action, the person for whom the action is performed, and the objects the action will be performed upon.

The verbs are typically

past tense: expressing action of a prototypical performer;

present tense: expressing "performative" action (first person: "I do"; third-person singular: "he does"; or plural: "they do");

imperative: expressing a command directed at the object of a spell (second person: "do!"; third person: "let him do!");

subjunctive: expressing a command directed at the object of spell (second or third person: "you/he shall do"); or

optative: expressing a wish of the performer (first person: "may I do") or an action to be taken by the object of a spell (second or third person: "may you/he do").

Repetitions are very common and the verbs can be repeated with different objects:

he smashes → X
              Y
              etc.

or varied with the same object:

he smashes   → me
he burns
he chases
etc.

he smashes   → X
he is the enemy of
etc.

for the discomfiture and removal of → the Evil Spirit,
for the discomfiture and removal of → the male and female magicians
etc.

Similar structures are the following:

far from this   →   house
                        village
                        tribe
                        land

[protect]
from Lieful   →   destruction
                    wrath
                    armies

We send forth →   the Ahuna Vairiya →   between heaven and earth
                   the Ashem Vohū
                   etc.

This form is the least common:

Block	→	their perception
Tie down	→	their hands
Grind together	→	their jaws

He smashes me	→	with the Ahuna Vairiya	→	like with a weapon . . .
He burns me	→	with the Asha Vahishta	→	just like metal.

The objects to be removed are all the kinds of evils discussed earlier. They are typically found in lists of words of similar structure, in alliterating or rhyming pairs (or more), and as repetitions with or without variation, for example:

alliterating:

YASNA 61.2

kakhwardanāmca	kakhwardināmca
kakhwardaheca	kakhwardiyāsca

rhyming:

YASNA 61.3

azhi.cithra	hazasnāmca
verkō.cithra	tāyunāmca
bizangrō.cithra	zandāmca
	yātumatāmca
tarō.mata	mithrō.drujāmca
pairi.mata	mithrō.ziyāmca

combined effects:

VIDEVDAD 20.9	VIDEVDAD 11.9
paiti.perne ashire	perne aēshmem
paiti.perne agūire	perne nasūm
paiti.perne agrām	perne hām.raēthvem
paiti.perne ugrām	perne paiti.raēthvem
paiti.perne yaskahe	perne xrū
paiti.perne mahrkahe	perne xruuigni

paiti.perne dᾱzhu

paiti.perne tᾱfnu

paiti.perne sᾱranahe

paiti.perne sᾱrastiyehe

paiti.perne azhanahe

paiti.perne azhahwahe

paiti.perne kurugahe

paiti.perne azhiwᾱkahe

paiti.perne drukahe

paiti.perne astairiyehe

paiti.perne agashyå pūitiyå āhitayå

perne būidi

perne būidizha

perne kundi

perne kundizha

perne būshiyansta yā zairina

perne būshiyansta yā dargō.gawa

perne mūidi

perne kapastish

perne pairikām

yā āiti ātrem āpem zām gām urwarå

perne āhitīm

yā āiti ātrem āpem zām gām urwarå

"PERFORMATIVE" PRESENT SPELLS

Spells with a "performative" present depict the desired action as actually taking place, for instance (and see other examples below):

YASNA 57.14

Evil, fearful scourges now go
far from this house,
far from this village,
far from this tribe,
far from this land [of the one]
in whose home obstruction-smashing Sraosha with the rewards is satisfied.

In this passage from the Yasna dedicated to Sraosha, the evil of the night is being dispersed as if it were present and now leaving. The evil scourges named later as male and female magicians, demons, and enemy armies, are leaving the areas this incantation means to protect. The protected locales are listed in concentric circles from the home, to the village, to the tribe, and finally the Aryan lands. In this way there is some hope that every area is covered when addressing this protective spell in the night.

EXAMPLE OF A COMPLEX SPELL IN YASHT 3

Yasht 3.10–16 is a spell against diseases and all kinds of evil influences. It is one of the most impressive spells of this kind, and I will analyze it in some detail.

This particular spell can be broken into three parts:

1. Yasht 3.10–12, in which the verb is in the present tense: "he smashes," the repetition of such verbs as "I break," etc.;
2. Yasht 3.13, which refers to the myth that tells of when this magic was first used, the myth of origin; and
3. Yasht 3.14–16, which uses the verb in the subjunctive (future), which serves to command the desired result.

YASHT 3.10	YASHT 3.10
yō janad aēshām daēwanām	He who smashed of these *daēwa*s
hazangrāi hazangrō pairi	a thousand for a thousand,
baēwarāi baēwanō paiti	ten thousand for ten thousand,
yaska jainti	he smashes diseases,
mahrka jainti	he smashes destructions,
daēwa jainti	he smashes *daēwa*s,
paitiyāra jainti	he smashes adversaries,
ashemaogō anashawa jainti	he smashes the obscurantist, who sustains no Order,
mashiyō.sāsta jainti	he smashes the false teacher of men.

YASHT 3.11	YASHT 3.11
azhi.chithra jainti	He smashes the brood of snakes.
verkō.chithra jainti	He smashes the brood of wolves.
bizangrō.chithra jainti	He smashes the brood of two-footed [wolves].
tarō.mata jainti	He smashes the despisers.
pairi.mata jainti	He smashes the ones of distraught minds.
tafnu jainti	He smashes the fevers.
spazga jainti	He smashes the slanderers.
anākhshta jainti	He smashes the sowers of discord.
duzhdōithra jainti	He smashes the ones with the evil eye.

YASHT 3.12

draogō.vākhsh draojishta jainti

jahi yātumaiti jainti

jahi kakhwardine jainti

vātō paourwō apākhtara jainti

vātō paourwō apākhtara
apa.nasiyata
yasca mē aētaēshām yad
bizangrō.chithranām

YASHT 3.12

He smashes the most lying, the one
with lying speech.
He smashes the evil woman
possessed by sorcerers.
He smashes the evil woman, the
female magician.
He smashes the southerly [and]
northerly wind.
Southerly [and] northerly wind,
get lost!
And any of these broods of two-
footed [wolves], [get away from]
me!

YASHT 3.13

yō janad aēshām daēwanām
hazangrāi hazangrō pairi
baēwarāi baēwanō pairi
paourwa.naēmād patad dyaosh

daēwanām draojishtō
angrō mainyush pouru.mahrkō

YASHT 3.13

He who smashed of these *daēwa*s
a thousand for a thousand,
ten thousand for ten thousand.
He fell headlong from in front of
the sky
the most lying of *daēwa*s,
the Evil Spirit full of destruction.

YASHT 3.14

adawata angrō mainyush
pouru.mahrkō
āwōiya mē bāwōiya asha vahishta
yaskanām yaskō.temem janād

yaskanām yaskō.temem dbaēshayād

markanām markō.temem janād

YASHT 3.14

He lied, the Evil Spirit full of
destruction:
Woe to me! Blast you, Best Order!
He shall smash the most disease-
inflicting of diseases.
He shall be the enemy of the most
disease-inflicting of diseases.
He shall smash the most destructive
of destructions.

markanām markō.temem dbaēshayād	He shall be the enemy of the most destructive of destructions.
daēwanām daēwō.temem janād	He shall smash the most *daēwic* of *daēwa*s.
daēwanām daēwō.temem <u>dbaēshayād</u>	He shall be the enemy of the most *daēwic* of *daēwa*s.
paitiyāranām paitiyārō.temem janād	He shall smash the most adverse of adversaries.
paitiyāranām paitiyārō dbaēshayād	He shall be the enemy of the most adverse of adversaries.
ashemaogō anashawa janād	He shall smash the obscurantist, who sustains no Order.
ashemaogō anashawa dbaēshayād	He shall be the enemy of the obscurantist, who sustains no Order.
mashiyō.sāsta.sāstō.temem janād	He shall smash the falsest teacher of men.
mashiyō.sāsta.sāstō.temem dbaēshayād	He shall be the enemy of the falsest teacher of men.

YASHT 3.15   YASHT 3.15

azhi.chithra azhi.chithrō.temem janād	He shall smash the one most brood of snakes with respect to being the brood of snakes.
azhi.chithra azhi.chithrō.temem dbaēshayād	He shall be the enemy of the one most brood of snakes with respect to being the brood of snakes.
verkō.chithra verkō.chithrō.temem janād	He shall smash the one most brood of wolves with respect to being the brood of wolves.
verkō.chithra verkō.chithrō.temem dbaēshayād	He shall be the enemy of the one most brood of wolves with respect to being the brood of wolves.
bizangrō.chithra bizangrō.chithrō .temem janād	He shall smash the one most brood of two-footed [wolves] with respect to being the brood of two-footed [wolves].

bizangrō.chithra bizangrō.chithrō .temem dbaēshayād	He shall be the enemy of the one most brood of wolves with respect to being the brood of wolves.
tarō.mata janād	He shall smash the despisers.
tarō.mata dbaēshayād	He shall be the enemy of the despisers.
pairi.mata janād	He shall smash those of distraught minds.
pairi.mata dbaēshayād	He shall be the enemy of those of distraught minds.
tafnu tafnō.temem janād	He shall smash the one most feverish with respect to fever.
tafnu tafnō.temem dbaēshayād	He shall be the enemy of the one most feverish with respect to fever.
spazga spazgō.temem janād	He shall smash the one most slanderer with respect to slander.
spazga spazgō.temem dbaēshayād	He shall be the enemy of the one most slanderer with respect to slander.
anāxshta anāxshtō.temem janād	He shall smash the one most sower of discord with respect to discord.
anāxshta anāxshtō.temem dbaēshayād	He shall be the enemy of the one most sower of discord with respect to discord.
duzhdōithra.duzhdōithrō.temem janād	He shall smash the one with the evilest eye with respect to the evil eye.
duzhdōithra.duzhdōithrō.temem dbaēshayād	He shall be the enemy of the one with the evilest eye with respect to the evil eye.

YASHT 3.16

YASHT 3.16

draogō.vākhsh draojishtō janād	He shall smash the most lying, the one with lying speech.

draogō.vākhsh draojishtō dbaēshayād	He shall be the enemy of the most lying, the one with lying speech.
jahi yātumaiti janād	He shall smash the evil woman possessed by sorcerers.
jahi yātumaiti dbaēshayād	He shall be the enemy of the evil woman possessed by sorcerers.
jahi kakhwardine janād	He shall smash the evil woman magician.
jahi kakhwardine dbaēshayād	He shall be the enemy of the evil woman magician.
vātō paourwō apākhtara janād	He shall smash the southerly [and] northerly wind.
vātō paourwō apākhtara dbaēshayād	He shall be the enemy of the southerly [and] northerly wind.

The myth referred to here is the Zoroastrian cosmogonic myth, for instance, as in the Pahlavi Bundahishn: after Ohrmazd (Ahura Mazdā), the Life-giving Spirit, had chanted the Ahuna Vairiya prayer, the first spell to ever have been recited (Bundahishn 1.29), Ahriman, the Evil Spirit, fell back, unconscious, into hell (Bundahishn 1.30–32). The reference is thus to the first time the Ahuna Vairiya prayer was used as a spell to counteract evil and render it powerless. This is an instance of part of the Gāthās being used as the most powerful spell.

Altogether, over twenty evils are cursed, first in Yasht 3.10–12 in simple form and then again in Yasht 3.14–15, but in superlative forms. In the first part, the verb "he smashes" is in the simple "performative" present tense. The second verb is in the commanding subjunctive "he shall be smashed," and each evil is repeated with the verb "he shall be an enemy to." Thus, for instance:

yaska jainti	He smashes diseases
yaskanām yaskō.temem janād	He shall smash the most disease-inflicting of diseases.
yaskanām yaskō.temem dbaēshayād	He shall be the enemy of the most disease-inflicting of diseases.

This brings us to the phonetic elements that help to express an emotional state. There is the insistent repetition of the present *jainti* and the subjunctive *janād* alternating with the rhyming *dbaēshayād*. In addition, in the second part, all the nouns are uttered twice in increasingly long form: *yaska* > *yaskanām* > *yaskō.temem*.

The phonetic elements work together to develop the necessary emotional state in the hearer. In the Avestan original, even if one does not understand the language, one can still sense the powerful effect of the word arrangement. The verb occurs at the end of each rhythmic unit, creating a forceful pattern in its repetition, with the nouns and adjectives rhyming and alliterating.

CHAPTER 10

USES FOR AVESTAN INCANTATIONS

INVOKING GODS IN THE SPELL

Spells against evildoers meant to ward off their curses usually contained requests to gods or goddesses for assistance. The god or goddess who was invoked was always closely involved in the protection of the person or item the priest sought to protect. Therefore, particular deities were invoked in both the spells and curses. In the Yasna, Haoma, who was both a god and a plant, attended to most of the curses. Haoma's juices were indispensable for the performance of the sacrifice. He was often invoked because he appeared to listen well at the sacrifice and gave boons generously, notably health. Sraosha, who, as we saw in Chapter 7, protected the creation at night, was for that reason frequently invoked to alleviate night terrors. Ardwī Surā Anāhitā was the goddess who presided over the waters with their cleansing power, but she also protected against miserly men, robbers, wolves, and lack of space. Ārmaiti, the earth, was concerned with warding off damage to homes and fields. The *frawashi*s were invoked for many forms of protection.

Ahura Mazdā, the highest god, was not invoked in this manner. Most often he appeared as instructing others, for example Zarathustra, in the use of magic against demons and magicians. His names, however, were used as potent talismans to avert evil, as we shall see. Avestan incantations invoked the names of the gods so that they could empower a spell or curse. In the Avesta, we also find other forms employing help from the gods, such as one in which a god utters a curse, as we have seen in the case of Haoma (Yasna 11.3).

CONTAINING ANGRY GODS

The gods were all called upon for help in the performance of magical rituals, but care had to be taken that the sacrifices did not offend them.[1] There was a risk involved in the use of spells, as we have already seen in the case of a spell backfiring. Attention to detail was critical, but, even then, bad luck might ruin a carefully considered ritual.

The gods that needed appeasing most received the majority of attention, and they appeared to be the most rewarding of all to worship, however dangerous they might have been. The Yashts contain dire warnings to those who would offend the gods:

YASHT 2.12

Woe to you! It puts [itself?] into [your?] body.
Woe to you! It will strike the Priest,
the Priest like the Charioteer.
All for our disobedience[?]
with the strength of the destroyers[?],
whoever receives it as ripping[?].
We sacrifice to the seven Life-giving Immortals,
who bestow good command and give good gifts,
[command?] even over the opponents,
the *daēnā* of those who sacrifice to Ahura Mazdā,
[and] the water in the shape of a horse,
the Orderly one set in place by [Ahura] Mazdā.[2]

The gods Mithra, Verthragna, Sraosha, and Rashnu, and to some extent Tishtriya, were dangerous, however beneficial. They were unpredictable at times, and easily slighted. In addition, they appeared to respond to the first army that used the spells to invoke them, rather than choosing the side that they favored. The entourage of Mithra was the most dangerous, but because they were the most warlike gods, the warrior called upon them for his success in the battlefield. Yasht 10.29 sums up the ambiguous feeling expressed by the Yashts concerning this type of god:

YASHT 10.29

You are bad and the best, O Mithra, for the lands.
You are bad and the best, O Mithra, for the people.
You command peace and lack of peace, O Mithra, for the lands.

There were ways, however, to manage the worship of unpredictable gods. Yasht 10.98 contains a spell to protect the worshipper, imploring protection from the angry god:

YASHT 10.98

May we not here come up against the thrust of Mithra,
who provides wide grazing grounds, when he is angered.
May you not, when angered, reject us, O Mithra,
you who provide wide grazing grounds.

Clearly, this passage addresses the problem of a god who has lost control because of anger, and needs to be placated. The Rigveda contains several examples of similar spells that simultaneously call on a dangerous god to destroy enemies, and attempt to divert the anger of the god from the petitioner:

RIGVEDA 2.33.5

If someone should call him with invocations, thinking,
"I will appease Rudra with songs of praise"—
may the softhearted god who is easy to invoke,
the tawny god whose lips are full—
may he not suspect us of that and give us over into the power of his anger.[3]

Rudra, a Vedic god who was easily angered, was frightening because he might misunderstand the supplicant. In the cases of Mithra and Verthragna, however, sometimes simply being in the path of these gods when angered could result in devastation.

YASHT 10.69

May we not here come up against the thrust of the lord when angered,
whose one thousand thrusts go against the opponent,
who has ten thousand watchers,
he the one rich in life-giving strength, all-knowing, not deceivable.

The spells that shielded the priest or sacrificer were defensive, and, although it may seem that one should not need protection from one's allies, in this case it was necessary because of the tremendous power of the gods.

The cautionary measures needed to protect one from annoyed gods were seen as early as the Gāthās. Thus, the Gathic sacrificer pleads with the gods:

YASNA 28.9

May we not, O Mazdā, anger you all, as well as Order and [*your*] thought,
the best, with those requests to you, we who have taken our places to fulfill
our obligations [in the form] of praises . . .

as does the Young Avestan sacrificer at the end of his first great invocation:

YASNA 1.21

If I have ever offended you, through thought, speech, [or] act,
whether because it pleased me or whether it did not,
I present myself to you [as guilty] of this and say it forth in praise [of you].
I make it known to you, if I have ever omitted [anything] from this of yours,
the sacrifice and the hymn.[4]

YASNA 1.22

O all greatest models! O models of Order, sustainers of Order!
If I have offended you either through thought, speech, [or] act,
whether because it pleased me or whether it did not,
I present myself to you [as guilty] of this and say it forth in praise [of you].
I make it known to you, if I have barred you from this,
the sacrifice and the hymn.

This was followed by the sacrificer's profession of faith:

YASNA 1.23

I choose to sacrifice to Ahura Mazdā in the tradition of Zarathustra,
discarding the *daēwa*s and holding the guidance of Ahura [Mazdā].

USE OF THE HOLY NAMES

Among potent magical words, the most powerful are probably the names of
gods, which in the Avesta are used in apotropaic spells, and are known from
other cultures as well.[5] Ancient Egyptian spells often made use of the names
of the gods, and Jan Assmann comments in this connection that this is a "decisive point between magic and theology: the divine name or names. The cryp-

tonomy of the creator is a very traditional concept and much older than the theological discourse."[6]

Surprisingly the Avesta contains only two lists of divine names that can be specifically used for the purpose of supernatural protection, namely those of Ahura Mazdā and Vayu (invoked in Yashts 1 and 15). Their names were used to ward off different sorts of evil. It is hard to fathom why only these two gods are invoked by name, especially because the two are very different. Perhaps Vayu had the status of a high god in some areas of Iran.[7] The names, which are illustrative of the gods, are spells in themselves, being known to those who have access to this special knowledge.

Vayu (Old Indic Vāyu) was, together with Mithra, one of the few gods that made the transition into the Iranian pantheon. He was an important god in the Avesta, as Dumézil found that he was in the Vedas. He is found in ritual lists,[8] ranking with Mithra and Verthragna as a martial god. Vayu was described as a brave warrior "girded high, broad-chested, with broad thighs, solid, with tall legs and full of light spreading further than the dawn" (Yasht 15.55). His garb was martial and totally made of gold. He had a golden wagon with golden wheels, and even golden weapons. His raiment was all gold, and he was said to have a crown, helmet, necklace, garments, belt, and shoes of gold (Yasht 15.57). He is lauded in Yasht 15 for his ability to conquer opponents and his generosity in giving boons. Vayu's position as a potent war god made him central to the battles on earth. His power was used in connection with incantations for success in combat. Even Ahura Mazdā worshipped Vayu, asking as a boon "that I may smash down [all] of the creatures of the Evil Spirit" (Yasht 15.3).

Vayu's special position was presumably due to the fact that, as the god of the space between earth and heaven (above) and hell (below), he could partake of both worlds and so was an ambivalent god. According to the Avestan interpretation, he was called Vayu because he could fly both in the realm of Ahura Mazdā and in that of Angra Mainyu, the Evil Spirit. He was called "the Reacher" for the same reason. In addition, he could conquer both realms, so he was called "All-Conqueror." His power to span both the worlds of Ahura Mazdā and Angra Mainyu made him appear to be more powerful than the other gods, and perhaps he was at an earlier stage:[9]

YASHT 15.42–44

We sacrifice to that of him that belongs to the Life-giving Spirit, wealthy [and] munificent.

I am called Vayu, O Orderly Zarathustra.
Thus I am called "Vayu" because I fly through both worlds,
both the one that the Life-giving Spirit set in place
and the one the Evil Spirit set in place.
I am called the Reacher, O Orderly Zarathustra.
Thus I am called Reacher because I reach both establishments,
both the one that the Life-giving Spirit set in place
and the one the Evil Spirit set in place.

I am called All-Conqueror, O Orderly Zarathustra.
Thus I am called All-Conqueror because I conquer both worlds,
both the one that the Life-giving Spirit set in place
and the one the Evil Spirit set in place.
I am called Worker-of-Good, O Orderly Zarathustra.
Thus I am called Worker-of-Good because I work
the good things of Ahura Mazdā the creator [and] the Life-giving Immortals.

Since he was a warlike god, most of Vayu's names have to do with the battlefield. He was described as the one who goes behind, the one who throws forth, the one who throws down, the one who strikes, the one who robs, the one who finds glory, the bravest, the firmest, the most solid, the most power-ful, the one who throws about well, the one who conquers here and now, the one who cannot be overcome, the one who makes the demons go away, the one who is more hostile, the one who creates commotion (on the battlefield), and the one who causes burning (Yasht 15.45–47). Although these names are explicitly martial, he even went by names of weapons such as the Sharp Spear, the Broad Spear, and the Brandished Spear (Yasht 15.48). Like Mithra, Vayu was called the "one who produces doubt among all horses and men," a clear reference to his position as a god directly involved with battlefield activities (Yasht 15.53). Vayu could be invoked outside of the battlefield, or when one was faced with the dangers of battles, demons, or illnesses.

Ahura Mazdā, the creator of the material world and its creatures, was one of the gods to pray to when one wished to overcome demons, hostile men, and sorcerers (Yasht 1.5–6). All of these characters required the use of magic against them. Although Ahura Mazdā was said to be "obstruction-smashing" and an overcomer of demons, his names hinted at a gentler, creative god who protected against evils of a supernatural sort. Many of his names had to do with intelligence, insight, and healing. Ahura Mazdā was known as the pro-tector, the defender, the knower, the Life-giving Spirit, rich in healing, the High Priest, the Lord, Wisdom, glorious, Orderly, the seer, the pursuer, the giver, the protector, the defender, the knower, rich in power, having most power at will, having power in his name, non-deceivable, the dispeller of deceit, the watchman, the overcomer of hostilities, the fashioner, the provider of good breathing space, the invigorating glow, the vitalizing strength, the most generous, and the one glowing from afar (Yasht 1.12–15).

Ahura Mazdā had a few martial-sounding names, such as the overcomer of hostilities, the conqueror here and now, the strongest, the exalted, and the most powerful. When he dealt with demons, Ahura Mazdā was not very lenient. He advised that power obtained by these names be used (Yasht 1.27) to

> Block their perception!
> Tie down their hands!
> Grind together their jaws!

The bulk of his names, however (and he has many more than Vayu),[10] point to his creative and moderate temperament. Ahura Mazdā promises that if a man utters these names "while standing up or lying down, girded or with a loosened girdle (*kusti*), going forth from the place, the tribe or from the land, or coming to another land," then neither rage-driven man, nor stings, daggers, arrows, knives, cudgels, or stones will reach him (Yasht 1.16–18). The names of Ahura Mazdā were thought to be effective against all types of demons, especially magicians and the Lie. Thus, his names were a source of protection against the supernatural, as opposed to the more practical dangers of the battlefield.

The difference between the two gods and their names is thus reflected in the protection the supplicant was seeking. Ahura Mazdā, the creator of the material world and its creatures, was one of the gods to pray to when a person feared supernatural evils. Vayu, on the other hand, was invoked specifically in connection with down-to-earth problems such as war.

HEALING SPELLS

While healing practices were required to repair the ailing world, they had to be accompanied by words to be wholly effective. Words had a wide range of other functions, however, and the force of words was considered crucial for maintaining the good existence and combating evil.

Among the healing gods, Haoma, as an herbal medicine employed in the sacrifice, brought help to both the gods and to humans and was therefore approached for relief from a number of ailments:

YASNA 71.17

We sacrifice to the invigorant and the good-mindedness.
We sacrifice to the good-mindedness and the invigorant,
for withstanding the darkness,
for withstanding weeping and illness [?].
We sacrifice to the invigorant . . . ,
and we sacrifice to fitness and healing,
and we sacrifice to furthering and growth
for withstanding agues and paralyses.

We also note the typical progress in expelling the demon from everywhere, proceeding outward from the "house" via ever-larger social units.

AN INVISIBILITY SPELL

Yasht 4.4–10 contains directions for making the body invisible and the spirit powerful. With this power, the performer waited until sunset and would strike toward the north, the home of the demons, to destroy many of them. This feat was especially difficult because the demons were thought to be more powerful after sunset. The invisibility of the performer was an advantage, as the demons would not be able to strike back. The ritual was performed by drawing lines, probably circles, around the performer of the ritual while reciting the following spell:

YASHT 4.4

Whither on the crooked path away from the sustainers of Order?[11]
Whither [on that] of the ones possessed by the Lie?
Then Ahura Mazdā said:
If he pronounces my Life-giving Holy Word
or memorizing or reciting or pronouncing [it] draws a line,
[then] he would hide his body [and then] he would hide his body and soul.

YASHT 4.5

Whichever [you may be], you and the Lie,
having forward going,
or whichever having backward going,
or whichever in roadless places,

whichever [you may be], you and the Lie,
I shall smash [you] with Aryan feet[?]
I [herewith] bind you and the Lie.
I [herewith] strike down you and the Lie.
I have carried [you] out [and brought you] down below.

YASHT 4.6

He draws a figure with three lines.
[Three times] I say forth the Orderly Man.
He draws six lines.
Six times I say forth the Orderly Man.
He draws nine lines.
Nine times I say forth the Orderly Man.

YASHT 4.7

He strikes back at the names of these Lies, cutters of corpses.
Smash the brood of the mumblers!
And burn the scorched dead—
[you,] Zarathustra the libationer—
from the terrible hell,—
each according to his own wish,
howsoever his pleasure.

YASHT 4.8

After the sun has set, he strikes the northern direction.
Afterward, as long as the sun has not yet risen,
he destroys the Carrion with [his] stunning weapon,
[inflicting it with] a bloody wound,
for the satisfaction and glorification
of those worthy of sacrifice in the world of thought.

YASHT 4.9[12]

O Zarathustra, do not teach this sacred thought
other than to [your] father or son,
brother or sibling,
or the priest who guards the roads.

Having good busy women, having a good *daēnā*
[is he] who, of good *daēnā*, delimits [?] a place
[and] straightens all the lines.

This spell contains six distinct parts, each with a specific function. The first part, Yasht 4.4, declares the intention of performing magic and gives the method. It was magic by means of the ancient sacred thought (*manthra* of Ahura Mazdā) and by the ritual act of drawing a single line (to begin with). The body and perhaps the soul would be hidden with this magic.

The second part, Yasht 4.5, is a curse in the form of a "performative" threat: "I am binding you, I am striking you down."[13]

The third part, Yasht 4.6, again employs a curse and a ritual action, as in the first part, but this time the lines are drawn in multiples of three, so that we finally get nine lines.

The fourth part, Yasht 4.7, is again a curse, a "performative" present followed by the two imperatives addressed not to the demon but to the participant, adding, apparently, the priest identified with Zarathustra, who, as we have seen, was the first to make the demons go underground (Yasna 9.15)[14] and sent the demons and the Evil Spirit himself back to the terrible hell (Videvdad 19.47). The reference to Zarathustra's deed is explicit in the phrase "from the terrible hell," which is used in Videvdad 19.47.[15]

The fifth part follows the pattern of instruction, again in the "performative" present. It asks the priest to do the most dangerous of deeds: to attack the northern direction at the dead of night. For the authors of the Avesta, the north represented the home of evil, and, like many cultures, they believed that demons were most potent at night.

The sixth and last part contains the typical warning given at the end of this sort of powerful spell, specifying to whom this ritual may be imparted.

THE USE OF ANCIENT TEXTS AS SPELLS

In the Young Avestan spells and curses we shall consider below, we will find abundant use of Old Avestan quotations, ranging from the four sacred prayers[16] to individual lines from the Gāthās and the Yasna Haptanghāiti. The Old Avestan formulas were utilized in these spells for the potency that they were thought to possess, a fact known from other cultures as well. Thus, S. J. Tambiah has found that old language acquires a certain authority beyond what may be possible with ordinary speech. He notes that this is a common phenomenon, not just in magic, but also in religion.[17] Similarly, the Jews use

Hebrew, the Hindus use Sanskrit, and Muslims use classical Arabic as powerful, sacred sound. It is not the antiquity of the language that matters, according to Tambiah, but the fact that the old languages were the languages of the founders or mythmakers of the religion.[18]

Of all the Old Avestan texts, however, the Ahuna Vairiya was the first to have been recited and by its primordial nature was the most powerful spell ever to have been used: by Ahura Mazdā and Zarathustra to lay low the Evil Spirit, and by Zarathustra to drive the demons underground, depriving them of their sacrifices:

YASNA 9.14–15

Renowned in the Aryan Expanse,[19]
you were the first, O Zarathustra, to chant the Ahuna Vairiya
with pauses [?] and repeated four times,
the last time with stronger enunciation.
You made all the *daēwa*s hide in the ground, O Zarathustra,
who before that went about in the shape of men on this earth,
[you] the strongest, the firmest, the most active, the fastest,
who were the greatest obstruction-smasher
of the creations of the two spirits.

YASHT 19.81

Then a single Ahuna Vairiya of yours,
which Orderly Zarathustra chanted,
with pauses[?] and repeated four times,
the last time with stronger enunciation.
drove all the *daēwa*s underground,
depriving them of sacrifice and prayer.

And the Ahuna Vairiya was used by Zarathustra in his attack against the Evil Spirit in Yasht 17.20, where the Evil Spirit wails:

YASHT 17.20

He smashes me with the Ahuna Vairiya,
[as] with a weapon like a stone the size of a house.
He burns me with the Asha Vahishta just like metal.

He chases me from this good earth,
who alone comes against me, Spitāma Zarathustra.

The two prayers and magical formulas, the Ahuna Vairiya and the
Ashem Vohū, are here used as supernatural weapons, one like a stone, the
other like fire.[20] It is clearly the primeval quality of the words first uttered by
the primordial god, Ahura Mazdā, and by his first follower among men, Zarathustra, that makes these spells so powerful. The same holds true for the frequent use of other Gathic passages in spells throughout the Young Avesta, as
for instance in the following spell to exorcise the Carrion demon:

VIDEVDAD 9.46

Then Ahura Mazdā said:
Say forth these words said twice in the Gāthās.
Say forth these words said three times in the Gāthās.
Say forth these words said four times in the Gāthās.
Then that Carrion demon will fly back,
just like this, O Spitāma Zarathustra:
like an arrow well shot,
or like felt after a season,
or like seasonal wool.[21]

That this is a common situation is shown by Bronislaw Malinowski's obser-
vation that the ancient words of the Trobrianders also had the most magical
potency.[22] Another important point made by Malinowski is that to safeguard
their special powers, the words had to be passed down through qualified practitioners. The same restrictions concerning who could use spells also held true
for the Avesta: the result of misusing a good spell could be disastrous. Commonly, the Yasna and Yasht passages that form spell-like compositions are
accompanied by warnings against misuse. One is that the spell should not be
taught to someone who is not a close relative of Zarathustra or who is not a
high priest, as we saw in Yasht 4.9. Another injunction in the same passage
states that this knowledge must be kept secret from witches, who would misuse it.

Sometimes there are restrictions as to the sex or condition of fertility of the
worshipper:

YASHT 17.54

Thus said good Ashi, the tall:
May no one partake in these libations of mine
with which they repay[?] me [for my favors]:
neither a man with blocked semen,
nor a whore beyond her period,
nor a tender child,
nor girls not yet approached by men.

The words must be spoken with precision. Many passages mention "correctly spoken words," such as these two:

YASHT 18.8

We offer up in sacrifice the Ahuna Vairiya.
We offer up in sacrifice the Asha Vahishta,
the most beautiful, Life-giving, Immortal one.
We offer up in sacrifice the correctly spoken words,
endowed with obstruction-smashing strength, healing.
We offer up in sacrifice the healing words,
obstruction-smashing when correctly spoken.

YASHT 5.17

Ahura Mazdā the creator sacrificed to her
in the Aryan Expanse of the Good Lawful One,
with *haoma* [mixed] with milk [and] with *barsom*,
with the skill of his tongue, with words correctly spoken.

In the case of a prayer or supplication, the god could turn down a request, but in the case of a spell there were consequences, regardless of the position of the performer. This did not mean that the unauthorized person using the spell would obtain whatever he or she desired. In most cases, a bad result was expected, and sometimes innocent members of the community were affected.

Yasna 61.1–4 is another example of the use of an ancient spell for bolstering the power of the larger spell of which it is a part. In this spell, three of the ancient formulas are used as weapons against evil, which makes it powerful. It mainly attacks all kinds of sorcerers and even the Evil Spirit himself.

The spell, again, has three parts. In the first part, the ancient and powerful spells are summoned and sent forth with the verb in the present tense. Next, we have a pattern where the evil ones are mentioned in the plural first, then in the singular. At the end of Yasna 61.4, any evil people who have not been covered are mentioned in a way that can encompass all evil people:

YASNA 61.1–4 AND YASNA 72.1–4

We send forth the Ahuna Vairiya
    between heaven and earth,
and we send forth the Ashem Vohū
    between heaven and earth,
and we send forth the Yenghē hātām well sacrificed
    between heaven and earth,
and we also send forth
the qualified Orderly man
and the qualified good Propitiation
    between heaven and earth,
for the discomfiture and removal
    of the Evil Spirit with his creations,
      the one full of destruction, whose creations are bad,
for the discomfiture and removal
    of the male and female magicians,
for the discomfiture and removal
    of the male and female magician,
for the discomfiture and removal
    of the sorcerers and sorceresses,
for the discomfiture and removal
    of the sorcerer and sorceress,
for the discomfiture and removal
    of thieves and violators,
for the discomfiture and removal
    of the *zanda*s[23] and those possessed by sorcerers,
for the discomfiture and removal
    of those who destroy the contract
      and the one whose contract contains the Lie,
for the discomfiture and removal
    of those who smash the Orderly ones
      and those who are hostile to the Orderly ones,
for the discomfiture and removal

of the obscurantist and the un-Orderly, false teacher,
for the discomfiture and removal
of each and every one of those possessed by the Lie,
whose thoughts are not according to the divine model,
whose words are not according to the divine model,
whose acts are not according to the divine model,
O Zarathustra of the Spitāmas.

This part of the Yasna was traditionally spoken just at the time when the sun is about to appear. The demons are stronger at night, and this spell attempts to dispel any who have not yet fled. The poet names as many evils as possible, with the hope that none will find a means to remain. Because words make up spells and are the most important aspect of magic, to be the most effective they must cover as much ground as possible. Otherwise there is a chance that evil will be able to escape the effect of the spell. The spell in Yasht 3.10–16 quoted above displays the same insistence on detail, covering most conceivable evils, yet in a way that is nonspecific in the sense that it does not use names. Spells that name demons also exist, and they will be discussed below.

CHAPTER II

EXORCISMS

EXORCISTIC SPELLS AND CURSES

Part of the requirement for being a qualified purifier (it was not necessary to be a priest, although most often priests performed this service) was to know the proper formulas for driving out the evil spirits. These formulas follow the pattern of the spells we have seen elsewhere in the Avesta: a series of commands are issued to the demons so that they will depart to the north. Videvdad 10 is one of the finest examples of a complete exorcistic spell found in the Avesta. Although there is no command language used in this exorcism, it achieves the same result. This is a good example of the performative language that Tambiah identifies in many spells. It states an action, and by this statement the act is as good as done. Of course, this is because of the nature of the spell. It is not ordinary language, but formal language that in this case performs the act of expelling demons.

In the case of exorcising the carrion demon from the body, the demon is pushed by the spell and the ritual pouring of water, from one part of the body to the next, until by slow degrees it is expelled.

VIDEVDAD 8.41–42

And if the good waters come onto the top of the head in front
where among these parts does this female demon Carrion run in?
Then Ahura Mazdā said:
straight against that man, between his eyebrows;
among these parts this female demon Carrion runs in.

And if the good waters come
straight against that man, between his eyebrows,
where among these parts does this female demon Carrion run in?

Then Ahura Mazdā said: in the back of his head;
among these parts this female demon Carrion runs in.

And so on:

VIDEVDAD 8.43–57

back of the head	his jaw
his jaw	his right ear
his right ear	his left ear
his left ear	his right shoulder
his right shoulder	his left shoulder
his left shoulder	his right armpit
his right armpit	his left armpit
his left armpit	his chest
his chest	his back
his back	his right nipple
his right nipple	his left nipple
his left nipple	his right ribs
his right ribs	his left ribs
his left ribs	his right buttock
his right buttock	his left buttock
his left buttock	his hips

VIDEVDAD 8.58

If it is a male, then you should first pour onto the front, then the back.
If it is a female, then you should first pour onto the back, then the front.

VIDEVDAD 8.59–60

And if the good waters come straight against his hips,
where among these parts does this demon Carrion run in?
Then Ahura Mazdā said: his right thigh;
among these parts this female demon Carrion runs in.

And if the good waters come straight against his right thigh,
where among these parts does this female demon Carrion run in?
Then Ahura Mazdā said: his left thigh;
among these parts this female demon Carrion runs in.

And so on:

VIDEVDAD 8.61–68

his left thigh	his right knee
his right knee	his left knee
his left knee	his right calves
his right calves	his left calves
his left calves	his right leg
his right leg	his left leg
his left leg	his right ankle[?]
his right ankle	his left ankle
his left ankle	

VIDEVDAD 8.69–72

Orderly creator . . .
And if the good waters come straight against his left ankle,
where of these parts does this female demon Carrion run in?
Then Ahura Mazdā said:
it burrows[?] under the sole of the foot, like the wing of a fly.

Pressing down the toes once and lifting the heels
you should pour water on the sole of his right foot.
Then the female demon Carrion runs onto the sole of his left foot.
You should pour water on the sole of his left foot.
Then the female demon Carrion burrows under the toes, like the wing of a fly.

Pressing down the heels once and lifting the toes
you should pour water on his right toe.
Then the female demon Carrion runs onto his left toe.
You should pour water on his left toe.

Then the female demon Carrion burrows under the toes . . .

The concern with detail is important, because to be careless in reciting a spell is an invitation for evil to find a means to reenter or to remain in a place or thing. The exorcist names each part of the body as he purifies it. In addition, the purifier/exorcist must be skilled and learned:

VIDEVDAD 9.47–48

And if the man who pours is not someone who is learned
in the purification procedure of the Mazdayasnian *daēnā*,
how shall he overcome this lie-demon
who rushes upon a living person from dead matter?
How shall he overcome this carrion
which contaminates a living person from dead matter?

Then Ahura Mazdā said:
Just like this, O Zarathustra of the Spitāmas,
this lie-demon, Carrion, grows much stronger than she was before.
She is these illnesses. She is these destructions, just like before.

Similarly, the Evil Spirit, Angra Mainyu, is driven out of the house, etc.,
and finally from every creature of the gods.

VIDEVDAD 10.5–7

And after the words said twice,
say forth these words, victorious power and healing power:
I overcome and chase the Evil Spirit,
from the house, from the town, from the tribe, from the land,
from my own body,
from the dead man,
from the dead woman,
from the house-lord of the house,
from the town-lord of the town,
from the tribe-lord of the tribe,
from the land-lord of the land,
from every being of the Orderly one.

I overcome and chase the Carrion,
I overcome and chase the direct pollution,
I overcome and chase the indirect pollution,
from the house, from the town, from the tribe, from the land,
from my own body,
from the dead man,
from the dead woman,
from the house-lord of the house,

from the town-lord of the town,
from the tribe-lord of the tribe,
from the land-lord of the land,
from every being of the Orderly one.

Orderly creator . . .
Which are these words which are those said three times in the Gāthās.
Then Ahura Mazdā said:
These are these words said three times in the Gāthās.
Say these words forth three times.

The use of verses from the ancient Gāthās (and the Yasna Haptanghāiti)
is seen again in this exorcism, together with instructions for how often they
are to be recited. The rare naming of the individual demons is another interesting feature of this exorcism, and apparently each demon had an evil mis-
sion to perform, although the meaning of many of these ancient names is now
unknown:

VIDEVDAD 10.8–11

Order is the best good . . . [= the Ashem Vohū]
You, who have the greatest life-giving strength . . . [Yasna 33.11]
Indeed, it is for one with best command . . . [Yasna Haptanghāiti[1] 35.5]
together with the ones of bad preferences . . . [Yasna 53.9]

And after the words said three times
say forth these words, rich in obstruction-smashing power and healing
    power:
I overcome and chase Indra,
I overcome and chase Saurwa,
I overcome and chase Nānghaithya,
from the house, from the town, from the tribe, from the land,
from my own body . . . from every being of the Orderly one.

I overcome and chase Taurwi,
I overcome and chase Zairica,
from the house, from the town, from the tribe, from the land,
from my own body . . . from every being of the Orderly one.

VIDEVDAD 10.11–12

Orderly creator . . .
Which are these words which are those said four times in the Gāthās?
Then Ahura Mazdā said:
These are these words said four times in the Gāthās.
Say these words forth four times:

In the way that [an existence] is the choice one by [the example of] the first
    existence . . . [= Ahuna Vairiya]
O Mazdā, thus say *my* poems conferring fame . . . [Yasna 34.15]
Let speedy Airyaman come here for support . . . [= Airyēmā Ishiyō]

VIDEVDAD 10.13–14

And after the words said three times,
say forth these words, rich in obstruction-smashing power and healing
    power:
I overcome and chase Wrath with the bloody club,
I overcome and chase the *daēwa* Evil-fashioner,
from the house, from the town, from the tribe, from the land,
from my own body . . .
from every being of the Orderly one.

I overcome and chase the greedy *daēwa*s,
I overcome and chase the *daēwa* Vātiya,
from the house, from the town, from the tribe, from the land,
from my own body . . . from every being of the Orderly one.

VIDEVDAD 10.15–17

These are these words said twice in the Gāthās.
These are these words said three times in the Gāthās.
These are these words said four times in the Gāthās.

These are these words which strike a blow at the Evil Spirit.
These are these words which strike a blow at Wrath with the bloody club.
These are these words which strike a blow at the giant *daēwa*s.
These are these words which strike a blow at all the *daēwa*s.

These are these words which are the opponents of that lie-demon, that
    Carrion,

who rushes upon a living person from what is dead.
These are these words which are the opponents of that lie-demon, that
   Carrion,
which contaminates a living person from what is dead.

There are also general spells for the cleansing of many objects. Cows, trees, the house, the fire, the water, and the earth can be cleansed, each with a particular formula. The purification of the waters and the earth, for example:

VIDEVDAD 11.5

I shall purify this water.
Then I shall say forth these words:
Thus, we are sacrificing [to] the waters . . . [Yasna Haptanghāiti 38.3]
I shall purify this earth.
Then I shall say forth these words:
Thus, we are sacrificing [to] this earth together with its women . . . [Yasna
   Haptanghāiti 38.1]

The earth and the women, presumably all the female divinities mentioned in the surrounding text, are mentioned together here because of the link they share as the mothers of creatures.

The following spell to exorcise several kinds of demons and illnesses uses repeated imperatives that contribute to the power of the spell while listing all the evils to be exorcised:

YASHT 3.7

Diseases, run away!
Destructions, run away!
Demons, run away!
Adversaries, run away!
Unorderly obscurantist, run away!
Men [who are] tyrants, run away!

YASHT 3.8

Brood of snakes, run away!
Brood of wolves, run away!

Brood of two-footed [wolves], run away!
Despiser, run away!
You of distraught mind, run away!
Fever, run away!
Slanderer, run away!
Sowers of discord, run away!
You with the evil eye, run away!

YASHT 3.9

You most lying with lying speech, run away!
Evil woman consorting with sorcerers, run away!
Evil woman, female magician, run away!
Southerly [and] northerly wind, run away!
Southerly [and] northerly wind, get lost!
And any of these broods of snakes, [get away from] me!

Humans are also cleansed in these not so specific formulas, but they must be purified by reciting the list of demons who must be banished again, with the requisite imperatives directed at particular demons (Videvdad 11.9–13).

The list of demons given in Videvdad 11 is important because many of these demons have not been named before. The exorcism is patterned in such a way that first there is a declaration that the exorcist can overcome the demon named. Then the demon is "chased" from the person or items to be exorcised (Videvdad 11.10). More instructions follow in Videvdad 11.11, which prescribe the use of the Gathic spells, and how many times they are to be repeated.

In Videvdad 11.12–13, the final expulsion takes place with a direct command, "Behind my back," followed by more instructions. This exorcistic passage, which is one of the most powerful in the Avesta, is applicable to many circumstances. It appears to be an all-purpose cleansing spell, as many exorcisms are in the Avesta. In each case, we see that the demon who causes the disease or uncleanness is targeted rather than the disease itself. The "filth demon" who is mentioned throughout this exorcism appears to be a female demon of the disembodied kind, but there is a strong possibility that the prostitute (or a menstruating woman) is being referred to here as well. The items that the "filth demon" seeks to contaminate are precisely those that can be defiled by a menstruating woman, and which must be protected from her touch and even sight. The spell is expanded, compared with the preceding one, by a first section in the performative present tense followed by a second section in the imperative with the same nouns as in the first section in a pattern similar to the one we saw above in Yasht 3:

VIDEVDAD 11.8–10

Then you should recite these words . . . You should recite eight
    Ahuna Vairiyas:
In the way that [an existence] is the choice one by [the example of] the first
    existence . . . [= Ahuna Vairiya]
Whom, I wonder, O Mazdā . . . (Yasna 46.7)
May you not destroy the bony living beings of Order!

I overcome Wrath.
I overcome the Carrion.
I overcome direct contamination.
I overcome indirect contamination.
I overcome blood.
I overcome Blood-smasher.
I overcome Būidi.
I overcome Būidizha.
I overcome Kundi.
I overcome Kundizha.
I overcome yellow-hued Sloth.
I overcome Sloth with long arms.
I overcome Mūidi.
I overcome Kapasti.
I overcome the witch who approaches the fire, the water, the earth, the cow,
    the plant.
I overcome the filth demon who approaches the fire, the water, the earth, the
    cow, the plant.

I overcome you, Evil Spirit of bad establishments [and chase you]
from the fire, from the water,
from the earth, from the cow, from the plant,
from the Orderly man, from the Orderly woman,
from the stars, from the moon, from the sun,
from the Endless Lights,
from all good things established by Ahura Mazdā, with their seed from
    Order[?]

VIDEVDAD 11.11–13

Then you should recite these words . . . You should recite four
  Ahuna Vairiyas:
In the way that [an existence] is the choice one by [the example of] the first
  existence . . . [= Ahuna Vairiya]
May you not destroy the bony living beings of Order!

Behind my back, Wrath!
Behind my back, Carrion!
Behind my back, direct contamination!
Behind my back, indirect contamination!
Behind my back, blood!
Behind my back, Blood-smasher!
Behind my back, Būidi!
Behind my back, Būidizha!
Behind my back, Kundi!
Behind my back, Kundizha!
Behind my back, yellow-hued Sloth!
Behind my back, Sloth with long arms!
Behind my back, Mūidi!
Behind my back, Kapasti!
Behind my back, the witch who approaches the fire, the water, the earth, the
  cow, the plant!
Behind my back, the filth demon who approaches the fire, the water, the
  earth, the cow, the plant.

Behind my back, you, Evil Spirit, whose creatures are bad. [I chase you]
from the fire, from the water,
from the earth, from the cow, from the plant,
from the Orderly man, from the Orderly woman,
from the stars, from the moon, from the sun,
from the Endless Lights,
from all good things established by Ahura Mazdā, with their seed from
  Order!

VIDEVDAD 11.14–16

Then you should recite these words . . . You should recite four
  Ahuna Vairiyas:

In the way that [an existence] is the choice one by [the example of] the first
   existence . . .
Whom, I wonder, O Mazdā . . .
May you not destroy the bony living beings of Order!

I overcome Wrath . . .

VIDEVDAD 11.17

Then you should recite these words . . . You should recite five Ahuna Vairiyas:
In the way that [an existence] is the choice one by [the example of] the first
   existence . . .
Whom, I wonder, O Mazdā . . .
May you not destroy the bony living beings of Order!

Other exorcistic spells are characterized by their use of imperatives to
drive off the demon causing the illness or other misfortune. The naming of
the demon is important in order to use the imperative, and Tambiah suggests
that it is also a means of calling the demon, or "hitting with sound," as the Sinhalese call it. The Sinhalese exorcism ceremony ends, says Tambiah, with "a
mantra which enacts the expulsion of the demon itself."[2]

The Avesta uses the same scheme of naming and calling all possible evils in
exorcistic spells. Exorcism is a means of driving away the demons by the uti-
lization of both spells and magical rituals, by which a demon is invoked, then
ordered to leave the body or village, etc.

Tambiah proposes that the naming of the demon or demons responsible for
the disease is therapeutic. After confronting the demon, and having faith that
the magician can exorcise it, the patient can begin to recuperate. The emotional confrontation of a demon is a factor that places these spells into the
category of protective exorcisms.

Let us first look at the exorcistic spells in Videvdad 20 after the installation
of Thrita as first human healer. These spells attack disease demons and the sorcerers who send disease to humans. The passage invokes the ancient Gathic
spells and alternates command language with the optative for imploring the
help of the spell:

VIDEVDAD 20.7 (CF. CHAPTER 7)

Disease, I tell you to go back!
Destruction, I tell you to go back!

Burning, I tell you to go back!
Fever, I tell you to go back!
etc.
Evil eye, I tell you to go back!

VIDEVDAD 20.8

. . . by the increase of which we may overcome the Lie,
May we overcome the Lie with growth,
command with strength for *me*, O Ahura.[3]

VIDEVDAD 20.9–10

May I conquer and chase *ashiri*,
may I conquer and chase *agūiri*,
may I conquer and chase *agra*,
may I conquer and chase *ugrā*,
may I conquer and chase disease,
may I conquer and chase destruction,
may I conquer and chase raging fever,
may I conquer and chase fever,
may I conquer and chase *sārana*,
may I conquer and chase *sārastiya*,
may I conquer and chase *azhana*,
may I conquer and chase *azhahwa*,
may I conquer and chase *kuruga*,
may I conquer and chase *azhiwāka*,
may I conquer and chase *druka*,
may I conquer and chase *astariya*,
May I conquer and chase the woman with the evil eye, who is rot and filth,
[diseases] which the Evil Spirit whittled forth
against this body, that of mortal men.

May I conquer and chase every disease and destruction,
all sorcerers and witches,
all women possessed by the Lie.

VIDEVDAD 20.11 (AIRYAMAN ISHIYA)

Let speedy Airyaman come here for support
for men/heroes and women/heroines, for the support of Zarathustra's
good thought, by which his vision-soul may gain a well-deserved fee.
I am now asking for the reward of Order, which Ahura Mazdā shall deem [?]
    worthy of being sped hither.

VIDEVDAD 20.12

Let the Airyaman Ishiya smash every disease and destruction,
all sorcerers and witches, all women possessed by the Lie.

VIDEVDAD 20.13–14

Ahuna Vairiya
Whom, I wonder, O Mazdā . . .
Who is the obstruction-smasher . . . [Yasna 44.16]
Protect us all around from the one hostile to us,
O Mazdā, O Ārmaiti, O Life-giving one!
Get lost, deceiving Lie!
Get lost, you *daēwa*-spawn!
Get lost, you *daēwa*-sown!
Get lost, you *daēwa*-made one!
Disappear, O Lie!
Run away, O Lie!
Run away and lose yourself, O Lie!
You disappear in the northern [direction]!
May you not destroy the bony living beings of Order!

Still another variety of exorcistic spell common in the Avesta is one initiated by the priest, who first sanctifies a man and then calls upon the gods to
release that man from the clutches of various demons. This is very close to an
outright exorcism with the exception that it is not couched in the normal command language of exorcism, yet the pattern of naming various demons who
are specifically connected with death is exorcistic in nature. Of the two examples below, Yasht 4.3 and Yasna 65.7, the first is meant to be administered
by a priest, and the second is a direct appeal to the gods. Although they are
similar, Yasht 4.3 is decidedly exorcistic, whereas Yasna 65.7 is not aimed at
death-causing demons, but at those who would make the good man go against

the good religion. Their verbal pattern, however, is similar in that there is a long list that does not repeat the verb, but are all connected with the main verb, e.g. "to release from," and "do not give us over to":

YASHT 4.3

Thus the first I pronounce [is] the Orderly Man.
If the first ones I pronounce [are] among the Orderly men,
this, O straightest Rashnu,
this for the Life-giving Immortals,
whoever is among the beings worthy of sacrifice in the world of inspiration,
they will release the Orderly Man
from the Carrion,
from the Violator[?],
from the Biter[?],
from the Cutter[?],
from the Dissolver[?],
from the army with wide front,
from [the army] with banners, raised far and wide,
from the false teacher possessed by the Lie, . . .
from the false teacher,
from the sorcerer,
from the witch,
from the Twister[?].

YASNA 65.7

Do not [give] us [over] to the one with evil thought,
nor to the one with evil speech,
nor to the one with evil acts,
nor to the one with evil *daēnā*,
nor to him who is hostile to his companion,
nor to him who is hostile to the *magu*,
nor to him who is hostile to the members of the community,
nor to him who is hostile to the members of the family . . .[4]

Curses differ from spells because they are addressed directly to the target of the curse, in the second person or the third person, using the imperative or subjunctive of command or the optative of wish. They are related to spells, and the people authorized to speak them are the same people who are empowered to use spells. A very significant element is the importance of the follower's declarations against the sorcerers and demons. Zarathustra again becomes the model for the follower of Mazdā. As he forswore the company of the *daēwa*s, so would the follower. Yasna 12.5–6 maintains that in the company of Ahura Mazdā, Zarathustra repeatedly forswore the *daēwa*s in their conversations. The worshipper adds: "And thus do I too, as a Mazdayasnian and adherent of Zarathustra, forswear the company with the *daēwa*s, like the Orderly Zarathustra used to forswear them." The intention of such statements, swearing allegiance to Ahura Mazdā and forswearing the *daēwa*s, is important to establish that the worshipper is loyal to the gods and scornful of the demons. The intention is consequential for setting the scene for the other, more powerful verses.

Hindu sages were feared for their prolific cursing, and some of them, such as Agastya Muni, were positively abusive in their use of curses. In the Mahābhārata, the ancient religious epic of India, the king of Vidarbha, fearing that he might inadvertently offend Agastya, cried to his wife: "He is a powerful seer. If angered, he may burn me with the fire of his curse!"[5] This was a typical reaction when faced with displeasing a sage, because it was assumed that a curse was forthcoming.

Most of the curses examined in this section are closely related to the exorcism of demons and their diseases. It is apparent that the authors of the Avesta imagined their curses to be different from those of the sorcerer because they considered them defensive. The way they saw it, the sorcerer sought to use demonic forces against innocent people. Like the spells we have looked at, curses in the Avesta were legitimized by religious authorities. Moreover, they addressed unknown persons who had trespassed against Order and the gods. However, they still hoped to achieve a violent end for their foes.

The Videvdad contains several spells and curses that have to do with driving away demons by name or driving out illnesses. Here we again encounter the formula of using the vocative and imperative forms, which are familiar from other curses we have encountered, mostly in the Yashts:

VIDEVDAD 8.21

Keep us from our hater, O Mazdā and life-giving Ārmaiti!
Perish, O fiendish Lie!
Perish, O brood of the fiend!
Perish, O creation of the fiend!
Perish, O world of the fiend!

Perish away, O Lie! Rush away, O Lie!
Perish away, O Lie!
Perish away to the regions of the north,
never more to give unto death the living world of Righteousness!

In Yasht 3.17 we find a similar curse, although it is spoken as a warning by the Evil Spirit himself:

YASHT 3.17

The Lie will get lost,
the Lie will be lost,
the Lie will run [away],
it will lose itself in the north.
You get yourself lost!
May you not destroy the bony living beings of Order!

To command evil to retreat to the north is the most powerful curse we find in the Videvdad, as well as in the Yashts. The north, as I have mentioned, is where the lair of the Evil Spirit is located. "Hell" was cold for the authors of the Avesta, which is understandable in light of how destructive Iranian winters can be.

These passages illustrate the use of commands to dispel evil. In Yasht 14, there is a clear description of a kind of incantation that utilizes the holy words of Ahura Mazdā. Spells cast by the use of a magical feather are included, as well as instructions explaining the secrecy of these rites, and telling who may perform them appropriately. There is also, for the first time, a clear indication of demon worship. Up until this time the worship performed by evil people seemed to be a rival worship which, as we see in the Yasht verses that deal with boons, was directed at the gods. In Yasht 14, Ahura Mazdā complains, however, that as long as the demon-worshippers are worshipping demons, his worship is hindered. Then the author gives some intriguing hints on the actual practice of demon worship: the blood sacrifice, the use of the juniper plant and salt, and, in Yasht 14.56, a possible description of the sacrifice. In addition, there is now an element of fear attached to certain deities, and warnings that negligence or improper worship can result in punishment for the worshipper as well as the evil ones.

Other curses are more direct and are aimed at enemies or demons. Here is an example of a powerful curse against enemies:

YASHT 1.27

A thousand healings, ten thousand healings!
Come to my help, O Mazdā,
[to the help?] of the well-fashioned, well-shaped Force,
of the Victory set in place by Ahura Mazdā,
of the victorious Superiority,
and of Life-giving Ārmaiti.
And with Life-giving Ārmaiti
do you all break the hostility of these!
Block their inner hearing!
Tie down their hands!
Grind together their jaws!
Tie fetters[?] onto them!

These may again represent curses against an unknown enemy, although it is conceivable that a general-purpose curse of this sort could be used for a particular, known person.

The last example we will look at is the direct curse. This form of spell in the Avesta is characterized by the use of optative forms (may X not . . .). This type of curse was useful against entities that were both known and unknown. These curses were used to empower the wish of the person uttering the spell. This kind of curse could be used against a sorcerer, witch, or demon whose identity was unknown, especially those who sought to stay hidden from the public. Yasna 9.21 is a spell, again under the power of Haoma, to reveal the presence of the robber and wolf:

YASNA 9.21

This I ask you as the fifth request,
O death-averting Haoma:
May we be the first to notice the thief and the robber,
the first to notice the wolf!
May no one first notice us!
May we notice all first!

This is followed in Yasna 9.29 by a series of curses in the form of exhortations in the optative, against particular types of evil:

YASNA 9.29

May you not be able to walk forth with the legs,
may you not at all be able to grasp with the hands!
May he not see the earth with his eyes,
may he not see the cow with his eyes,
who does sinful things to our thought,
who does sinful things to our body!

This is followed in Yasna 9.30–32 by a series of imperative verbs, but with different targets:

YASNA 9.30–32

Against the yellow dragon, the Sima spurting venom,
for the benefit of Orderly one who wishes to obtain[6] his body,
strike your weapon, O tawny Haoma!
Against the robber seeking to bloat [his possessions], bloody, raging,
for the benefit of the Orderly one who wishes to obtain [his] body,
strike your weapon, O tawny Haoma!
Against the man possessed by the Lie, the tyrant
who [arrogantly] tosses his head,
for the benefit of Orderly one who wishes to obtain his body,
strike your weapon, O tawny Haoma!
Against the un-Orderly obscurantist, who destroys this existence,
who gives heed through word of this *daēnā*,
but does not succeed in acts,
for the benefit of Orderly one who wishes to obtain his body,
strike your weapon, O tawny Haoma!
Against the whore versed in sorcery,
whose activities are for pleasure, who offers her lap,
whose thought flutters forth
like a cloud traveling with the wind,
who wishes to harm the body for an Orderly one!
for the benefit of Orderly one who wishes to obtain his body,
strike your weapon, O tawny Haoma!
When it is for him,
for the benefit of the Orderly one who wishes to obtain his body,
strike your weapon, O tawny Haoma!

In a society where disease, natural disasters, and attacks by hostile forces were a constant threat, magic became an important means of defense. The curse provided people with a means of dealing with evil that was either not understood, or simply impossible to handle any other way. Because people believed in the power of magic, dealing with people suspected of sorcery and witchcraft was another means of defense. E. E. Evans-Pritchard noted, "Witchcraft and sorcery are opposed to, and opposed by, good magic."[7] He reported that the Azande considered sorcery evil not because of its destructive potential, but because it went against moral and legal conventions. This is an important point to ponder as we examine many of the curses and spells in the Avesta that call for death and destruction for the enemies of the good people. Evans-Pritchard commented: "Good magic with destructive functions of this kind only acts against criminals,"[8] concluding that therefore this is not considered immoral, as is the destruction caused by sorcery. He gave an example of an Azande curse in the same class as the Avestan one above, with verb forms stating a wish:

> May misfortune come upon you,
> thunder roar, seize you, and kill you.
> May a snake bite you so that you die.
> May death come upon you from ulcers.
> May you die if you drink water.
> May every kind of sickness trouble you.

This is a curse of revenge. It was not considered bad magic, because only the guilty were punished. Bad magic, on the other hand, was believed to be malicious and unfairly directed at the innocent.

SPELLS AND CURSES IN THE GĀTHĀS

To conclude our investigation, let us look at the oldest Iranian texts. Spells and curses in the Gāthās are scarce compared to what we find in the Young Avesta, but in the matter of punishing their enemies in this world, the Gathic sacrificers employed curses.[9] Several passages in the Gāthās are suggestive of spells and curses. In Yasna 43.8, Zarathustra declares, "I wish to command hostilities for the one possessed by the Lie."[10] In Yasna 49, an angry poet-sacrificer wishes death upon his enemy Benduwa, the Binder [?]: "Find with your good thought death for him!" Others are full-fledged curses, similar to those found in later compositions. The use of curse language, such as the use of the optative or an imperative in a statement of ill wishes, is found in the Gāthās on several occasions besides the eschatological passages that we have already seen. Thus, Yasna 46.5, with its optative "may he bleed him":

YASNA 46.5

He who would honor [a guest] who comes to him by placing him there [in his home?], either [because] in charge of him, being of [the same?] good lineage either by virtue of the conclusion of a deal or by virtue of contracts . . . —a sustainer of Order who, living by a straight utterance, [honors] one possessed by the Lie—being the judge [of these things]—should [always] tell that to the family. In the case of noncompliance[?], may he bleed him, O Mazdā Ahura!

However, especially Yasna 53.8-9, with its imperatives and abusive termi-nology coupled with ridicule, clearly gives examples of the early use of curses, which become more prominent in the Young Avestan compositions:

YASNA 53.8

On account of those [utterances/performances] of theirs, let them be there [at the judgment, as men] of bad virility, dupes, and ridiculed all of them! Let *them* be howled upon!
By those who have good commands let *them* now be smashed and bled![?][11]
—And let [*this one?*] give peace by these [actions of ours?] to the settled towns!—
Let torment [?] huddle *them* off as their greatest [share?], the one with the fetter of death, and let it be soon!

YASNA 53.9[12]

The foul [?] one together with the ones of bad preferences/wool [?] is composing [?] for you the frayed ropes [?] of one having forfeited his body with a puny invocation [?] with crippled Order.
Where is an Ahura who follows Order, who might deprive them of their livelihood and freedom to roam?
That, O Mazdā, is *your* command, by which you shall give the better of this existence to the poor living a straight life.

The intense curses in these strophes take on a special importance in view of the fact that they conclude the entire Old Avesta, followed only by Yasna 54.1, the Airyēmā Ishiyō, which, as we saw, is the ultimate healing spell. The position of the curse is reminiscent of what Skjærvø has called the "parting shot" motif found in the Yashts, which occurs at the end of some hymns, notably Yasht 19 with its repeated performative present tenses ("overcomes") and sub-junctives ("shall overcome"):

YASHT 19.95–96

His companions will come forth,
those of obstruction-smashing Astwad-erta,
[companions] of good thought, good speech,
good deeds, good *daēnā*,
who none of them have ever once spoken
something wrong with their own tongue.
Before them Wrath with the bloody club, of evil Fortune, will retreat.
With his Order, *he* shall overcome
the evil Lie, the one of darkness, of evil seed.
He overcomes even evil thought.
Good Thought overcomes it.
He overcomes the wrongly spoken speech.
The word correctly spoken overcomes it.
Wholeness and Immortality shall overcome both hunger and thirst.
Wholeness and Immortality shall overcome the evil hunger and thirst.
The Evil Spirit, who performs only evil deeds,
now in command of nothing, shall retreat.

The most important aspect of the Gāthās for the authors of the Young Avesta was their mythical antiquity, which conferred authority to the words. The spells of the Gāthās became the magical formulas containing the greatest power in the Young Avesta. Zarathustra was the first human to use the powerful magical formulas, whereas Ahura Mazdā is the primeval magician who instructed him. The Evil Spirit is the primeval and powerful sorcerer whom they had to conquer, along with his minions, who often included traitorous humans. The authors of the Avesta used Old Avestan texts in the most powerful spells. In Yasna 9.14–15, Zarathustra uses the Ahuna Vairiya to drive the demons underground, and previously it was used by Ahura Mazdā himself to lay low the Evil Spirit (Yasna 19.15).

Avestan spells often invoked particular gods such as Haoma and Sraosha. The many names of Ahura Mazdā, along with those of Vayu, were used to ward off demons and sorcerers. Although the gods could be appealed to for help in spells, they could also be the cause of havoc if offended. Therefore, there were also spells to ward off angry gods.

We have seen that exorcistic spells and curses were used in purity rituals. It is important to note that purity rituals in the Avesta were actually exorcistic because their aim was to drive out the pollution demons. In the case of disease, the demon was targeted rather than the disease itself. Fever, for example, was considered a demon. Driving off the demon often involved calling out long lists of demons, and sometimes gods were called upon to assist. Cursing was used often in exorcisms, and demons were commanded to die or to get lost to the north, their cold abode. Finally, there are Old Avestan passages that contain curses based on both language and meaning. The applications of magic in the Avesta were varied and of great doctrinal importance because they aided the gods in the battle against evil.

CHAPTER 12

CONCLUSION

WHEN WORKING WITH TEXTS ALONE, one encounters several seemingly insurmountable challenges. Texts tell us something about the composers, the society they lived in, and their worldviews. However, one must remember that the author's gender, social rank, and economic standing in society will temper those worldviews. While we know much about what the authors of the Avesta thought about witches, for example, we do not know who these individuals really were, or how they fulfilled their spiritual needs. Were witches women who practiced healing arts? Were they women who might have used magical rituals and spells to attempt to help their customers? Did they sometimes fulfill their customer's desire to gain revenge or to settle a grudge? Perhaps some did all of these things. The texts do seem to point to several possibilities of this sort.

Texts are notorious for viewing women and lower classes as outsiders to the priestly tradition. Many scholars and researchers are addressing these problems by studying folk traditions in the field. This is something we obviously cannot do when studying ancient traditions with almost no available data, yet we can use modern field studies to attempt to pick apart some of the hints we can glean from the texts. By studying the concept of evil in the Avestan texts, I have approached a subject that deals very much with those in the non-priestly class. The so-called evildoers were people who threatened the priests and their views on purity and pollution. Some cases seem to point to diatribes against rival worshippers, but many of the passages evidently attack folk traditions whose followers worshipped gods or spirits who the authors of the Avesta considered demons and who might have used spells and curses against others. I have noted that the Avestan authors considered their magic defensive, while other magic was offensive. They took some pains to make this point, but they still sought to crush those whom they considered enemies.

The anthropological model can help in deciphering some of the puzzles presented in the texts, but no single tool will prove sufficient, especially when approaching textual material. Every discipline has its own set of challenges, and, for the study of early Iranian material, the texts have proven to be the most problematic. Difficulties in the interpretation of the texts have resulted in philologists and historians taking the lead in researching these traditions. Because of this, well-studied concepts in the study of religion may be somewhat new in this field. I have attempted to approach the texts without the artificial separation between "religion" and "magic." These terms are notoriously difficult to define, but I have separated them by their general functions, rather than trying to assess their value. Religious acts are centered on the praise and worship of the divinity, and magic functions to fulfill the practical needs of the society by removing demons and undoing their injuries to the good world, which are death, disease, and other harms. Magic and religion are never totally separate realms. Magic often contains prayers and praise, but there is a difference in the aim of the prayer versus the aim of the spell or curse.

Viewing magic and religion as dichotomies, as did many before the advent of modern anthropology, is practically unimaginable today. For every example we can find to set these two terms apart, another example will appear to link them. Arnold van Gennep's magico-religious model has been helpful in that while it makes a distinction between the two, it acknowledges that they are two parts of a whole.[1] Some traditions employ one aspect more than they do the other, but all religions employ magic to some extent. In the case of the Gāthās, to view them apart from their magical intentions and uses is to skew their meaning, coloring them with our own modern, Western outlooks. While some scholars will object even to the use of words like "magic" and "sorcery," as well as to the concepts themselves, we cannot ignore them because the Avestan texts make use of these concepts repeatedly. The Avestan passages I have included indeed make a clear distinction between what the authors consider sorcery and witchcraft, as opposed to good magic.

Like many other traditions, the Avestan people found the need to contend with situations beyond their control with the magico-religious. It is important for the scholar in the study of religion to understand the cultural and social functions of magic. In the case of the Zoroastrians of the Avesta, understanding their system of magic and its supporting theology may give us a rare glimpse into their religious lives.

We have seen that magic had an important function in assuaging fears of problems that seemed beyond human control, such as disease and bad weather. Belief in demonic forces allowed them to answer the questions of the origin of evil and evil events. More importantly, it gave them an instrument for fighting back. There was meaning for their suffering in that it was part of the battle humans had to wage against evil as allies of God. For the authors of the Avesta, disease, death, misfortune, and even crime were the work of unseen demons or the result of evil magic. In almost all cases, the solution was to employ good magic against evil magic.

The authors of the Avesta conceived of a world where good and evil existed in subtle, unseen forms, as well as in material forms. These two realms were connected so that they could interact. As evil in subtle forms could affect the material world, so the material actions of a skilled good magician could affect the nonmaterial world of evil. In the Avestan worldview, the powers of good could be augmented by the sacrifice. Likewise, the powers of evil could have equivalent, if malevolent, sacrifices for their increase. As both good and evil powers were able to act through magic, the practitioner had to follow rules carefully to ensure success.

As Tambiah explains, the special language of spells was the source of knowledge from which the priest-magician drew his power. We have seen that, in the Avesta, the successful use of magic depended on the practitioner's linguistic competence. The spells had to be pronounced perfectly and by the right person. This leads us to the necessity of secrecy in magic. Spells and magical rites had to be performed only by the elite and priests. Many of the spells of the Yashts specify that only a close relative of Zarathustra—that is, a priest (many of the priests claimed descent from Zarathustra)—be allowed to learn the spell and magical ritual. This was especially true in the case of the most powerful magic, such as feather and line magic.

The Avesta makes it clear that the power of magic in the wrong hands could go out of control. We saw that even the gods could go berserk in response to a mistake, or if a witch got hold of the offerings meant to placate a god invoked for magic. On the other hand, exorcisms could be performed by a wider section of society, but the Videvdad warns firmly about the dire consequences of an unqualified person performing an exorcism.

The conflict between the good gods with their allies and the bad gods with their allies was on both a cosmological and a microcosmic scale. The gods fought against the demons for their share of the sacrifice. The magician-priests of the good side and the sorcerers, witches, and evil magicians of the evil side were the human specialists in this battle. Therefore, ordinary humans had to appeal to them for help. The isolation of the practitioner of magic and the secrecy of his rituals has been compared to the priest and communal rites by Marcel Mauss in an effort to differentiate religion from magic. In the case of the Avesta, the priest for the community was also the magician, but his work was done in relative secrecy.[2] The Avesta presents a situation that Mauss did not anticipate.

Setting up strict rules as to what constitutes magic and what constitutes religion can thus be difficult, if not impossible. While we have examined several aspects of magic in Zoroastrianism, we still find the conventional trappings of religion. There was a priestly class and a congregation that they served. Yet there were also magical rituals that were performed in secrecy and in a language unknown to ordinary people. Perhaps the answer lies in the separation of the domain of the fight against evil from other practices of the Zoroastrian religion. If one considers anti-evil efforts separately from other religious practices in the Avesta, one must conclude that these specific spells and rituals fall into the realm of what we may define as magic. Religious rituals and prayers existed alongside these anti-evil efforts, and they worked together to produce a system that satisfied the needs of the community.

Another interesting feature of spells that this study has examined is the invoking of the supernatural by reference to primordial dramas of creation and other cosmic events. The antiquity, the mythic context, and the references to primordial founders of the magical acts endow spells with power and authority. It is well known that most oral traditions assume knowledge, and continued knowledge, of mythical references. The Avesta, like these other traditions, did not feel the need to repeat entire myths. Any oral society expected its members to be well versed in myth. Therefore, the mere mention of a part of a myth was sufficient to make a connection in the mind of a listener. This is the reason we so often find ourselves trying to interpret a cryptic reference to a mythic event. In some cases, as in that of the Gāthās, the language became unintelligible to most, but the power of the spell derived from the mysterious and ancient vocabularies. In spells, it is possible to find examples of the most ancient myths and legends. They serve as reminders of the way things were and the great people who fought early battles against evil.

Finally, the use of spells, curses, and exorcisms in the Avesta was associated with control and power over unseen beings such as demons, inexplicable events such as disease, drought, and death, or disorderly beings such as thieves, enemy armies, and wolves. Magic in the Avesta was phenomenal power that sought to control people, animals, nature, and, most of all, subtle evil forces. The war magic of the Yashts was directed toward people on the opposing side. It sought to make their arrows fall down and miss their mark, and to make the horses of the enemy rebel. Rain magic of the Videvdad and the Yashts sought to control the clouds, ocean, and stars for the production of rain.

Most of the spells, curses, and exorcisms of the Avesta are directed at sorcerers, witches, magicians, and their followers, or the unseen host of demons who were created to oppose humans and harass them at every opportunity.

The Zoroastrian attitude toward sorcery must be seen within the Old Iranian dualism, in which good, defined as Order, life, and growth, was eternally pitched against evil, defined as disorder, death, and destruction. Thus, death and disease, conditions brought about by demons and sorcerers, were the ultimate forms of disorder. When the body became ill, there was a disordering of the functions of the body, and this was what made it sick. Death implies total disorder, as the body literally becomes disordered and disjointed. Death was therefore the ultimate weapon of the Evil Spirit. The Avestan people, with their strong belief in "Order" as the highest principle, naturally found their enemy in "Disorder," a state represented by everything that ran counter to their ideas concerning order.

While most Westerners accept the idea that "sin," or evil, is a matter of immorality, the Avestan people viewed evil as anything that inhibited order. Disease, death, menstruation, and even old age were symptoms of the Evil Spirit inflicting harm on the good creation. From the poets of the Gāthās to the priest-magician of the Avesta, the goal was to uphold the order created by the gods, but at the same time to put down the disorder-causing demons. Worship was not enough. Just as in the oldest layer of the Indo-European religious traditions, the order of the universe was a matter of maintenance in which humans had to contribute, so human assistance was also necessary in the realm of eradicating evil and evil beings who caused disorder.

The belief in sorcerers and other practitioners of evil magic in the Avesta was also a necessary explanation for evil. As the great original sorcerer, the Evil Spirit, fought a war with the great good magician, Ahura Mazdā, their human representatives continue this war. This dualistic outlook makes a clean distinction between good and evil, for the two have separate and powerful sources. Both sides were in many ways similar. Their rites—that is, their spells, sacrifices, and other rituals—were similar to the point where the Avesta acknowledged that demons could, and did, attempt to worship the good gods, as well as the demon gods. The apparent similarity of the rituals of the good priests and those of the sorcerers created a situation that appeared to be too close for comfort.

The good priest, by his thoughts, words and deeds, wished to bring prosperity and health to his community. The sorcerer was thought to be plotting to bring about the opposite effect. In the first chapter of the Videvdad, when Ahura Mazdā makes good things for the lands, the Evil Spirit immediately makes bad things for them. In Chapter 1 of the Bundahishn, which contains the Zoroastrian creation story, the Evil Spirit reacts to every creative act of the Good Spirit by creating the opposite:

BUNDAHISHN 1.44–50

From his own selfdom, from the existing light, Ohrmazd fashioned forth
the form of his own creatures, in the form of fire, white, round, visible from
afar. . . .
The Foul Spirit whittled forth from the existing darkness, his own body, his
creation in that black form the color of ashes, worthy of darkness, lying, like
the most sinful evil creature.
For from the existing darkness, the endless darkness, he produced lying
speech; it appeared from the evilness of that Foul Spirit . . .
From the existing light Ohrmazd produced straight/true speech. And from
straight/true speech the creator's ability to increase appeared, which he
fashioned from the endless light.

Ohrmazd creates life, and Ahriman creates death; Ohrmazd creates health,
and Ahriman creates disease; and so on. In this way, there is always an opposite reaction on the cosmic level. Therefore, on the human level, we have two
kinds of priests: the good and the evil, working two kinds of magic—good and
evil.

Any failure of the good sacrifice, with its good magic, to work the way
it was expected, was blamed on the activities of demons and their allies, the
sorcerers and other evildoers. In particular, they were represented as performing sacrifices aimed at producing disorder. The authors of the Avesta,
too, viewed human evils in terms of an inversion of social and cosmic order,
which accounts for their interpretation of these ills in terms of sorcery and evil
sacrifices.

Sorcery was aimed at disrupting the order established by Ahura Mazdā,
so it not only affected the world of the here and now, but it acted against the
cosmic scheme of order. Sorcery and other bad magic was seen as evil on a
very large scale, for it could cause the downfall of the universal structure. The
battle that started in the beginning of time between the two great spirits will
have to come to an end, according to the Pahlavi texts. To ensure that the good
god wins, the Evil Spirit's minions must be repressed. In this way, even a small
act of sorcery adds to the stock of points on the side of evil and diminishes the
chances that the good god will win.

Since, as has been noted, the original poets of the Avesta, whether imagined
to be on one side or the other, used very similar techniques, there was an even
greater urgency to vilify "the bad side." Indeed, they depict Ahura Mazdā as
having been the first to use magic, and his human representative, Zarathustra,

as the first human magician. Below, the Evil Spirit himself is made to complain about Zarathustra's awful magical power:

YASHT 17.18–19

Then Zarathustra of the Spitāmas came forth from there, speaking thus,
he, the first to praise best Order,
to sacrifice to Ahura Mazdā,
to sacrifice to the Life-giving Immortals,
at whose birth and growth the waters and plants rejoiced,
at whose birth and growth the waters and plants grew,
at whose birth and growth the Evil Spirit ran away
from the wide, round earth with distant borders.
Thus spoke the Evil Spirit full of destruction,
he who gives bad gifts:
"All those worthy of sacrifice [= deities]
could not catch up with [?] me against my will,
but Zarathustra, all alone,
reaches me against my will.
He smashes me with the Ahuna Vairiya,
as with as great a weapon
as a stone the size of a house.
He heats me with the Best Order (Ashem Vohū)
just like with hot metal.
He makes me flee from this good earth,
he who comes against me alone, Zarathustra of the Spitāmas.

According to the texts, magic of the sort created by Ahura Mazdā and used by Zarathustra was intended to help people against evil. The fact that the Evil Spirit and his minions took that same magic and perverted it for evil purposes offended the gods and priests, especially because it appeared to be a scornful imitation of their acts. Like the bad sacrifice, the Avestan people saw sorcery as a travesty and a mockery of their attempts to uphold order. Perhaps this, more than anything else, was the main reason for the attention paid to practitioners of supernatural evils: they were directly antagonistic because they were employing the magic invented by the gods against those gods and their creatures.

INTRODUCTION

1. Anglicized form of Zarathustra (Zaraθuštra), Grecized "Zoroaster."

2. Compare to H. S. Versnel's four categories in "Some Reflections on the Relationship Magic-Religion," 178–179.

3. Ibid., 185.

4. Ibid., 192.

5. For an examination of the word *mantra* and the often negative associations with magic that have been attached to it, see Burchett, "The Magical Language of Mantra." I hope to avoid these negative associations. I will be using the Sanskrit word *mantra* in the sense of "a mystical verse or magical formula," rather than the Avestan *manthra*, because it is more common.

6. Doniger, *The Origins of Evil in Hindu Mythology*.

CHAPTER ONE

1. For a detailed discussion, see: Skjærvø, "The Achaemenids and the *Avesta*"; Kellens, *Essays on Zarathustra and Zoroastrianism*, 25–30.

2. Henning was one of the first to propose that dualism was a "protest against monotheism," in *Zoroaster*, 46. The argument does not appear self-conscious until the Pahlavi texts, especially the later eighth- and ninth-century polemic texts such as the Shkand-gumānīg Wizār; see Menasce, ed. *Shkand gumanig vichar*.

3. Avestan *vī-daēwa dāta*—"the established (by Ahura Mazdā) rules for keeping the evil gods (*daēwa*s) away." The common rendering as "the law against the *daēwa*s" is wrong; see Benveniste, "Que signifie Vidēvdāt"; Skjærvø, "The Videvdad." Outside the Old Avesta, here, the term *daēwa* will be rendered as "demon." See Chapter 4, note 4, on the definition of "demon."

4. For a commentary on this phenomenon, see Luhrmann, "Evil in the Sands of Time."

5. Doniger, *The Hindus*, 597.

6. Ibid., 596–597. Doniger explains that the monism of the Upanishads seemed to the evangelists to be a "rough form of monotheism."

7. For a discussion on the common scholarly view of Zoroaster as an ethical prophet, see Skjærvø's "The State of Old Avestan Scholarship."

8. See, for example, Zaehner, *The Dawn and Twilight of Zoroastrianism*, 19.

9. Jong, *Traditions of the Magi*, 388.

10. Skjærvø, "Old Avestan Scholarship," 105. Skjærvø also mentions earlier scholars, such as Martin Haug, who was the first to assert, in 1893, that the Gāthās were Zarathustra's sole compositions; see Haug, *The Parsis*. Also important was A. V. Williams Jackson, whose 1899 work *Zoroaster: The Prophet of Ancient Iran* and others introduced this idea before Bartholomae. However, Bartholomae's scholarly influence was certainly the greatest.

11. Bartholomae, *Zarathuštra's Leben und Lehre*.

12. Weber, *The Sociology of Religion*, 55.

13. Ibid., 58.

14. Duchesne-Guillemin, *The Western Response to Zoroaster*, 100–101.

15. Gnoli, "Problems and Prospects of the Studies on Persian Religion," 69.

16. Ibid., 82.

17. Zaehner, *Dawn and Twilight*, 19.

18. See Skjærvø, "The Antiquity of Old Avestan," 27–35.

19. Beginning with Marijan Molé and Gherardo Gnoli. For his views developing "an approach to the texts unhindered by the 'theological a priori,'" see Skjærvø, "Old Avestan Scholarship," 107. See also Skjærvø's more recent articles, especially "Zarathustra: First Poet-Sacrificer."

CHAPTER TWO

1. Sarianidi, *Margiana and Protozoroastrianism*, 157; Hiebert, *Oasis Civilization*, 177–178; Lamberg-Karlovsky, "Archaeology and Language," 74.

2. Skjærvø, "The Avesta as Source for the Early History of the Iranians," 163–164.

3. See the overview and synthesis of Lamberg-Karlovsky, "Enigmatic Civilizations: The Indus Valley and the Oxus," 172–217; "Eclipse in the East," 218–250; in *Beyond the Tigris and Euphrates: Bronze Age Civilizations*. See also the earlier discussions in Frye, *The Heritage of Persia*, 22–23.

4. On one campaign of Shalmaneser III (858–824 BCE) in 843, the city of Parsua (Parshuwash) is mentioned for the first time, and on another campaign in 835 he is said to have received tributes from twenty-seven kings of Parsua, before moving on to Amadāiya, presumably Media. See Grayson, *Assyrian Rulers of the Early First Millennium B.C.*, 40, 68.

5. The Medes are mentioned under Adad-nirari III (810–783 BCE). See Pritchard, *Ancient Near Eastern Texts*, 281; Boyce, *A History of Zoroastrianism*, vol. 2 (from here on, *HZ II*), 5–13; Waters, "The Earliest Persians in Southwestern Iran."

6. Boyce, *HZ II*, 9. Kuhrt, *The Persian Empire*, 34–35.

7. Kuhrt, *The Ancient Near East*, 543, 654; *The Persian Empire*, 30–35; Frye, *The Heritage of Persia*, 97–98.

8. Boyce, *HZ II*, 3; Skjærvø, "The Antiquity of Old Avestan," 37.

9. See Skjærvø, "The Avesta as Source"; Gnoli, *Zoroaster's Time and Homeland*, 160–161 for the dating of the Avesta; see Lamberg-Karlovsky, *Beyond the Tigris and Euphrates*, 227–228 for that of the Rigveda.

10. On the issues of the date and the oral nature of these texts, see Skjærvø, "Hymnic Composition in the Avesta," 199–206; Skjærvø, "Avestan Quotations in Old Persian?," 1–10; Skjærvø, "The Antiquity of Old Avestan," 15–41.

11. Molé, *Culte, mythe et cosmologie*, vii.

12. Skjærvø, "The Avesta as Source," 161.

13. The Avestan terms *spenta*, *sūra*, etc., sometimes translated as "holy," are here rendered as "life-giving." See, e.g., Skjærvø, "Praise and Blame in the Avesta," 32n11.

14. These so-called "seven climes (continents)" are explained at length by Mary Boyce in *HZ I*, 134–140. She notes that "[t]he Iranians and Indians both thought that the world was divided into seven regions, called in Avestan *karšuuar* (Pahl. *kešvar*), in Sanskrit *dvīpa*" (134).

15. The term *khwarnah* is here rendered as "Fortune" and in the plural as "gifts of Fortune," but the precise function in the Avestan myth has still not been established. Often it obviously refers to some luminous substance sent by those in the other world to this world, where it promotes growth.

16. Avestan *asha*, often translated as "truth" or "righteousness," is here rendered as "Order," and *ashawan* as "sustainer of Order, abiding by Order." In translations of the Aves-

tan, the word "Orderly" means "that which is in accord with *asha*." Similarly, *drugwant*, the one affected by the Lie, is rendered as "possessed of the Lie." For a discussion on the word *asha*, see: Skjærvø, "Truth and Deception in Ancient Iran," 407–413.

17. Skjærvø, "The Videvdad," 109–112; Vogelsang, "The Sixteen Lands of Videvdat 1."

18. Skjærvø, "The Videvdad," 111.

19. On the Arachosian "hypothesis," see Hoffmann and Narten, *Der Sasanidische Archetypus*, and the remarks by Skjærvø in his corresponding "Review," 107–108.

20. See Kent, *Old Persian*; Mayrhofer, *Supplement zur Sammlung der altpersischen Inschriften*; Schmitt, ed. *Die altpersischen Inschriften der Achaimeniden*.

21. This last inscription is the only Achaemenid inscription that contains references to sorcerers; see Skjærvø, "Avestan Quotations in Old Persian?," 33.

22. Numerous editions since Weissbach, ed. *Die Keilinschriften der Achämeniden*. Old Persian: Schmitt, ed. *The Bisitun Inscriptions of Darius the Great*; Aramaic: Greenfield and Porten, eds., *The Bisitun Inscription of Darius the Great*; Babylonian: Voigtlander, ed. *The Bisitun Inscription of Darius the Great*.

23. Frye, "Gestures of Deference."

24. Skjærvø, "Avestan Quotations in Old Persian?"; Boyce, *HZ* II, 41–43.

25. The inscriptions of Kerdīr in: MacKenzie, "Kerdir's Inscription."

26. The term "Zend Avesta" is used properly for the Zand and Avesta, that is, the Avesta with its Pahlavi translation and commentary.

27. Partial editions and/or translations: Menasce, ed. *Le troisième livre du Denkart*; Shaked, ed. *The Wisdom of the Sasanian Sages* (Dēnkard 6); Molé, ed. *La Légende de Zoroastre selon les textes pehlevis* (Dēnkard 7 and parts of 5).

28. Anklesaria, ed. *Zand-Ākāsīh*. There is a variant manuscript tradition referred to as the "Indian Bundahishn." See also a more recent transliteration with commentary, Pakzad, *Bundahishn: Zoroastrische Kosmogonie und Kosmologie*.

29. Translations: Williams, ed. *The Pahlavi Rivāyat*.

30. West, ed. *The Book of the Mainyo-i-Khard*.

31. Haug and West, eds., *The Book of Arda Viraf*; Gignoux, *Le livre d'Ardā Vīrāz*.

32. Menasce, ed. *Shkand Gumanig Vichar*.

33. Kellens, "Considérations sur l'histoire de l'Avesta," 472n41. See discussion in Hoffmann and Narten, *Der Sasanidische Archetypus*, 34–37.

34. Hoffmann and Narten, *Der Sasanidische Archetypus*, 15–16.

35. West, "Part 4: Contents of the Nasks."

36. According to J. Duchesne-Guillemin, we only have about one-quarter of the Sasanian Avesta (Duchesne-Guillemin, *La religion de l'Iran ancien*, 31).

37. Composed in approximately the thirteenth century CE. Eastwick translates it in Wilson, *The Parsi Religion*, 477–522.

38. Williams, ed. *The Pahlavi Rivāyat*; Dhābhar, ed. *The Persian Rivayats*.

39. See Skjærvø, "Chinese Turkestan."

40. Sims-Williams, "The Sogdian Fragments," 75–82.

41. Bailey, *Zoroastrian Problems*, 154; Shaki, "The Denkard Account of the History of the Zoroastrian Scriptures." Stausberg discusses this at length in "The Invention of a Canon."

42. This was stated in one of the letters of Manushchihr, a prominent ninth-century Zoroastrian theologian. See Bailey, *Zoroastrian Problems*, 161–174; Kellens, "Considérations sur l'Histoire de l'Avesta." See also E. W. West's introduction to the translation of Dēnkard 8 in "Part 4: Contents of the Nasks."

43. Complete (or almost complete) editions: Geldner, ed. *Avesta*; Westergaard, ed. *Zend-avesta*. Translation: Darmesteter, ed. *Le Zend-Avesta* (English version in Darmesteter and Mills, eds., *The Zend-Avesta*); Geldner, ed. *Avesta, Die heiligen Bücher der Parsen* (German translation based upon Bartholomae's Wörterbuch). Recent editions and translations: Humbach, Elfenbein, and Skjærvø, eds., *The Gāthās of Zarathushtra*; Humbach and Ichaporia, eds., *The Heritage of Zarathushtra*; Insler, ed. *The Gāthās of Zarathustra*; Azargushasb, ed. *Translation of Gathas*; Khazai, ed. *The Gathas*; Irani, ed. *The Gathas*; Kanga, ed. *Avesta Reader*.

44. *Hāiti* ("section") refers to the divisions of the text, not stages of the sacrifice. See Kellens and Pirart, *Les textes vieil-avestiques*; Narten, ed. *Der Yasna Haptanhāiti*; Hintze, "On the Literary Structure of the Older Avesta."

45. It was once concluded from this that Zarathustra had banned the sacrifice to other gods. This is an argument *e silentio*, which proves nothing.

46. Cf. Molé, *Culte, mythe et cosmologie*, 24–25.

47. Skjærvø, "The Videvdad," 120.

48. On the nature and structure of the *Yasht*s, as well as their relative chronology and other questions, see Skjærvø, "Hymnic Composition in the Avesta." Translations: Lommel, ed. *Die Yäšt's des Awesta*. Selections also in Malandra, ed. *Ancient Iranian Religion*. Several editions and translations of individual Yashts.

49. Gershevitch and Geldner, eds., *The Avestan Hymn to Mithra*.

50. Panaino, ed. *Tištrya*.

51. Hintze, ed. *Der Zamyād-Yašt*; Humbach and Ichaporia, eds., *Zamyād Yasht*. See also Skjærvø, review of *Der Zamyād-Yašt*.

52. Kreyenbroek, ed. *Sraoša in the Zoroastrian Tradition*.

53. Translation: Dhabhar, ed. *Zand-i Khūrtak Avistāk*.

54. Kotwal and Kreyenbroek, eds., *The Hērbedestān and Nērangestān*; Humbach and Elfenbein, eds., *Ērbedestān*.

55. Waag, ed. *Nirangistan*; Kotwal and Kreyenbroek, eds., *The Hērbedestān and Nērangestān*.

56. Haug and West, eds., *The Book of Arda Viraf*. This edition also contains the Hādōxt nask.

57. Jamaspasa, ed. *Aogemadaēcā*.

58. See Chapter 1, note 3, for the meaning of the term.

CHAPTER THREE

1. The origin of this word is disputed.

2. Molé, *Culte, mythe et cosmologie*, 79.

3. See Kellens' "Le rituel spéculatif du mazdéisme ancien," in Herrenschmidt and Kellens, "La Question du Rituel," 47–56. Also in translation in Kellens, *Essays on Zarathustra and Zoroastrianism*, 99–112. For a thorough discussion, see Skjærvø, "Tāhadī."

4. Benveniste, *Les Mages dans l'ancien Iran*, 18.

5. In his first dream, Astyages dreamed that his young daughter Mandane urinated such a great quantity that it flooded Asia. The Magi told him its meaning. Trying to change his future, he married her not to a Mede, but to a Persian, Cambyses, whom he considered too weak to be a threat. A year after the marriage, Astyages again consulted the Magi with another ominous dream. In the dream, a vine had grown from his daughter's vagina and had covered all of Asia. The Magi told him that the interpretation was that her son would one day usurp his throne. Her son was Cyrus the Great, who was the usurper of the Median throne

(Herodotus, *Histories* 1.107–108, 1.125). See Jong, *Traditions of the Magi*, 396. References for Greek and Latin literature are from his book.

 6. Xerxes had a series of dreams, all frightening, in which a ghostly figure approached him and gave advice and warnings. The Magi interpreted the dream—wrongly, as we know—as a sign that Xerxes would be victorious in his campaign against the Greeks. Herodotus, *Histories*, 7.19; see Jong, *Traditions of the Magi*, 396.

 7. See Jong, *Traditions of the Magi*, 398.

 8. Ibid.

 9. Ibid., 399.

 10. Seidel, "Charming Criminals," 157.

 11. Gignoux, "Les voyages chamaniques dans le monde iranien," 245.

 12. See Williams, *The Pahlavi Rivāyat*, vol. 2, 78–79.

 13. Gignoux, ed. *Le livre d'Ardā Vīrāz*.

 14. Skjærvø, "Kirdir's Vision."

 15. See discussion in Skjærvø, "Kirdir's Vision," 291–292.

 16. On the evil eye, see Chapter 7 of this book.

 17. Jong, *Traditions of the Magi*, 35.

 18. Henning, "An Astronomical Chapter of the Bundahishn."

 19. See the discussion of terminology below.

 20. Videvdad 9.47 explains this issue: "Orderly creator. . . . And if the man who pours is not someone who is not learned in the purification procedure of the Mazdayasnian daēnā, how shall he overcome this lie-demon who rushes upon a living person from dead matter? How shall he overcome this carrion which contaminates a living person from dead matter?"

 21. Modi, *The Parsees*, 197–200.

 22. The Letters of Manushchihr, dated about 881, are adamantly traditionalist; see Boyce, "Middle Persian Literature," 42–43. Translation: West, "Part 2: The Dadestan-i-Dinik."

 23. Modi, *The Parsees*, 260–261.

 24. Ibid. Modi explains that only priests, who are always men, can attend the "inner ceremonies," which include the *yasna* ceremony.

 25. For which the terms "white and black magic" are also used, but with obvious racial connotations.

 26. The best time seemed to be noon, when the sun is at its highest, see Afrīnagān ī Rapithvin, where Ahura Mazdā tells Zarathustra that the sacrifice performed at noon, "[l]ike the wind from the southern direction, Zarathustra of the Spitāmas furthers the entire existence and makes it grow and strengthens it and makes it come to 'bliss'" (Afrīnagān 4.6).

 27. Skjærvø, "Truth and Deception," 383–384.

 28. Skjærvø's translation, cf. Indian *māyā*. According to Skjærvø, the word seems to imply both magic and change, but also creativity.

 29. For a description of the *yasna* ceremony, see Kotwal and Boyd, *A Persian Offering*. For an analysis of the *yasna* ceremony and its myths, see Skjærvø, "The Avestan Yasna: Ritual and Myth."

 30. Kotwal and Boyd, *A Persian Offering*, 81–82, explain that during the pounding of the *haoma* for the sacrifice, Yasna 27, which contains curses against the demons, is chanted while the priest strikes the mortar with the pestle. It is significant that the priest strikes the rim of the mortar as he "strikes" the demon with the curse. See Chapter 10 on the use of ancient texts as spells.

 31. Literally "those who sacrifice to Ahura Mazdā."

CHAPTER FOUR

1. This is a very basic definition, but it can hold true for what is represented in the extant Zoroastrian literature.

2. See Kellens, "Ahura Mazda n'est pas un dieu créateur," 217-228.

3. In the Young Avestan texts it is sometimes seen as a dragon, the descendant of an Indo-Iranian and even Indo-European mythical dragon dedicated to causing chaos by preventing the orderly functioning of the cosmos, e.g., by withholding the heavenly waters. See Watkins, *How to Kill a Dragon*, 297-303.

4. Avestan *drəguuant* and Old Persian *draujana* can roughly correspond to the word "demon," but technically a *drəguuant* is a follower of the Lie, while a *daēwa* could describe one of the old Indo-European celestial gods who were demoted to demons, or more generally it could describe a demon.

5. Avestan *drug*, Old Persian *drauga*.

6. See Boyce, *HZ* I, 141-149, and more generally, Eliade, "The Regeneration of Time."

7. On this function of the sacrifice see Skjærvø, "Praise and Blame," 36-37.

8. On this aspect of the sacrifice, see Doniger, *Origins of Evil*, 194.

9. Gnoli, "Problems and Prospects," 82.

10. That is, they do not contain the phrase "Angra Mainyu" as such, but it is implicit in Yasna 45.2: "Thus, I shall proclaim the two spirits/inspirations at the beginning of [this?] existence of which two *the Life-giving one* shall tell him whom [you know to be?] *the Evil one*: Neither our thoughts, nor announcements, nor [guiding] thoughts, nor preferences, nor utterances, nor actions, nor vision-souls, nor breath-souls go together."

11. I.e., "sleeping entities" [fetuses].

12. Other interpretations of this passage include that of Helmut Humbach, who gives this translation of Yasna 30.4: "[A]nd when these two spirits confront each other [to vie for a person], then [that person] decides [of what nature will be] the primal [stage of his existence]: vitality and lack of vitality, and [on the other hand] of what nature [his] existence will be in the end: that of the deceitful [will be] the worst, but best thought will [be in store] for the truthful one" (Humbach, Elfenbein, and Skjærvø, eds., *The Gāthās of Zarathushtra*, 124). Humbach thus poses this as a choice for humans, not for the gods. It appears in his translation that the gods are vying for souls, rather than making personal choices for themselves.

13. *Dēn* is often translated as "religion." A more adequate translation in most instances may be "tradition."

14. The Indian Bundahishn has: "That omniscience and goodness is all of Ohrmazd. Some call it *dēn*, which means the same thing. All that was [there] for an unlimited time, for Ohrmazd and the *dēn* and the time of Ohrmazd were, are, and shall [always] be." See Chapter 2, note 28, on the Indian Bundahishn.

15. Note that the verb tenses imply repeated past action, here expressed by "again and again" and "would do."

16. The verb *dād* is the same that means "set in place" in Avestan. It is homonymous with the verb "give," and it is often impossible to decide which meaning is intended.

17. The world needs to be reborn every day and every new year, which is mediated by the sacrifice. The final sacrifices in this world and the other will produce the Final Body, a world that will no longer deteriorate, but be perfect forever and ever.

18. See Kellens' "Le rituel spéculatif du mazdéisme ancien" in Herrenschmidt and Kel-

lens, "La Question du rituel." For English translation, see Kellens, *Essays on Zarathustra and Zoroastrianism*, 99–112.

19. See Yasna 45.2, cited in note number 10, above.

20. For a detailed discussion of the Indo-European phenomenon of gods offering sacrifices or worship to other gods, see Patton, *Religion of the Gods*.

21. Skjærvø, "Rivals and Bad Poets," 354–355.

22. See Skjærvø, "Praise and Blame," 33–34.

23. Bruce Lincoln suggests that it is possible to interpret this verse as "Zarathustra's condemnation of an attempt to homologize cattle and the sun, in violation of the proper cosmological construct, whereby human : bovine :: sun : moon" (Lincoln, *Theorizing Myth*, 283n10). I have taken a more literal approach.

24. See Chapter 7 for more on the evil eye. See Chapter 7, note 1, on the literature.

25. The term is *ashi*, which is the inherited word for "eye" (Old Indic *akshi*), but in Iranian became part of the daevic vocabulary, contrasting with the ahuric *chashman* and *dōithra*. In the Young Avesta, we also find the demon *agashi* (*ayaši*) from *aga ashi* "evil eye," while one with the evil eye is called *duzh-dōithra*.

26. See Chapter 6, note 3, for explanation of terms.

27. See the discussion in Skjærvø, "Smashing Urine," 262.

28. Skjærvø, "Rivals and Bad Poets," 351.

29. Doniger, *Origins of Evil*, 99.

30. Skjærvø, "Old Avestan Scholarship," 110.

31. On the choice: Molé, *Culte, mythe et cosmologie*, 18–20; Kellens, *Le panthéon de l'Avesta ancien*, 59–80.

32. Boyce suggests that this is a metaphor for the moral, as opposed to a wicked person, comparing a moral man to a shepherd (*HZ* I, 211). This is a common image in Indo-European cultures. Watkins, for instance, talks about it in *How to Kill a Dragon*, 211–213. See also Bruce Lincoln's discussion of this point in *Death, War, and Sacrifice*, 153–156.

33. On the "binder," see Skjærvø, "Rivals and Bad Poets," 371–374.

34. See discussion in Boyce, *HZ* II, 232.

35. See Skjærvø, "Zarathustra: First Poet-Sacrificer," 161–162.

36. See Chapter 7 on bad sacrificers.

37. See Chapter 8 on the disposal of hair and nails.

38. See Boyce, *HZ* I, 274–275, on the counter-creation of the sixteen lands of the Videvdad.

39. The word *vīmanahya*, found in Videvdad 1.7, means "having one's thought go to all sides."

40. According to the Pahlavi commentary: excessive weeping and wailing.

41. Unfortunately, the opposing evils to the second, third, fourth, eighth, and twelfth lands created by Ahura Mazdā are undecipherable.

42. See Skjærvø, "Jamšid."

43. On healing the cosmos, see Skjærvø, "The Videvdad," 128–129.

44. On homosexuality, see Skjærvø, "Persian/Iranian Literature and Culture."

45. Bundahishn 4.5. Menstruation was a gift from Ahriman to Jeh the Whore. Also see Boyce, *HZ* I, 307–308. This will be discussed at length in Chapter 6.

46. See Chapter 7.

202 NOTES TO PAGES 44-54

CHAPTER FIVE

1. See Chapter 8 for coverage of diseases and their cures.

2. Cf. Yasna 30.5–6 cited above.

3. These were creatures thought to be created by the Evil Spirit. See Moazami, "Evil Animals in the Zoroastrian Religion."

4. See Skjærvø, "Of Lice and Men," passim.

5. Pahlavi *Tarsagāhīh* ("respect") is the standard rendering of Avestan Ashi, Goddess of the Reward. The quotation is from the Pahlavi version of Yasna 48.6: "Thus, by that respect of his, i.e., when he gave the lone-established kine a body, Ohrmazd made the plant grow, i.e., he increased it."

6. "Kine" is used as a gender-neutral term meaning "cow or bull."

7. In the myth, the "Life-giving Sacred Thought" is the chariot of the sun.

8. Many of the terms are not understood or only understood tentatively.

9. Yasht 17.54 excludes "girls not approached by men." If we look at Hindu notions concerning unmarried girls, this may be explained. An unmarried girl is considered inauspicious in Hinduism because she is not fertile. When she matures, begins to menstruate, and is married, she becomes auspicious. Yet, as in the Iranian examples, as a menstruating woman, she is potentially polluted. In the Yashts, virginity after marriage was especially repugnant (see Yasht 17.59).

10. Choksy notes that by the time of the Persian Rivayats, Ahriman is seen as seducing the first woman from the true path (Choksy, *Evil, Good and Gender*, 107).

11. For more on dogs, see Moazami, "The Dog in Zoroastrian Religion."

12. See references to the *barshnūm* ceremony in the discussion on exorcisms in Chapter 8.

13. See Chapter 8 on stillbirths and purification.

14. More will be said on the subject of dogs, but it is important to note that by the time of the composition of the Videvdad, dogs had a very high station as the watchers of demons, and were empowered by the god Sraosha to disperse them.

15. Videvdad 5.28: "Then Ahura Mazdā said: If it is a priest, then, O Zarathustra of the Spitāmas, this lie-demon, Carrion, rushes forth. If she reaches the eleventh, she contaminates the tenth. And if it is a charioteer, then, O Zarathustra of the Spitāmas, this lie-demon, Carrion, rushes forth. If she reaches the tenth, she contaminates the ninth. And if it is a husbandman, then, O Zarathustra of the Spitāmas, this lie-demon, Carrion, rushes forth. If she reaches the ninth, she contaminates the eighth." Videvdad 5.29: "And if it is a shepherd dog, then, O Zarathustra of the Spitāmas, this lie-demon, Carrion, rushes forth. If she reaches the eighth, she contaminates the seventh. And if it is a dog that protects the village, then, O Zarathustra of the Spitāmas, this lie-demon, Carrion, rushes forth. If she reaches the seventh, she contaminates the sixth." Videvdad 5.30–34 names various kinds of dogs and their power of contamination when dead. In 5.35 humans are again addressed: "O Orderly maker of the world of the living with bones, and if it is a two-legged villain possessed by the Lie, one who sustains no Order but darkens Order, how much does he contaminate of the living beings of the Life-giving Spirit? How much does he pollute?" Videvdad 5.36–37: "Then Ahura Mazdā said: Just as much as the frog, [which lies] dried out [and] dead for a year [at a time]. For alive, O Zarathustra of the Spitāmas, a two-legged villain possessed by the Lie, one who sustains no Order but darkens Order, contaminates the living beings of the Life-giving Spirit. Alive he pollutes them. Alive he strikes the water. Alive he blows out the fire. Alive he drives the cow in captivity. Alive he strikes the Orderly a blow that leaves him

unconscious and bereft of life breath. Not so if dead." Videvdad 5.38: "For alive, O Zara-thustra of the Spitāmas, a two-legged villain possessed by the Lie, one who sustains no Order but darkens Order, carries off from the Orderly Man what he has gained of food, clothing, wood, felt, and iron. Not so if dead."

16. My translation.

17. These are the Avestan *Amesha Spenta*s, the "Bountiful Immortals," or seven divine guardians of the creation. See Chapter 8 of Boyce, *HZ* I, particularly 195–199.

18. See Chapter 8 of this book for the ritual disposal of hair and nails.

19. See Panaino, ed. *Tištrya*; see also Skjærvø's corresponding review, "The Horse in Indo-Iranian Mythology."

20. Boyce calls him the "god of the rain star" (*HZ* I, 74).

21. The *kusti* signifies a person's entry into adulthood and responsibility. At this time, a person becomes fully responsible for sins, and above all, he or she is responsible for uphold-ing the religion. Failure to do one's part could cause the gods to become weakened. Modi says that in modern times, seven is the age at which children are initiated into the religion in the *navjote* ritual, but the age of initiation must be fifteen or younger. Videvdad 15.31.54 states that a child must not pass the age of fifteen without being initiated into the religion (Modi, *The Parsees*, 179).

22. "DPd" refers to an Old Persian inscription in Persepolis. See Kuhrt, *The Persian Empire*, 487.

CHAPTER SIX

1. Often referred to as "spiritual sphere" or similar, which is likely to evoke quite differ-ent and misleading associations. Its counterpart is the world of living beings or "the world that has bones," often referred to as the "material sphere" or similar.

2. See Chapter 7 on bad priests.

3. According to Skjærvø ("Rivals and Bad Poets"), originally *kawi* was "poet," then "competing > bad poet"; *karpan*- perhaps a "mumbler" or a kind of "sacrificer," then "com-peting > bad poet-sacrificer." According to the later tradition they tried to destroy the infant Zarathustra.

4. Avestan *asha-maoga*, Pahlavi *ahlomōgh*, approximately "heretic."

5. Typical modes of locomotion of the followers of the Lie.

6. A²Sa is an inscription of Artaxerxes II from Susa: Kent, A²Sa, 4–5; Schmitt, ed. *Die altpersischen Inschriften der Achaimeniden*, 192.

7. Stève, ed. *Nouveaux mélanges épigraphiques*, 90.

8. Haug and West, eds., *The Book of Arda Viraf*, 205–266.

9. Monchi-Zadeh, ed. *Die Geschichte Zarēr's*, 47.

10. Menasce, ed. *Le troisième livre du Denkart*, 178–179, 291, 315, 33.

11. We call this incest, but this word is imbued with negative implications with which the early Zoroastrians did not associate it. See Skjærvø, "Marriage."

12. Williams, ed. *The Pahlavi Rivāyat*, vol. 1, 56–57, 96–97; vol. 2, 14, 36.

13. Doniger, trans. *The Rig Veda*, 295.

14. Sorcerers who take the form of dogs or werewolves, according to Doniger in *The Rig Veda*, 296n10.

15. See, for example, Mēnōy ī Khrād 49.16, West's edition.

16. The translation of these terms as "whore" is traditional, as there is not direct evidence that these women, the *jahī*s and *jahikā*s, sold sexual services. The Pahlavi translations also do

not translate the term (Pahlavi *rōspīg*), but use the Avestan term. The only Avestan reference to sex for pay is with a menstruating woman in Videvdad 16.14: "he who with a woman . . . in menses and bleeding mingles his body in 'action' at a pre[arranged] price . . . what is the penalty for this?"

17. Doniger, ed. *The Rig Veda*, 294.

18. Schmitt, *Dichtung und Dichtersprache*, 110–111.

19. Skjærvø, "Truth and Deception, 401.

20. Menasce, ed. *Le troisième livre du Denkart*, 196, 296, 309, 314, 368–369.

21. Edgerton, *Sanskrit Grammar and Dictionary*, 175.

22. Hübschmann, *Armenische Grammatik*, 162.

23. MacKenzie defines *kēd* as "soothsayer, magician" (MacKenzie, *A Concise Pahlavi Dictionary*).

24. Sundermann, *Mitteliranische manichäische Texte Kirchengeschichtlichen Inhalts*, 108.

25. See Schaeder, *Iranische Beiträge*, 274–291; Zaehner, *Zurvan*, 38.

26. MacKenzie, "Kerdir's Inscription," 58. See also Skjærvø, "Kartīr," forthcoming in the *Encyclopædia Iranica*.

27. My translation.

28. Perhaps Jong was correct in surmising that there was no specific sect involved in these practices (Jong, *Traditions of the Magi*, 178). However, this we will never know.

29. Opposite of *āfrīn*, approximately "blessing."

30. Compare Yasna 32.3 cited above. "But you, O *daēwa*s, are all the seed issued from an evil thought, / and so is the great one who is sacrificing to you: issued from the Lie and your distraught mind."

31. Skjærvø, "Avestan Quotations in Old Persian?," 44.

32. Linke, "Manhood, Femaleness, and Power," 594.

33. Zaehner, *Zurvan*, 189. Choksy too, sees this link between the Whore and human women in *Evil, Good and Gender*, 62.

34. See Anklesaria's translation: Anklesaria, ed. *Zand-Ākāsīh*, 137. Zaehner translates this too in *Zurvan*, 188.

35. A bread offering.

36. Boyce, *HZ* I, 307.

37. On punishments and their enforcement, see Jany, "Criminal Justice in Sasanian Persia."

38. Similar sanctions appear in other religions. See Leviticus 15:19–24.

39. The period might last for three days, but the purification actually could not begin until after the fourth day.

40. Chapter 8 will more fully explain this purification rite.

41. According to Bailey, the word "bang" is of disputed meaning. It was a drug of some sort that relieved pain or produced unconsciousness. It was probably not related to "bhangā," or hemp. Bailey, *Zoroastrian Problems*, xxxvii–xxxviii.

CHAPTER SEVEN

1. See Jahn, *Über den Aberglauben des bösen Blicks bei den Alten*. See also McDaniel, "The Pupula Duplex."

2. There are other causes, as Bess Allen Donaldson explains: "Covetousness is feared as much as admiration or surprise, and is held to be responsible for as much bad fortune" (Donaldson, "The Evil Eye in Iran," 72).

3. The third eye of Shiva, for example, threatened to destroy the universe after it burned Kāma (Doniger, *Origins of Evil*, 161).

4. Gignoux and Tafazzulī, eds., *Anthologie de Zādspram*, 12.1–10, pp. 71–73.

5. Videvdad 8.10: "He runs a first mile or even more until someone of the existence with bones stands before him. He should raise his voice speaking loudly: I have stepped on the body of a dead thing. Seek purification for me, of weak mind, weak speech, weak action! The first time he comes running, if they do not purify him, they receive as their share a third of this [sinful] act."

6. Williams, ed. *The Pahlavi Rivāyat*, 217.

7. See Chapter 6 for the myth.

8. See Malinowski, *Magic, Science and Religion*, 71.

9. Videvdad 6.30–31: "O Orderly maker of the world of the living with bones, how much of this still water does this lie-demon, Carrion, reach with pain, rot, and pollution? Then Ahura Mazdā said: six steps on either of the four sides, so far this water is impure and undrinkable. . . . As long as this corpse needs to be brought out from the [water?], so long they should bring it out of the water and deposit it on dry earth."

10. Videvdad 8.74–75: "Then Ahura Mazdā said: This carrion-cooker shall be killed. They shall kill him. They shall carry off his pot. They shall carry off its stand. With two rays from the fire you shall kindle the firewood, either from these plants that contain the seed of fire or [you make] this fire with a bundle of this plant [called?] Fire-maker. One should carry it to all sides and make it go to all sides, so that one may blow it out as quickly as possible."

11. See Boyce, "Ātaš."

12. Doniger, *Origins of Evil*, 30–32.

13. In the Pahlavi literature the importance of the sexual union between Ahura Mazdā and his daughter Ārmaiti is set in the greater context of three fundamental incestuous unions, beginning with that of Ohrmazd and Spandārmad, from whom was born Gayōmard, the first human. When Gayōmard was killed by the Evil Spirit, his sperm fertilized the earth, Spandārmad, his mother. From that union were born Mashī and Mashyānī, the first human couple, brother and sister, from whom humanity descends. See Molé, *Culte, mythe et cosmologie*, 123. In Dēnkard 9.38.5–6, Wahman is said to result from the union of Ohrmazd with his daughter Spandārmad; see Skjærvø, "Ahura Mazdā and Ārmaiti," 408n38; Herrenschmidt, "Le *xwēdōdas* ou mariage «incestueux» en Iran ancien"; Skjærvø, "Homosexuality in Zoroastrianism."

14. Hintze, ed. *Der Zamyād-Yašt*, 28–32.

15. See Dhabhar, ed. *The Persian Rivayats*, 295–296; König, ed. *Die Erzählung von Tahmuras und Gamšid*; Skjærvø, "Jamšid."

16. On this passage, see Schwartz, "Viiāmburas and Kafirs."

17. See Skjærvø, "Praise and Blame," 47–53; Skjærvø, "Rivals and Bad Poets," 352.

18. See Chapter 8 for further discussion of surgery.

19. Skjærvø notes that "when the poet-sacrificer asks Ahura Mazdā to 'teach them a lesson with a blow,' he is asking Ahura Mazdā to bring the cosmic battle down to earth, targeting the poet-sacrificers possessed by the Lie in the poet-sacrificer's community—his rivals" (Skjærvø, "Truth and Deception," 388).

20. *Draonah* is the sacred bread offered during the *yasna* ceremony. See Kotwal and Boyd, *A Persian Offering*, 94.

21. See also Bruce Lincoln's discussion of the Pahlavi version in Lincoln, "Pahlavi *Kirrēnīdan*," 683.

22. See Chapter 8 on the use of magical lines.

23. Bundahishn 19.27. It is not always the case that the creatures are similar. Often it is only a functional opposition, such as the mongoose, which opposes the snake.

24. Bundahishn 23.6–8.

25. Bundahishn 19.33.

26. Doniger, ed. *The Rig Veda*, 218.

27. Ibid., 200.

28. Ibid., 194.

29. Cf. Indra's thunderbolt, the *vajra*.

30. Yasht 10.56: "[to him who] sacrifices to me with a sacrifice in which [your name] is spoken, with speech according to the models, an Orderly one, bringing a libation. I [Ahura Mazdā] will sacrifice to you, O Mithra, with libations, with a sacrifice in which [your name] is spoken, with speech according to the models, O you rich in life-giving strength!"

31. Kreyenbroek suggests that much of the imagery used to describe Sraosha in his militant aspect is borrowed from the Mihr Yasht; Kreyenbroek, *Sraoša in the Zoroastrian Tradition*, 166. Although there are similarities, they may derive from the fact that they were both militant deities. In the Yasna passages, Sraosha is certainly militant, bearing a club to strike the demons dead, but in the Yashts his militancy increases considerably.

32. Elder, "Crossroads."

33. Tambiah, "The Form and Meaning of Magical Acts," 199–229.

34. See Chapter 6 on witches and sorcerers.

35. Yasht 11.5: "in each and every one of back alleys, or in each and every one of roadless places, fearing hostility, not ever shall on this day, in this night the one possessed by the Lie, irritated, angered, irate, espy him with [his] eyes by any espying whatever, nor may the hostility of a robber who drives herds off reach [him] by any reaching whatever."

CHAPTER EIGHT

1. Larson and many others have pointed out that the system must be quite a bit older, at least as old as 500 BCE, by the time of the Buddha. Buddhist texts such as the Dhammacakkappavattana-sutta of the Saṁyutta-nikāya suggest that similar knowledge was current (Larson, "Āyurveda," 246).

2. Obeyesekere argues convincingly that āyurveda distinguished between mental illness caused by "humoural imbalance and psychic excitement with that caused by *bhutas* or demons" (Obeyesekere, "Ayurveda and Mental Illness," 294).

3. See Chapter 7 on demon worshippers.

4. See also Watkins, *How to Kill a Dragon*, 540.

5. The ritual fire or the sun (or both).

6. Someone like Sraosha. Skjærvø, "Smashing Urine," 277.

7. Either "let one of the other gods listen to my hymns and thereby receive the invigoration needed to perform his protective function" or "let Sraosha, a protector *par excellence*, come"; cf. Yasna 57.2. The fact that the person to come is left undetermined may indicate the former alternative, as otherwise we might expect "to me, to this one."

8. Zysk, *Religious Healing in the Veda*, 8.

9. Dhabhar, ed. *The Persian Rivayats*, 553.

10. Benveniste, "La doctrine médicale des Indo-Européens."

11. Puhvel, "Mythological Reflections."

12. Lincoln, *Myth, Cosmos, and Society*, 100–101.

13. Eliade, *Myth and Reality*, 24–28. Malinowski also argued that the myth of the first use of magic was an important element of exorcistic spells.

14. Lincoln, *Myth, Cosmos, and Society*, 107.

15. Saokā is a goddess of unknown function. Her name, if derived from *saok-* or *saoc* ("burn"), may mean "Burning." Perhaps she represents the burning fire of the sacrifice.

16. It is unclear what the authors meant by the thousand pregnant females. It may even have referred to human females.

17. Videvdad 22.2–3: "Then the villain looked at me, then the villain made against me, the Evil Spirit full of destruction, 99 diseases, 9,900 and 90,000. So may you heal me, Life-giving Sacred Thought, you of great munificence! For this I shall give you at one and the same time a thousand fleet, enduring horses [?]. I shall sacrifice [to you], of Good Saokā [Glow?], set in place by Ahura Mazdā, Orderly. For this I shall give you at once a thousand camels, . . . with . . . humps. I shall sacrifice [to you], of Good Saokā, set in place by Ahura Mazdā, Orderly."

18. Skjærvø, "Praise and Blame," 56.

19. See Boyce, "Airyaman"; Brunner, "Airyaman Išīya."

20. The name means perhaps he who has (provides?) Order with fat. Note the name of the last of Zarathustra's eschatological sons, Astwad-erta, literally "he by whom Order has bones," and recall that according to the Pahlavi books, at the resurrection, the bones will rise first and then receive fat to cover them (Wizidagiha i Zādspram 51).

21. A part of man that is prefabricated by Ahura Mazdā and sent down into this world to help develop the fetus, then returns to Ahura Mazdā when the person dies. The Frawashis play important roles in cosmology, eschatology, and anthropology. See Boyce, "Fravaši."

22. Dumézil, *The Destiny of the Warrior*, 26.

23. In fact, only one brother of Thrita's is known in the Avesta, and in the Pahlavi texts he is called the "seventh son." See discussion in Boyce, *HZ* I, 97–100.

24. Yasna 9.7: "Then he answered me, the Orderly death-averting Haoma: Āthviya was the second man to press me for the world of the living with bones. That reward was sent to him, that prize came to him that a son was born to him: Thraētaona of the house of life-giving strength."

25. See Boyce, *HZ* I, 98–99; Watkins, *How to Kill a Dragon*, 314.

26. See Chapter 11 on exorcisms for text.

27. Also called the white *hōm*, which will be used in the last sacrifice performed to heal the world permanently. Boyce, *HZ* I, 244.

28. On healing with water in the *Atharvaveda*, see Zysk, *Religious Healing in the Veda*, 10.

29. See Chapter 9 for examples.

30. Tambiah, "The Magical Power of Words," 176.

31. The meaning of Avestan *pakhrushta* is unknown, but may have implied some manner of constraint. The later tradition understood it approximately as "called" or "howled away" (cf. Yasna 5.53, Yasht 5.94–95).

32. Conjectural translation. The word may also refer to the demon. Similarly, *kakhwazhi* may refer to a place or a demon.

33. Tambiah, "The Magical Power of Words," 177.

34. Dēnkard 6.236: "For as long as a man thinks good deeds and righteousness the gods stay in his body and the demons are made powerless and depart, and when he thinks sinful things the demons rush into his body" (translation by Shaked, ed. *The Wisdom of the Sasanian Sages*, 93).

35. For a general discussion, see Abusch, "Witchcraft and the Anger of the Personal God."

36. Tambiah, "The Magical Power of Words," 179.

37. Good and Good, "Popular Illness Categories."

38. Ibid., 147.

39. Choksy, *Purity and Pollution in Zoroastrianism*, 123.

40. Greenfield, "Study of Palaeologan Magic," 136.

41. Yasht 4.6: "He draws three lines. [Three times] I say forth the Orderly Man. He draws six lines. Six times I say forth the Orderly Man. He draws nine lines. Nine times I say forth the Orderly Man."

42. These texts contain many words of uncertain meaning.

43. Phrase cited from other texts, e.g. Videvdad 19.47.

44. Phrase cited from other texts, e.g. Videvdad 2.11.

45. The interpretation of the phrase in question (also in Videvdad 3.20) is doubtful.

46. Videvdad 9.47–48: "Orderly creator . . . And if the man who pours is not someone who is learned in the purification procedure of the Mazdayasnian *daēnā*, how shall he overcome this lie-demon who rushes upon a living person from dead matter? How shall he overcome this carrion which contaminates a living person from dead matter? Then Ahura Mazdā said: Just like this, O Zarathustra of the Spitāmas, this lie-demon, Carrion, grows much stronger than she was before. She is these illnesses. She is these destructions, just like before."

47. For a detailed description of this ceremony, see Choksy, *Purity and Pollution in Zoroastrianism*.

48. Jany interprets the number of lashes symbolically as a measure of the severity of the crime, not as an actual number (Jany, "Criminal Justice in Sasanian Persia," 356).

49. See Faraone and Obbink, eds., *Magika Hiera: Ancient Greek Magic and Religion*, 14.

50. Videvdad 17.1–2: "Zarathustra asked Ahura Mazdā: O Ahura Mazdā, Orderly maker of the world of the living with bones, what mortal's sacrifice to the *daēwa*s causes the strongest destruction and death? Then Ahura Mazdā said: O Orderly Zarathustra! He who in this existence with bones combs his hair and cuts his hair and cuts his nails and then empties it out in holes and crevices."

51. See also Skjærvø, "Of Lice and Men," 272.

52. Lincoln, *Myth, Cosmos, and Society*, 91, and "Treatment of Hair and Fingernails."

53. Choksy believes it may be an owl (*Purity and Pollution in Zoroastrianism*, 81).

54. Shahbazi prefers to call this bird a falcon, which is a bird that has a flight pattern similar to the eagle ("On Vāreghna the Royal Falcon"). Falcons, however, are small birds, and the bird described in Yasht 14.21 gives the impression of being much larger. He flies "stroking the yawning hollows of the hills, stroking the heights of the mountains, stroking the depths of the rivers."

55. In the Islamic-period tradition, Kāy Us (= Kawi Usan) tries to fly up to heaven on eagles, but falls down again (for various reasons according to the various sources).

56. Watkins, *How to Kill a Dragon*, 313–320.

57. In Yasht 19.92, what Thraētaona carries is a victorious weapon, with which he performed these feats.

58. Watkins, *How to Kill a Dragon*, 313–320.

59. Yasht 5.45 describes him as "[t]he fleet Kawi Usan of great magic."

60. The precise meaning of the verb is not entirely certain.

61. Someone condemned to death for a capital crime.

62. Firdawsī, *The Epic of the Kings*, 39.

63. Davidson, *Poet and Hero*, 115n12.

CHAPTER NINE

1. See Chapter 8.

2. Malinowski, *Magic, Science and Religion*, 88.

3. Weber, *The Sociology of Religion*, 28.

4. Malinowski, *Coral Gardens and Their Magic*, 238.

5. Malinowski, *Magic, Science and Religion*, 73–74.

6. Tambiah, "The Magical Power of Words," 191.

7. Ibid.

8. See Austin, "How to Do Things with Words."

9. For similar structures in the spells of other ancient Indo-European languages, see Schmitt, *Dichtung und Dichtersprache in indogermanischer Zeit*, Chapter 8, "Indogermanische Zauberdichtung" on Indo-European spells.

CHAPTER TEN

1. See Kellens, "Les précautions rituelles."

2. Anāhitā? Cf. Yasht 5.133: "the sacrifice to the good waters, set in place by [Ahura] Mazdā, [those] of the lofty, unattached, Orderly water."

3. Doniger, ed. *The Rig Veda*, 221.

4. Cf. *Rigveda* 7.104.14 (Indra, Soma, etc.) "If I have ever had gods not according to Order or if I have ever only pretended to invigorate you, O Agni."

5. See, for example, Lesses, "Prince of the Presence."

6. Assmann, "Magic and Theology in Ancient Egypt," 7–8; Panaino, *Lists of Names*.

7. Zaehner, *Zurvan*, 83.

8. Dumézil, *Tarpeia*.

9. See Widengren, *Hochgottglaube im alten Iran*.

10. Panaino suggests that more names could have been added in the Islamic era as there were ninety-nine names of Allah (*Lists of Names*, 120–121).

11. This Yasht consists of a variety of spells and disjointed passages. The manuscript readings vary considerably, and the faulty grammar is often difficult to analyze. The translation of the beginning is conjectural.

12. Cf. Yasht 14.46.

13. Like all the short Yashts, the manuscript tradition of Yasht 3 is very corrupt, and many of the forms are interpreted conjecturally. In this case the form *bandāmi* ("I am binding") is clear, however, while "I am smashing down" is a conjecture.

14. See Skjærvø, "Zarathustra: First Poet-Sacrificer," 163–164, and "The Avestan Yasna," 66.

15. Videvdad 19.47: "They ran thither all a-chatter, the evil-giving *daēwa*s possessed by the Lie, to the bottom of the existence of darkness, that of the terrible Hell."

16. They are Yasna 27.13, Yathā ahū vairiyō (also called the Ahuna Vairiya); Yasna 27.14, Ashem Vohū (also called Asha Vahishta); Yasna 27.15, Yenghē Hātām; and Yasna 54.1, Airyaman Ishiya.

17. Tambiah, "The Magical Power of Words," 180.

18. Ibid., 181.

19. Airyana Vaējah, the mythical homeland of the Iranians.

20. On the Indo-Iranian and even Indo-European age of the formulas employed and the situation depicted, see Skjærvø, "Eastern Iranian Epic Traditions III: Zarathustra and Diomedes."

21. The fabric references are unexplained.

22. Malinowski, *Coral Gardens and Their Magic*, vol. 2, 223.

23. The meaning of this word is unknown. It probably has nothing to do with Middle Persian *zandīg* ("Manichean").

CHAPTER ELEVEN

1. The Yasna Haptanghāiti, the "sacrifice in seven sections," is an Old Avestan composition in archaic metric prose.

2. Tambiah, "The Power of Words," 176–177.

3. Yasna 31.4: "[C]ommand with strength for me, by the increase of which we may overcome the Lie."

4. Compare to this similar passage from *Rigveda* 7.104.23: "Do not let the demon of the sorcerers get close to us! Let the light blot out the fiends that work in couples!" Doniger, *Rig Veda*, 295.

5. Mahābhārata, Vol. 2, trans. J. A. B. van Buitenen (Chicago: University of Chicago Press, 1975), 413. For the burning effect of spells and curses, see also Zarathustra's use of the Ashem Vohū cited above and the Rigvedic passages cited in Skjærvø, "Zarathustra in the Avesta and in Manicheism."

6. I.e., keep it unharmed?

7. Evans-Pritchard, *Witchcraft, Oracles and Magic*, 387.

8. Ibid., 389.

9. See more on the subject of blame in Skjærvø, "Praise and Blame in the Avesta: The Poet-Sacrificer and His Duties."

10. Yasna 43.8: "Thus, I declare myself to him first as Zarathustra, the real one; (second) that I wish to command hostilities for the follower of the Lie, but for the follower of Order I wish to be support and strength, because I would like to receive the adornments of one who commands at will; and (third) that to the extent that I can I am praising you, O Mazdā, and hymning you." See also Skjærvø, "Zarathustra: First Poet-Sacrificer," 176–177.

11. Skjærvø, "Smashing Urine," 277–278.

12. See Skjærvø, "Praise and Blame in the Avesta," 55.

CHAPTER TWELVE

1. van Gennep, *The Rites of Passage*, 13.

2. Mauss, *A General Theory of Magic*, 20–23.

Abusch, Tzvi. "Witchcraft and the Anger of the Personal God." In *Mesopotamian Magic: Textual, Historical, and Interpretative Perspectives,* edited by Tzvi Abusch and Karel van der Toorn, 83-121. Groningen: Styx Publications, 1999.

Anklesaria, Behramgore Tehmurasp, ed. *The Pahlavi Rivayat of Aturfarnbag and Farnbag-Srosh.* Bombay: M. F. Cama Athornan Institute, 1969.

———. *Pahlavi Vendidad.* Bombay: Shahnamah Press, 1949.

———. *Zand-Ākāsīh: Iranian or Greater Bundahisn.* Bombay: Rahnumae Mazdayasnan Sabha, 1956.

Assmann, Jan. "Magic and Theology in Ancient Egypt." In *Envisioning Magic,* edited by Peter Schäfer and Hans G. Kippenberg, 1-18. Leiden: Brill, 1997.

Austin, J. L. *How to Do Things with Words.* The William James Lectures. Cambridge: Harvard University Press, 1962.

Azargushasb, Fīrūz, ed. *Translation of Gathas, the Holy Songs of Zarathushtra, from Persian into English.* San Diego: Council of Iranian Mobeds of North America, 1988.

Bailey, H. W. *Zoroastrian Problems in the Ninth-Century Books.* Ratanbai Katrak Lectures. Oxford: Clarendon Press, 1943.

Barthélemy, A. *Gujastak Abalish: Relation d'une Conference Theologique.* Paris: F. Vieweg, 1887.

Benveniste, Emile. "La doctrine médicale des Indo-Européens." *Revue de l'Histoire des Religions* 130 (1945): 5-12.

———. "Le *Memorial de Zarer;* poeme pehlevi mazdeen." *Journal Asiatique* 220 (1932), 245-293.

———. *Le vocabulaire des institutions indo-européennes,* 2 vols., Paris, 1969.

———. *Les Mages dans l'ancien Iran.* Publications de la Société des Études Iraniennes, 15. Paris: G.-P. Maisonneuve, 1938.

———. "Que signifie Vidēvdāt." In *W. B. Henning Memorial Volume,* edited by M. Boyce and I. Gershevitch, 37-42. London: Lund Humphries, 1970.

———. "Une Apocalypse Pehlevie, le Zamasp-Namak." *Revue de l'Histoire des Religions* 106 (1932), 337-380.

Boyce, Mary. "Airyaman." *Encyclopædia Iranica,* vol. 1, London: Routledge and Kegan Paul, 1985, 694-695.

———. "Ātaš." *Encyclopædia Iranica,* vol. 3, 1989, 1-11.

———. "Dahm Yazad." *Encyclopædia Iranica Online,* December 15, 1993, available at www.iranicaonline.org.

———. "Fravaši." *Encyclopædia Iranica,* December 15, 2000, available at www.iranicaonline.org.

———. *A History of Zoroastrianism,* vol. 1, *The Early Period.* Leiden: E. J. Brill, 1989.

———. *A History of Zoroastrianism,* vol. 2, *Under the Achaemenians.* Leiden: E. J. Brill, 1982.

———. "Middle Persian Literature." In *Iranistik,* edited by B. Spuler, 31-66. Leiden: E. J. Brill, 1968.

———. *A Persian Stronghold of Zoroastrianism.* Oxford: Clarendon Press, 1977.

Boyce, M., with F. Grenet. *A History of Zoroastrianism*, vol. 3, *Under Macedonian and Roman Rule*. Leiden: E. J. Brill, 1991.

Brunner, C. J. "Airyaman Išīya." *Encyclopædia Iranica*, vol. 1, 1985, 695.

Bulsara, Sohrab Jamsheedjee. *Aerpatastan and Nirangastan*. Bombay: British India Press, 1915.

Burchett, Patton E. "The Magical Language of Mantra." *Journal of the American Academy of Religion* 76, no. 4 (2008): 807–843.

Choksy, Jamsheed K. *Evil, Good and Gender: Facets of the Feminine in Zoroastrian Religious History*. Toronto Studies in Religion, vol. 28. New York: Peter Lang, 2002.

———. *Purity and Pollution in Zoroastrianism: Triumph over Evil*. Austin: University of Texas Press, 1989.

Curtis, Vesta Sarkhosh, and Sarah Stewart, eds. *Birth of the Persian Empire*. The Idea of Iran, v. 1. London: I. B. Tauris in association with the London Middle East Institute at SOAS and the British Museum, 2005.

Darmesteter, James, ed. *Le Zend-Avesta*. Annales du Musée Guimet. Paris: E. Leroux, 1892.

Darmesteter, James, and Lawrence Heyworth Mills, eds. *The Zend-Avesta*. Sacred Books of the East. Oxford: Clarendon Press, 1880.

Davidson, Olga M. *Poet and Hero in the Persian Book of Kings*. Myth and Poetics. Ithaca: Cornell University Press, 1994.

Dhabhar, Bamanji Nasarvanji, ed. *The Nyaishes or Zoroastrian Litanies*. New York: AMS Press, 1965.

———. *The Persian Rivayats of Hormazyar Framarz and Others*. Bombay: K. R. Cama Oriental Institute, 1932.

———. *Zand-i Khūrtak Avistāk*. Bombay: Fort Printing Press, 1927.

Donaldson, Bess Allen. "The Evil Eye in Iran." In *The Evil Eye: A Casebook*, edited by Alan Dundes, 66–77. Madison: University of Wisconsin Press, 1992.

Doniger, Wendy. *The Hindus: An Alternative History*. New York: Penguin Press, 2009.

———. *The Origins of Evil in Hindu Mythology*. Berkeley: University of California Press, 1980.

———, ed. *The Rig Veda: An Anthology: One Hundred and Eight Hymns*. Penguin Classics. New York: Penguin Books, 1981.

Duchesne-Guillemin, Jacques. *La religion de l'Iran ancien*. Paris: Presses Universitaires de France, 1962.

———. *The Western Response to Zoroaster*. Oxford: Clarendon Press, 1958.

Dumézil, Georges. *The Destiny of the Warrior*. Chicago: University of Chicago Press, 1970.

———. *Tarpeia: essais de philologie comparative indo-européenne*. Les Mythes Romains 3. Paris: Gallimard, 1947.

Edgerton, Franklin. *Buddhist Hybrid Sanskrit Grammar and Dictionary*. William Dwight Whitney Linguistic Series, vol. 2. New Haven: Yale University Press, 1953.

Elder, George. "Crossroads." In *The Encyclopedia of Religion*, edited by Mircea Eliade. New York: Macmillan, 1987.

Eliade, Mircea. *Myth and Reality*. Translated by Willard R. Trask. World Perspectives. New York: Harper & Row, 1975.

———. "The Regeneration of Time." In *The Myth of the Eternal Return*. Princeton: Princeton University Press, 1991.

———. *The Sacred and the Profane*. San Diego: Harcourt Brace Jovanovich, 1987. First published 1957.

Erdosy, George. *The Indo-Aryans of Ancient South Asia: Language, Material Culture and Ethnicity*. Indian Philology and South Asian Studies, vol. 1. Berlin: Walter de Gruyter, 1995.

Evans-Pritchard, E. E. *Theories of Primitive Religion*. London: Oxford University Press, 1965.

———. *Witchcraft, Oracles and Magic Among the Azande*. Oxford: Clarendon Press, 1937.

Faraone, Christopher A., and Dirk Obbink, eds. *Magika Hiera: Ancient Greek Magic and Religion*. New York: Oxford University Press, 1991.

Firdawsī. *The Epic of the Kings: Shah-Nama, the National Epic of Persia*. Translated by Reuben Levy. Persian Heritage Series. London: Routledge & K. Paul, 1967.

Frye, Richard Nelson. "Gestures of Deference." In *Opera Minora*, edited by Y.M. Nawabi. Shiraz: Asia Institute of Pahlavi Language, 1977.

———. *The Heritage of Persia*. London: Weidenfeld and Nicholson, 1962.

Geiger, Wilhelm, and Ernst Kuhn, eds. *Grundriss der iranischen Philologie*. 2 vols. Strassburg: K. J. Trübner, 1895–1904. Reprinted 1974.

Geldner, Karl F., ed. *Avesta, die heiligen Bücher der Parsen*. Stuttgart: W. Kohlhammer, 1886–1895.

———, ed. *Avesta: The Sacred Books of the Parsis*. Stuttgart: W. Kohlhammer, 1886.

———. *Die Zoroastrische Religion*. Turbingen: J. C. B. Mohr, 1911.

Gershevitch, Ilya, and Karl F. Geldner, eds. *The Avestan Hymn to Mithra*. University of Cambridge: Oriental Publications. Cambridge: Cambridge University Press, 1959.

Gignoux, Philippe, ed. *Le livre d'Ardā Vīrāz*. Bibliothèque Iranienne. Paris: Editions Recherché sur les civilisations, 1984.

———. *Les quatre inscriptions du Mage Kirdīr*. Collection des sources pour l'histoire de l'Asie Centrale pré-islamique, série II, vol. 1; Studia Iranica, cahier 9. Paris: Peeters, 1991.

———. "Les voyages chamaniques dans le monde iranien." In *Monumentum Georg Morgenstierne*, 244–265. Leiden: E. J. Brill, 1981.

Gignoux, Philippe, and Abū al-Qāsim Tafazzulī, eds. *Anthologie De Zādspram: Édition critique du texte pehlevi*. Studia Iranica, cahier 13. Paris: Association pour l'avancement des études iraniennes, 1993.

Gnoli, Gherardo. "Problems and Prospects of the Studies on Persian Religion." In *Problems and Methods of the History of Religions*, edited by U. Bianchi et al., 67–101. Leiden: E. J. Brill, 1972.

———. *Zoroaster's Time and Homeland: A Study on the Origins of Mazdeism and Related Problems*. Naples: Istituto Universitario Orientale, 1980.

Good, Byron J., and Mary-Jo Delvecchio Good. "Toward a Meaning-Centered Analysis of Popular Illness Categories: 'Fright-Illness' And 'Heart Distress' In Iran." In *Cultural Conceptions of Mental Health and Therapy*, edited by Anthony J. Marsella and Geoffrey M. White. Dordrecht: D. Reidel, 1982.

Grayson, Albert Kirk. *Assyrian Rulers of the Early First Millennium B.C.*, vol. 2, *The Royal Inscriptions of Mesopotamia: Assyrian Periods*. Toronto: University of Toronto Press, 1991.

Greenfield, Jonas, and Bezalel Porten, eds. *The Bisitun Inscription of Darius the Great: Aramaic Version*. Corpus Inscriptionum Iranicarum. London: Lund Humphries, 1982.

Greenfield, Richard P. H. "A Contribution to the Study of Palaeologan Magic." In *Byzantine Magic*, edited by Henry Maguire, 117–154. Washington, D.C.: Dumbarton Oaks, 1995.

Haug, Martin. *The Parsis: Essays on Their Sacred Language, Writings, and Religion*. New Delhi: Cosmo, 1978.

Haug, Martin, and Edward William West, eds. *The Book of Arda Viraf: The Pahlavi Text Prepared by Destur Hoshangji Jamaspji Asa*. Bombay: Govt. Central Book Depot, 1872.

Henning, W. B. "An Astronomical Chapter of the Bundahishn." *Journal of the Royal Asiatic Society of Great Britain and Ireland* 3 (1942): 229–248.

———. *Zoroaster: Politician or Witch-Doctor?* London: Oxford University Press, 1951.

Herodotus. *The Histories*. Translated by Aubrey De Sélincourt. Penguin Classics. New York: Penguin Books, 1972.

Herrenschmidt, Clarisse. "Le *xwēdōdas* ou mariage «incestueux» en Iran ancien." In *Épouser au plus proche: Inceste, prohibitions et stratégies matrimoniales autour de la Méditerranée*, edited by Pierre Bonte, 113–125. Paris: Editions de l'Ecole des hautes Études en Sciences Sociales, 1994.

Herrenschmidt, Clarisse, and Jean Kellens. "La question du rituel: Le mazdéisme ancien et achéménide." *Archives des Sciences Sociales des Religions* 85 (1994): 45–67.

Hiebert, Fredrik T. *Origins of the Bronze Age Oasis Civilization in Central Asia*. Bulletin of the American School of Prehistoric Research. Cambridge: Peabody Museum of Archaeology and Ethnology, Harvard University, 1994.

Hintze, Almut, ed. *Der Zamyād-Yašt*, Beiträge zur Iranistik, bd. 15. Wiesbaden: Dr. Ludwig Reichert Verlag, 1994.

———. "On the Literary Structure of the Older Avesta." *Bulletin of the School of Oriental and African Studies, University of London* 65, no. 1 (2002): 31–51.

Hoffmann, Karl, and Johanna Narten. *Der Sasanidische Archetypus: Untersuchungen zu Schreibung und Lautgestalt des Avestischen*. Wiesbaden: L. Reichert, 1989.

Hübschmann, Heinrich. *Armenische Grammatik: Erster Teil: Armenische Etymologie*. 3rd ed. Hildesheim: G. Olms, 1972.

Huff, Dietrich. "Archaeological Evidence of Zoroastrian Funerary Practices." In *Zoroastrian Rituals in Context*, edited by Michael Stausberg, 593–630. Leiden: E. J. Brill, 2004.

Humbach, Helmut, and J. H. Elfenbein, eds. *Ērbedestān: An Avesta-Pahlavi Text*. Münchener Studien zur Sprachwissenschaft. Munich: R. Kitzinger, 1990.

Humbach, Helmut, J. H. Elfenbein, and Prods O. Skjærvø, eds. *The Gāthās of Zarathushtra: And the Other Old Avestan Texts*. Indogermanische Bibliothek, vol. 1. Heidelberg: Universitätsverlag C. Winter, 1991.

———. *The Gāthās of Zarathushtra: And the Other Old Avestan Texts*. Indogermanische Bibliothek, vol. 2. Heidelberg: Universitätsverlag C. Winter, 1991.

Humbach, Helmut, and Pallan R. Ichaporia, eds. *The Heritage of Zarathushtra: A New Translation of His Gāthās*. Heidelberg: Universitätsverlag C. Winter, 1994.

———, eds. *Zamyād Yasht: Yasht 19 of the Younger Avesta: Text, Translation, Commentary*. Wiesbaden: Harrassowitz, 1998.

Humbach, H., and Prods Oktor Skjærvø. *The Sassanian Inscription of Paikuli*. Three parts. Wiesbaden: Reichert, 1978–83.

Insler, Stanley, ed. *The Gāthās of Zarathustra*. Acta Iranica 8. Leiden: E. J. Brill, 1975.

Irani, K. D., ed. *The Gathas: The Hymns of Zarathushtra*. New Delhi: K. R. Cama Oriental Institute, 1999.

Jackson, A. V. Williams. *Zoroaster: The Prophet of Ancient Iran*. London: Macmillan, 1899.

Jahn, Otto. *Über den Aberglauben des bösen Blicks bei den Alten*. Leipzig: S. Hirzel, 1855.

Jamaspasa, Kaikhusroo M., ed. *Aogemadaēcā: A Zoroastrian Liturgy*, Veröffentlichungen der Iranischen Kommission. Wien: Verlag der Österreichischen Akademie der Wissenschaften, 1982.

Jany, János. "Criminal Justice in Sasanian Persia." *Iranica Antiqua* 42 (2007): 347–386.

Jong, Albert de. *Traditions of the Magi: Zoroastrianism in Greek and Latin Literature.* Religions in the Graeco-Roman World. Leiden: E. J. Brill, 1997.

Kanga, M. F., ed. *Avesta Reader: Text Translation, and Explanatory Notes with Sanskrit Cognates.* Pune: Vaidika Samśodhana Mandala, 1988.

Kellens, Jean. "Ahura Mazda n'est pas un dieu créateur." In *Études irano-aryennes offertes à Gilbert Lazard,* edited by Charles-Henri de Fouchécour and Philippe Gignoux, 217–228. Paris: Association pour l'avancement des études iranniennes, 1989.

———. "Characters of ancient Mazdaism." *History and Anthropology* 3 (1987): 239–262.

———. "Considérations sur l'histoire de l'Avesta." *Journal Asiatique* 286, no. 2 (1998): 451–519.

———. *Essays on Zarathustra and Zoroastrianism.* Translated and edited by Prods Oktor Skjærvø. Bibliotheca Iranica, Zoroastrian Studies Series. Costa Mesa, Calif.: Mazda Publishers, 2000.

———. *Le panthéon de l'Avesta ancien.* Wiesbaden: L. Reichert, 1994.

———. "L'eschatologie mazdéenne ancienne." In S. Shaked and A. Netzer, eds., *Irano-Judaica,* vol. 3, *Studies Relating to Jewish Contacts with Persian Culture throughout the Ages,* 49–53. Jerusalem: Benzvi Institute, 1994.

———. "Les précautions rituelles et la triade du comportement." In *Zoroastrian Rituals in Context,* edited by Michael Stausberg, 283–290. Leiden: E. J. Brill, 2004.

———. "Quatre siècles obscurs." In Societas Iranologica Europaea, *Transition Periods in Iranian History, Actes du symposium de Fribourg-en-Brisgau (22-24 mai 1985),* 135–139. Studia Iranica, cahier 5, Paris: Peeters, 1987.

———. "Qui était Zarathustra?" In *Les civilisations orientales: figures de Proue.* Université de Liège, Faculté de philosophie et lettres, Conférences, G7. Liège: Université de Liège, 1984.

Kellens, Jean, and Eric Pirart. *Les textes vieil-avestiques.* Wiesbaden: L. Reichert, 1988.

Kent, Roland G. *Old Persian: Grammar, Texts, Lexicon.* American Oriental Series. New Haven: American Oriental Society, 1950.

Khazai, Khosro, ed. *The Gathas: The Sublime Book of Zarathustra.* Brussels: European Centre for Zoroastrian Studies, 2007.

König, Götz, ed. *Die Erzählung von Tahmuras und Gamšid.* Iranica bd. 14. Wiesbaden: Harrassowitz, 2008.

Kotwal, Firoze M. P., and James W. Boyd. *A Persian Offering: The Yasna, a Zoroastrian High Liturgy.* Studia Iranica, volume 8. Paris: Association pour l'avancement des études iraniennes, 1991.

Kotwal, Firoze M. P., and Philip G. Kreyenbroek, eds. *The Hērbedestān and Nērangestān.* 4 vols. Hērbedestān, vol. 1. Studia Iranica. Paris: Association pour l'avancement des études iraniennes, 1992.

Kreyenbroek, Philip G., ed. *Sraoša in the Zoroastrian Tradition.* Orientalia Rheno-Traiectina. Leiden: E. J. Brill, 1985.

Kuhrt, Amélie. *The Ancient Near East, c. 3000-330 B.C.* Routledge History of the Ancient World. London: Routledge, 1995.

———. *The Persian Empire.* London: Routledge, 2007.

Lamberg-Karlovsky, C. C. "Archaeology and Language: The Indo-Iranians." *Current Anthropology* 43, no. 1 (2002): 63–88.

———. *Beyond the Tigris and Euphrates: Bronze Age Civilizations.* Be'er Sheva': Ben-Gurion University of the Negev Press, 1996.

Larson, Gerald James. "Āyurveda and the Hindu Philosophical Systems." *Philosophy East and West* 37, no. 3 (1987): 245–259.

Lesses, Rebecca. "The Adjuration of the Prince of the Presence: Performative Utterance in a Jewish Ritual." In *Ancient Magic and Ritual Power*, edited by Marvin W. Meyer and Paul Allan Mirecki, 185–206. Leiden: E. J. Brill, 1995.

Lincoln, Bruce. *Death, War, and Sacrifice: Studies in Ideology and Practice*. Chicago: University of Chicago Press, 1991.

———. *Myth, Cosmos, and Society: Indo-European Themes of Creation and Destruction*. Cambridge: Harvard University Press, 1986.

———. "Pahlavi *Kirrēnīdan*: Traces of Iranian Creation Mythology." *Journal of the American Oriental Society* 117, no. 4 (1997): 681–685.

———. *Theorizing Myth: Narrative, Ideology, and Scholarship*. Chicago: University of Chicago Press, 1999.

———. "Treatment of Hair and Fingernails among the Indo-Europeans." *History of Religions* 16, no. 4 (1977): 351–362.

Linke, Uli. "Manhood, Femaleness, and Power: A Cultural Analysis of Prehistoric Images of Reproduction." *Comparative Studies in Society and History* 34, no. 4 (1992): 579–620.

Lommel, Herman, ed. *Die Yäšt's des Awesta*. Quellen der Religionsgeschichte. Göttingen: Vandenhoeck & Ruprecht, 1927.

Luhrmann, T. M. "Evil in the Sands of Time: Theology and Identity Politics among the Zoroastrian Parsis." *Journal of Asian Studies* 61, no. 3 (2002): 861–889.

MacKenzie, David N. *A Concise Pahlavi Dictionary*. London: Oxford University Press, 1971.

———. "Kerdir's Inscription." In *The Sasanian Rock Reliefs at Naqsh-i Rustam: Naqsh-i Rustam 6, the Triumph of Shapur I*, edited by Georgina Herrmann, 35–72. Berlin: D. Reimer, 1989.

Malandra, William W., ed. *An Introduction to Ancient Iranian Religion: Readings from the Avesta and Achaemenid Inscriptions*. Minnesota Publications in the Humanities. Minneapolis: University of Minnesota Press, 1983.

Malinowski, Bronislaw. *Coral Gardens and Their Magic*. Indiana University Studies in the History and Theory of Linguistics. Bloomington: Indiana University Press, 1965.

———. *Coral Gardens and Their Magic: A Study of the Methods of Tilling the Soil and of Agricultural Rites in the Trobriand Islands*. Vol. 2. London: G. Allen & Unwin, 1935.

———. *Magic, Science and Religion and Other Essays*. Garden City: Doubleday Anchor Books, 1948.

Mauss, Marcel. *A General Theory of Magic*. Translated by Robert Brain. London: Routledge & Kegan Paul, 1972.

Mayrhofer, Manfred. *Supplement zur Sammlung der altpersischen Inschriften*. Veröffentlichungen Der Iranischen Kommission, vol. 7. Vienna: Verlag der Österreichischen Akademie der Wissenschaften, 1978.

McDaniel, Walton Brooks. "The Pupula Duplex and Other Tokens of An 'Evil Eye' In the Light of Ophthalmology." *Classical Philology* 13, no. 4 (1918): 335–346.

Menasce, Jean Pierre de, ed. *Le troisième livre du Denkart*. Bibliothèque des oeuvres classiques persanes, 4. Paris: C. Klincksieck, 1973.

———, ed. *Shkand gumanig vichar: la solution decisive des doutes*. Collectanea Friburgensia, nouvelle série, fasc. 30. Fribourg en Suisse: Librairie de l'Université, 1945.

Moazami, Mahnaz. "The Dog in Zoroastrian Religion: Vidēvdād Chapter XIII." *Indo-Iranian Journal* 49, no. 1 (2006): 127–149.

———. "Evil Animals in the Zoroastrian Religion." *History of Religions* 44, no. 4 (2005): 300–317.

Modi, Jivanji Jamshedji. *The Religious Ceremonies and Customs of the Parsees.* Oriental Religions. New York: Garland, 1979.

Molé, Marijan. *Culte, mythe et cosmologie dans l'Iran ancien.* Annales du Musée Guimet. Paris: Presses universitaires de France, 1963.

———, ed. *La Légende de Zoroastre selon les textes pehlevis.* Travaux de l'Institut d'études iraniennes de l'Université de Paris. Paris: C. Klincksieck, 1967.

Monchi-Zadeh, Davoud, ed. *Die Geschichte Zarēr's.* Acta Universitatis Upsaliensis. Uppsala: Almqvist & Wiksell International, 1981.

Narten, Johanna, ed. *Der Yasna Haptaŋhāiti.* Wiesbaden: L. Reichert, 1986.

Obeyesekere, Gananath. "Ayurveda and Mental Illness." *Comparative Studies in Society and History* 12, no. 3 (1970): 292–296.

Pākzād, Fazl Allāh, ed. *Bundahišn: Zoroastrische Kosmogonie und Kosmologie.* Series Majmū'ah-'i Pizhūhishhā-yi Īrān-i Bāstān. Tehran: Markaz-i Dā'irat al-Ma'ārif-i Buzurg-i Islāmī, 2005.

Panaino, Antonio. *The Lists of Names of Ahura Mazdā (Yašt I) and Vayu (Yašt XV).* Serie Orientale Roma, 94. Rome: Istituto Italiano per l'Africa e l'Oriente, 2002.

———, ed. *Tištrya.* Serie Orientale Roma. Rome: Istituto Italiano per il Medio ed Estremo Oriente, 1990.

Patton, Kimberley C. *Religion of the Gods: Ritual, Paradox, and Reflexivity.* Oxford: Oxford University Press, 2009.

Pritchard, James Bennett. *Ancient Near Eastern Texts Relating to the Old Testament.* 3rd ed. Princeton, N.J.: Princeton University Press, 1969.

Puhvel, Jaan. "Mythological Reflections of Indo-European Medicine." In *Indo-European and Indo-Europeans*, edited by G. Cardona, H. Hoenigswald and A. Senn, 369–382. Philadelphia: University of Pennsylvania Press, 1970.

Sarianidi, V. I. *Margiana and Protozoroastrism.* Athens: Kapon Editions, 1998.

Schaeder, Hans Heinrich. *Iranische Beiträge.* Schriften der Königsberger Gelehrten Gesellschaft. Halle: Max Niemeyer Verlag, 1930.

Schmitt, Rüdiger, ed. *The Bisitun Inscriptions of Darius the Great: Old Persian Text.* Corpus Inscriptionum Iranicarum. London: School of Oriental and African Studies, 1991.

———. *Dichtung und Dichtersprache in indogermanischer Zeit.* Wiesbaden: Harrassowitz, 1967.

———, ed. *Die altpersischen Inschriften der Achaimeniden.* Wiesbaden: Reichert Verlag, 2009.

Schwartz, Martin. "Viiāmburas and Kafirs." *Bulletin of the Asia Institute* 4 (1990): 251–255.

Seidel, Jonathan. "Charming Criminals: Classification of Magic in the Babylonian Talmud." In *Ancient Magic and Ritual Power*, edited by Marvin W. Meyer and Paul Allan Mirecki, 145–166. New York: E.J. Brill, 1995.

Shahbazi, A. "On Vāreghna the Royal Falcon." *Zeitschrift der Deutschen Morgenländischen Gesellschaft* 134 (1984): 314–317.

Shaked, Shaul, ed. *The Wisdom of the Sasanian Sages: Dēnkard VI.* Persian Heritage Series. Boulder: Westview Press, 1979.

Shaki, M. "The Denkard Account of the History of the Zoroastrian Scriptures." *Archiv Orientalni* 49 (1981): 114–125.

Sims-Williams, Nicholas. "The Sogdian Fragments of the British Library." *Indo-Iranian Journal* 18, no. 1 (1976): 43–82.

Skjærvø, Prods Oktor. "The Achaemenids and the *Avesta*." In *Birth of the Persian Empire*, edited by Vesta Sarkhosh Curtis and Sarah Stewart, 52–84. New York: I. B. Tauris, 2005.

———. "Ahura Mazdā and Ārmaiti, Heaven and Earth, in the Old Avesta." *Journal of the American Oriental Society* 122, no. 2 (2002): 399–410.

———. "The Antiquity of Old Avestan." *Nāme-ye Irān-e Bāstān* 3, no. 2 (2003–2004): 15–41.

———. "The Avesta as Source for the Early History of the Iranians." In *The Indo-Aryans of Ancient South Asia: Language, Material Culture and Ethnicity*, edited by George Erdosy, 155–176. New York: Walter de Gruyter, 1995.

———. "Avestan Quotations in Old Persian?" In *Irano-Judaica*, edited by S. Shaked and A. Netzer, 1–64. Jerusalem: Yad Ben-Zvi Press, 1999.

———. "The Avestan Yasna: Ritual and Myth." *FEZANA*, Summer 2005: 57–60.

———. "Chinese Turkestan." *Encyclopædia Iranica*, vol. 5, 1992, 463–469.

———. "Eastern Iranian Epic Traditions III: Zarathustra and Diomedes—an Indo-European Epic Warrior Type." *Bulletin of the Asia Institute* 11 (1997): 175–182.

———. "Homosexuality in Zoroastrianism." *Encyclopædia Iranica Online*, December 15, 2004, available at www.iranicaonline.org.

———. "The Horse in Indo-Iranian Mythology." *Journal of the American Oriental Society* 128, no. 2 (2008): 295–302.

———. "Hymnic Composition in the Avesta." *Die Sprache* 36, no. 2 (1994): 199–243.

———. "Jamšid." *Encyclopædia Iranica Online*, June 23, 2008, available at www.iranica online.org.

———. "Kirdir's Vision: Translation and Analysis." *Archäologische Mitteilungen aus Iran* 16 (1983): 269–306.

———. "Of Lice and Men." In *Festschrift George Buddruss*, edited by R. Söhnen-Thieme and O. V. Hinüber, 269–286. Reinbek: Wezler, 1994.

———. "Persian/Iranian Literature and Culture." In *Gay Histories and Cultures: An Encyclopedia*, edited by George E. Haggerty, 677–680. New York: Garland, 2000.

———. "Praise and Blame in the Avesta: The Poet Sacrificer and His Duties." In *Studies in Honour of Shaul Shaked*, 29–67. Jerusalem: Hebrew University of Jerusalem, 2002.

———. "Review: *Der Sasanidische Archetypus*." *Kratylos* 36 (1991): 104–109.

———. "Review: *Der Zamyād-Yašt*." *Journal of the American Oriental Society* 117, no. 3 (1997): 610–612.

———. "Rivals and Bad Poets: The Poet's Complaint in the Old Avesta." In *Philologica et linguistica: historia, pluralitas, universitas*, edited by Maria Gabriela Schmidt and Walter Bisang, 351–376. Trier: Wissenschaftlicher Verlag Trier, 2001.

———. "Smashing Urine: On Yasna 48.10." In *Zoroastrian Rituals in Context*, edited by Michael Stausberg, 253–281. Leiden: E. J. Brill, 2004.

———. "The State of Old Avestan Scholarship." *Journal of the American Oriental Society* 117, no. 1 (1997): 103–114.

———. "Tāhadī: Gifts, Debts, and Counter-Gifts." In *Classical Arabic Humanities in Their Own Terms*, edited by R. Gruendler and M. Cooperson, 493–520. New York: Brill, 2008.

———. "Truth and Deception in Ancient Iran." In *The Fire Within*, edited by F. Vajifdar and C. Cereti, 383–434. Tehran: Sorya, 2003.

———. "The Videvdad: Its Ritual-Mythical Significance." In *The Age of the Parthians*, edited by Vesta Sarkhosh Curtis and Sarah Stewart, 105–141. New York: I. B. Tauris, 2007.

———. "Zarathustra: First Poet-Sacrificer." In *Paitimāna: Essays in Iranian, Indo-European, and Indian Studies in Honor of Hanns-Peter Schmidt*, edited by Siamak Adhami, 157–194. Costa Mesa, Calif.: Mazda Publishers, 2003.

———. "Zarathustra in the Avesta and in Manicheism. Irano-Manichaica IV." In *La Persia e l'Asia centrale da Alessandro al X secolo*, 597–628. Rome: Accademia nazionale dei Lincei, 1996.

Stausberg, Michael. "The Invention of a Canon: The Case of Zoroastrianism." In *Canonization and Decanonization*, edited by Arie van der Kooij, K. van der Toorn, and J. A. M. Snoek, 257–277. Leiden: E. J. Brill, 1998.

Stève, M. J., ed. *Nouveaux mélanges épigraphiques: inscriptions royales de Suse et de la Susiane.* Ville Royale De Suse. Nice: Editions Serre, 1987.

Sundermann, Werner. *Mitteliranische manichäische Texte Kirchengeschichtlichen Inhalts*, Schriften zur Geschichte und Kultur des Alten Orients. Berlin: Akademie-Verlag, 1981.

Tambiah, S. J. "The Form and Meaning of Magical Acts." In *Modes of Thought: Essays on Thinking in Western and Non-Western Societies*, edited by Robin Horton and Ruth Finnegan, 399. London: Faber, 1973.

———. "The Magical Power of Words." *Man* 3, no. 2 (1968): 175–208.

van Gennep, Arnold. *The Rites of Passage.* Translated by Monika B. Vizedom and Gabrielle L. Caffee. Chicago: University of Chicago Press, 1960.

Versnel, H. S. "Some Reflections on the Relationship Magic-Religion." *Numen* 38, no. 2 (1991): 177–197.

Vogelsang, Willem. "The Sixteen Lands of Videvdat 1." *Persica* 16 (2000): 49–66.

Voigtlander, E. N. von, ed. *The Bisitun Inscription of Darius the Great: Babylonian Version.* Corpus Inscriptionum Iranicarum. London: Lund Humphries, 1978.

Waag, Anatol, ed. *Nirangistan: der Awestatraktat über die rituellen Vorschriften.* Iranische forschungen. Leipzig: J. C. Hinrichs, 1941.

Waters, Matthew William. "The Earliest Persians in Southwestern Iran: The Textual Evidence." *Iranian Studies* 32, no. 1 (1999): 99–107.

Watkins, Calvert. *How to Kill a Dragon: Aspects of Indo-European Poetics.* New York: Oxford University Press, 1995.

Weber, Max. *The Sociology of Religion.* Translated by Ephraim Fischoff. Beacon Paperbacks. Boston: Beacon Press, 1964.

Weissbach, F. H., ed. *Die Keilinschriften der Achämeniden.* Vorderasiatische Bibliothek. Leipzig: J. C. Hinrichs, 1911.

West, Edward William, ed. *The Book of the Mainyo-i-Khard, or the Spirit of Wisdom: The Pazand and Sanskrit Texts, as Arranged in the Fifteenth Century by Neriosengh Dhaval.* Amsterdam: APA Oriental Press, 1979.

———. "Part 2: The Dadestan-i-Dinik." In *Pahlavi Texts.* Oxford: Clarendon Press, 1892.

———. "Part 4: Contents of the Nasks." In *Pahlavi Texts.* Oxford: Clarendon Press, 1892.

Westergaard, N. L., ed. *Zendavesta, or the Religious Books of the Zoroastrians.* Copenhagen: Berling Brothers, 1852.

Widengren, Geo. *Hochgottglaube im alten Iran; eine religionsphänomenologische untersuchung.* Uppsala universitets Årsskrift. Uppsala: Lundequistska bokhandeln, 1938.

Williams, A. V., ed. *The Pahlavi Rivāyat accompanying the Dādestān i Dēnīg.* 2 vols. Historisk-Filosofiske Meddelelser, 2. Copenhagen: Munksgard, 1990.

Wilson, John. *The Parsi Religion*. 2nd ed. Haryana: Vintage Books, 1989.

Zaehner, R. C. *The Dawn and Twilight of Zoroastrianism*. History of Religion. London: Weidenfeld and Nicolson, 1961.

———. *Zurvan: A Zoroastrian Dilemma*. Oxford: Clarendon Press, 1955.

Zysk, Kenneth G. *Religious Healing in the Veda*. Transactions of the American Philosophical Society. Philadelphia: American Philosophical Society, 1985.

Verse stanza line numbers are set in bold. Italicized page numbers refer to verse translations. In most instances verse translations are also discussed on italicized pages.